The Flea Market Handbook

Robert G. Miner

The Flea Market Handbook

SECOND EDITION

WALLACE-HOMESTEAD BOOK COMPANY
Radnor, Pennsylvania

Copyright © 1990 by Robert G. Miner
Second Edition   All Rights Reserved
Published in Radnor, Pennsylvania 19089, by
Wallace-Homestead Book Company

Designed by Tracy Baldwin
Manufactured in the United States of America

Library of Congress Cataloging in Publication Data
Miner, Robert G.
    Flea market handbook / Robert G. Miner.—2nd ed.
      p.   cm.
    Includes bibliographical references.
    ISBN 0-87069-559-2
    1. Flea markets—Handbooks, manuals, etc. I. Title.
HF5482.M56   1990
658.8'7—dc20   89-51677
                                              CIP

2 3 4 5 6 7 8 9 0   9 8 7 6 5 4 3 2 1 0

 o my son, Dave Miner, who lends help,
encouragement, design ability, strong arms,
and even love to my projects—no matter how
screwy they seem.

ontents

The Flea Market Handbook

ntiques: The Small Business that Can Make You Rich!

Reading Guide. Read this chapter before you decide to dispose of the stuff in your attic and garage. Let it help you decide whether to start a business selling junk, antiques, and/or collectibles in the flea market. To do this, you need:

- A firm desire to start your own business.
- A strong interest in a field of collectibles.
- A reasonable proximity to a flea market.
- The ability to learn quickly from experience.

Everybody who works for someone else thinks of starting a business. What a great idea! No boss, set your own hours, lots of fun doing business the way *you* think it should be done. Sounds so great there must be a catch somewhere!

It's Easy to Say No

There are several catches, and they've probably all occurred to you. The main one is that, by the time you're ready to take the plunge, you're probably tied down with responsibilities of family and home ownership. Payments are due each month on the mortgage and car loan, and you think of hungry little mouths that need to be fed. The challenge of going it alone and still having to pay bills seems too formidable to contemplate! Even in today's world, with financial responsibility shared by both partners, it's hard to see how even *one* of you can forego a weekly paycheck to get something of your own started.

Then there's the money needed to pay the expenses of a new business, like payroll, rent, and utilities, before the business can pay its own way. Starting a business usually requires a considerable investment of either your money or somebody else's. One reason most people never start a business is that they can't see how to finance the big step. To take on the responsibility for paying back the large sum of money a new business eats up seems too much to contemplate!

We resist the idea of borrowing money from a bank or from relatives, so most people just sigh and say, "Well, someday when my ship comes in . . ."

Another reason people shy away from starting a business is lack of experience in their chosen field. By the time they've built experience they're settled into the routines of life and they're glued to the status quo. It's a vicious circle!

Finally, there's the thought expressed by older people who say, "Yes, the kids are grown, we don't have all those responsibilities, we could take a little time to get a business going, but it's just too late."

Why do people work so hard to think up excuses for not doing what they *want to do*—like it's either too early or too late? Instead of thinking you're too young or too old, read this book and find out how at any age you *can* go into your own business and not risk a big investment of anything but your spare time. As the business grows you'll decide how far you want to go with it.

Say Yes!

What this book says is that your ship could be here—right now! It's at the dock and ready for you to get aboard!

I know this is true because after retiring from a 30-year publishing career at the age of 54, I became a flea market dealer on weekends. I then started (with a partner) an antiques mall at 57. At the grand old age of 60 I became a professional auctioneer. I never learned to say "no!"

But wait! A couple of years later I started a mail order antiques business and had the time of my life making a profit from it. Along the way, I wrote the first edition of this book, published it myself, and sold several thousand copies.

Now I'm writing a new book and looking forward to further adventures in the Virgin Islands! Maybe I'm lucky nobody told me it was too late. If I can do it, so can you. If you're 20- or 30-years younger than I was when I started, you have even less excuse than I did to refuse to give a little spare time to your own business in antiques!

Of course, all of this assumes you like antiques or collectibles. If your idea of a day of fun is shopping at K-Mart, toss this book and forget the whole thing! But if you enjoy yard sales and flea markets—read on!

I say you *can* get rich in the antiques business. I certainly do not *guarantee* you will. You might not even like it, and maybe you'll be terrible at it, in which case, after you've given it a try, you'll quit and go back to playing tennis on Sundays. How come I'm so damn sure you can make money in antiques? Because, in addition to my own experience, I know lots of people who've done it. What are the rewards?

First, many folks who buy and sell antiques on a part time basis find the additional income provides a touch of class to their lives. Without it they'd be close to the poverty level. Add the flea market and they're doing okay. I know older couples who have chosen to supplement their Social Security pensions with profits from antiques trading and now are living very well. In addition, they have an activity that's fulfilling. After your retirement do you want to sit around with nothing to do? You'll dry up and blow away!

There are young married couples who need income to supplement their earnings from regular weekday jobs. They work flea markets partly for income but mostly because, according to them, they love it—it's pure recreation!

One couple I know built a part-time flea market business out of the man's hobby of collecting sports memorabilia and his wife's knowledge of primitives. They soon began to operate a regular inside shop in a good market. The man has become a licensed professional auctioneer, thereby adding yet another source of income and vocational satisfaction. At this point they're both fully employed and do their antiques business and auctioneering as part-time activities.

Another gentleman had a lifelong interest in coin collecting that led him to setting up at flea markets. The next step was a regular indoor space at an antiques mall, followed by a move to a retail glass-front store located in a wealthy suburb. In it, he not only sells his coins but has expanded into old advertising material and a general line of small antiques.

A lady who came into our antiques mart as a brand-new dealer (she skipped the flea market stage!) was so successful that she graduated to a larger mart, helped her son enter the antique furniture business, and got her husband so involved that he decided to become a professional auctioneer. (If you can't beat 'em, join 'em!) She did all this in the space of less than eight years!

I've known married couples, single people, single parents with children, retirees, yuppies, radicals, and conservatives all of who have found their own thing to do in the flea market. Some have gone on to greater things.

Getting Started

Chances are you wouldn't be reading this if you hadn't already done something that leads people into becoming antiques dealers! You've collected *something*. That collection, be it glassware, antique toys, dolls, paper collectibles, kitchen utensils, or whatever can be your ticket to a new full or part time career. You have a *field* of interest, something you know about. Maybe you're not the world's number one expert in your collecting specialty, but you know *something*, and you *like* the field or you wouldn't be collecting in it.

You don't need cash to start your business, or at least no more than it takes to make up a "bank" with which to make change during the first few hours of your first selling day. You'll probably take in enough cash to coast the rest of the day and even make a few buys to bolster your inventory.

The No-Cash Method

I think of the antiques business as a "zero capital" business because it takes virtually no cash investment to start. Nit-pickers point out what they call an error. They say starting with your own collection is "investing" your objects, be they lamps, dolls, or glass and china; and this is an investment as much as cash is.

They're playing with words. They call it investing, I say you're trading these objects, which you already own, for cash. You then use the cash to accumulate more objects for sale. If you sell right and buy right, the value of your collection, which is now your inventory, will go up. You'll increase the total value of your capital and that's what getting rich is all about! You just keep doing the same thing at higher and higher levels. After a while you draw down a profit.

A Point of View

"I couldn't bear to part with my dolls!" That's typical of what many collectors say when they're asked whether they've thought about the antiques business. They're collectors, first, last, and always and probably never will be dealers.

"I don't have a collection, this is inventory." That's what Ben Alexander, the late, great Central Pennsylvania dealer in antique tools told me one day when I remarked that I thought he had the best collection I'd seen.

The interesting thing is that Ben, whose love and knowledge of old tools was unrivaled, treated each implement as though he were its curator. When I asked him about his philosophy of antiques dealing, he replied that a collection is limited by space, but an inventory, continuously turning over, is infinite in size and value with its dimension in time. "I can always say, 'Sure I once had one of those.' and it's just as real a part of my 'collection' as if I still had it! And, if I've never had it, I know someday I will!"

The dealer can't afford the luxury of a static collection, but he can take joy in *owning* the objects of his "Movable Collection" as their temporary curator. That's what he is! Many dealers, like Ben, exhibit the same devotion to their inventory as a collector does.

Put it this way: the professional antiques dealer is a temporary custodian who can always say, "I had one of those," and remember every detail of the object with great pleasure. In addition he can say, "I want one of those," and work hard to acquire a rare object of interest, knowing all the while that it will become a part of his inventory and eventually he'll sell it and use part of the money to acquire something else even more desirable.

Collecting is selfish, while being a dealer means bringing pleasure to others. Dealing in antiques is more fun than hoarding. You should adopt a professional attitude from the very first day and leave behind the tendency to collect. It's easier said than done, but the rewards are great. The key to the whole transition is to learn to say "inventory" instead of "collection."

The Antiques Business

Antiques dealing is "small business," mostly consisting of one-man or one-woman shops. Part-timers (school teachers, government employees, factory and office workers, for example) sell from $5,000 to $25,000 worth of antiques in a year. Their profit? Probably close to half their annual sales. Both sales and profits are related to two things:

How many days per month do you work at it?

How many sales dollars are plowed back into inventory?

At the bottom step of the ladder is the little guy who operates mostly out of his home, attends an occasional flea market or antiques show as a dealer, and scouts for specific types of items for which he has a waiting clientele. He's in the five to twenty-five thousand dollar class, and sometimes almost as much a collector as dealer.

On the next rung are dealers who've been at it a long time—mostly doing shows. Some have shops, a few are in marts, and a few specialists deal out of their homes. They sell $50,000 to $100,000 worth of antiques a year. They deal with clients who depend upon them to find and authenticate such objects as period furniture and estate jewelry. They're able to make occasional killings like buying a piece for $100 and selling it for $10,000.

They are also content to buy something for a client for a thousand and sell it to him for eleven hundred. Nothing wrong with a 10 percent markup if the sale is certain, doesn't cost anything for care and feeding, and is for a good client. The hundred dollar profit may be a reward for an hour's work or even less, so who can object?

The operator whose annual sales are over $100,000 is in the big leagues. He or she may even have employees (not many) who sweep the shop and strip furniture so the proprietor doesn't have to get his hands dirty. Many people like this learned the business at the knee of a mom or dad who had been in it for a lifetime.

I'll show you how you can start small, with only your own collection as inventory and, within a period of three to five years, build to a $10,000 to $20,000 annual sale with up to $5,000 to $10,000 per year profit—part-time.

Then, having reached the $10,000 to $20,000 per annum point, the rest will be up to you. If you want to get bigger, you'll have to switch to a full-time basis. But if you can make a profit of a thousand a week with chances of doing better, why not go full time?

Along the way you'll find all kinds of interesting opportunities. You may decide, as I did, that auctioneering is something you want to do. It's possible to be either a part-time or full-time auctioneer.

Appraising is a closely related activity to which many antiques experts find themselves inevitably drawn. Once you've developed expertise in a field of antiques you'll find you know values in your field better than most people. You'll command a price for applying your knowledge of the market to appraising collections for legal or insurance purposes.

If you like management, you may see a chance to develop an antiques co-op—a collection of dealer shops under one roof—managed and promoted by you. In it you can have your own shop and profit from managing the entire enterprise.

You may find yourself tempted to open a flea market with a hundred or five hundred dealers. There's money in owning a flea market or antiques mart.

In this book I'll discuss all of these opportunities. It'll take time to investigate them all, but you should be aware of what they are and explore them as you take up your new profession of selling antiques.

Getting Smart

You can start selling next Sunday at the local flea market without knowing a darned thing and probably end your first day with a wad of cash and a blurry memory of having had lots of fun.

That's fine for a first day, but if you don't make an effort to learn more about what you're doing, how to buy and sell, how to manage inventory, improve your display, and understand the psychology of the trade and its people, you'll not progress beyond the status of beginner.

You could be fair game for every charlatan that comes down the flea market path. You'll be a sucker for a crafty auctioneer, a sitting duck for every picker and hauler who comes along, and your name will pass from dealer to dealer as the sucker who can be taken.

The only way to prevent this is to get smart—about what sells in your area and for how much, what's new and what's passé, what the next hot item might be, and when to get out of a line of merchandise that's dead. We'll cover all this and more.

Your First Inventory

Take a look at your collections. You're not going to sell *all* of any bunch of stuff you take to the market in any one day, so don't worry about not having enough! As a matter of fact, I've concluded that a good day in the market means you've sold between five and ten percent of what you've put up for display. You should know something of the value of most of your things. If you don't know the value of something, either leave it home or hide it in the car until you find out how to price it.

Try to sell everything you put on display, but be happy to sell ten percent. Don't despair when your things that will be the hardest to replace, sell first. Predawn vultures, dealers looking for inexperienced exhibitors, will try to strip your prized possessions and pay nothing for them before you get them out of their packing boxes! Steel yoursel and *act* professional, even if it hurts.

Contemplating the sale of your things may be in the same category as selling your children. Try to think of the items you will sell as objects for which there isn't space left at home! After a few sales you'll take the money and buy new objects. You'll have fun selling, and you'll find buying new inventory is more fun than hoarding!

Where to Do Business

Once you've decided what to put up for sale, your next decision is where to do it. Or at least, where to *begin* to do it. Don't consider setting up an antiques shop. That's only for experienced dealers. You can contemplate that step a few years from now, but even then, think long and deep first. It was once a pretty good business, but except for experienced antiques dealers with a loyal clientele, isn't any more.

I wouldn't consider shop operation without an inventory of at least thirty-thousand dollars, retail. Even then, stand ready to take a loss for two years and to be able to support yourself during that time without a profit. An experienced business advisor warns that one should have a year's living expenses in the bank before contemplating starting any new full-time business, regardless of your ability to obtain financing.

Before contemplating shop operation with high fixed expenses, develop your business skills, then your clientele, after which you might think about the fixed cost of a lease.

Many dealers first cut their teeth in flea markets, then switched to antiques shows. There are hundreds of such shows advertised each year in trade papers. To start in the business by doing shows is difficult. Space in the good ones is sold out to selected dealers far in advance, and a poor show is a ticket to disaster. After a couple of years of learning the antiques business, you can decide whether you want to do shows and which ones to try. Your name will then spend time on a waiting list before you're offered space in a better show.

Getting started in the antiques business is like going to school. You don't begin with graduate school. You start in kindergarten or at most first grade. Your primary education will be garage sales and flea markets followed by high school which can be an indoor flea market or a dealer co-op. After that it's on to college level—antiques shows or an antiques mart.

The opening of a single owner antiques shop should be thought of as graduate school. You've made it, and now you're ready to start working on your thesis! By this time you've come to be well-known for a specialty or two and have collected a growing list of clients.

Tag Sales

Consider a tag sale, garage sale, or yard sale if you're thinking of expanding your horizons. Gather items, both collectibles and junk, serviceable and worn out, throw it on card tables and boards stretched between chairs in the yard, and sell for prices that range from a dime to a few dollars. It's a great way to get rid of junk and find out whether you like dealing with people who think they're sharper than you are.

Use a classified ad in the local paper. It's the best way to reach the steady stream of Saturday yard shoppers who chart their day by arranging the tag sales into a logical route and setting out at 7:00 A.M. with their numbered list and a pocket full of money they're eager to spend. Your ad said "9:00 A.M. to 3:00 P.M.," but they'll start showing up at seven. Get used to it. If you chase the early ones away, you'll lose half of them who won't come back later. It's better to arise at 5:00 A.M., have breakfast and get your stuff out by 6:30 or 7:00. Most of the early shoppers will be dealers looking for things you don't know the value of but which they know are worth thousands. The dealer scores big about once every ten years. It's a bit like a fisherman dragging his lure around a lake for two weeks a year hoping to find a record muskie!

Your tag sale will draw dealers, pickers, haulers, collectors, and nosy people. It's fun and good experience, and it has the great advantage of getting rid of a lot of junk. Don't put out period antiques or anything you want to sell for market price! Save them for the flea market where you'll get better prices.

Advice for your tag sale: Write a descriptive ad. Don't use meaningless phrases like "Thousands of bargains." Say "3-HP Mower, runs." Or, "Six willow ware plates." This advice applies to any advertising you'll do now or in your later expanded retail career. It's worth repeating: Make advertising descriptive with specific offerings. It'll pay off for you.

Second, be sure to price and tag before the sale. Many people will pay the tag price (written, it's official!) who would haggle the hell out of you if it's not written. Make your prices fair, but a bit over what you think people will pay. This encourages offers. Throughout this book you'll find the advice: Get an offer. Don't be disappointed when the vase you thought should sell for $10 and which you've priced at $11 pulls as offer of $5. Go to the price you want to stick with and quote it: "I'll take nine." Of course, if the customer counters with $6, then you'll have to come up with an answer, and the haggling begins!

Some people won't offer. They'll ask questions like "Could you take less?" "What's your best price?" "Do you give a senior citizen's discount?" Any of these questions indicates your customer wants to bargain. Go to it! It's not only the essence of tag sale buying, but a stylish method of dealing for any antique. Never be afraid to bargain. Never be ashamed of the price you start with, but have an ending price in mind!

It's amazing how often people sell things at home in tag sales but never take the next step of trying space in a flea market. A couple of homes in the Pennsylvania town where we recently lived had a tag sale a month! The quality and prices of their offerings were higher than one would expect, and since they were located on busy streets, they should be congratulated for finding rent-free space! They probably sold enough to make the rent or mortgage payment for the month!

One warning: A monthly yard sale is almost sure to draw the attention of state tax inspectors, and sales tax laws usually require the collection and forwarding of taxes if there's a regularly repeated offering of merchandise. A monthly tag sale will likely be construed as a retail operation subject to sales tax laws. I don't think such an investigation will land you in jail. The tax lady probably will advise you to apply for a tax license. If you don't heed the advice, her second warning could be more stringent.

Your Local Flea Market

During the last forty years, there's been an amazing growth in the number of flea markets in every state of the union. You might think of them as a country phenomenon, but you'll find them in metropolitan areas such as New York City where there's a regular Sunday market on Sixth Avenue in midtown.

But it's in rural America where the flea market has come into its own. Dealers used to handle mostly secondhand and antique merchandise. But as sources for the older things have dried up, there are fewer antiques and more new merchandise. Importers offer products made specifically to sell through flea markets. They're generally inferior in quality and consist largely of electronic gadgets, car stereo, dolls, lawn furniture, automotive gadgets, costume jewelry, sun glasses, household goods, and appliances. Much is plastic and there are lots of knockoffs of branded merchandise. It doesn't interest me and I haven't made a study of it or sold any of it. There are many suppliers from whom you can get the stuff, and I can only assume it retails profitably or the commerce would not continue.

There are food stands for fresh vegetables from local market growers (mostly excellent) plus salty and sugary prepared foods such as pizzas, hot dogs and soft ice cream. My physician says these are too high in chloresterol and that I should therefore not eat them. Wherever people gather they will eat. Plants and other horticultural items are often excellent bargains.

The flea market that's best for your antiques and collectibles will have at least half of its stands devoted to antiques and collectibles. Such a market draws a throng of collectors and dealers every weekend. Some, like the large ones in Adamstown, Pennsylvania or Brimfield, Massachusetts, prohibit the exhibition of any merchandise that is not antique or at least collectible. Those, of course, are the best.

I doubted the veracity of one market's claim that its manager would throw out anyone who dealt in new merchandise until one Saturday I saw a dealer given the heave-ho because he was selling reproductions. The manager of the market announced the "event" over the public address system after which the offending dealer packed up and left.

Big Business

There are probably 20,000 flea markets in the country. Most seem to be doing well. What you want is the largest market within driving distance of your home where your line fits and where you'll find shoppers in large numbers every Sunday or whenever it's open.

Numbers alone may not produce sales for you. Before you start, visit markets within convenient driving radius. Spend a couple of hours in each one. Note the types of dealers and what customers seem to be buying. Make a judgement based on what you see. Even if you make a mistake in selecting your first market you won't be badly hurt. Daily space rent runs between $5.00 and $20.00! One or two sales and you've made your rent, and your chances to make a great deal more than that are very good.

A Case History

My wife and I were introduced to tag sales when we lived for almost twenty years in Fairfield County, Connecticut. It was a time when life styles were changing for descendants of old families and traditional furnishings were out of fashion. New homes of younger married people didn't have room for old family treasures, so antiques went out into the yard on Saturday to make way for a new style of living that included back yard barbecuing, and sailing, and thumbs turned down on antiques collecting.

Furniture, glassware, clocks, lamps, and books began to come on the market in tag sales. Our idea in "collecting" was mostly to furnish our suburban home in things that seemed comfortable but which were less expensive than comparable items from Sloan's and Altman's. We also just happened to like old things, so we hit the local tag sales, tentatively at first, then heavily as we caught the collecting fever.

It's fair to say that half of our Westport home was furnished in "secondhand" items. As we collected we began to study antiques. We learned that a chair which we paid almost nothing for was an eighteenth-century Windsor. A table, after we stripped it of nine coats of paint, was a country piece made of hand-planed butternut with hand-wrought iron pivots in the dropleaf mechanisms. An ancient iron implement, sold to me by a man who used it to chip ice from his driveway in winter, turned out to be a seventeenth-century oven peel. We began a collection of copper cooking utensils that had once been used in kitchens of hotels and great estates as well as in galleys of ocean going vessels.

The Yard Sale

After moving to Pennsylvania many years later, we felt overloaded with "stuff." It was logical that I should finally join a friend in what was billed as a "neighborhood yard sale." There were four of us who set up our stuff on the empty front apron of an abandoned service station on Main Street.

Mostly modern tools, toys and books were displayed by the participants in the sale that day. I decided to try some leatherbound books and extras from my collection of antique carpenter's tools. I also displayed some kitchen equipment from the 1920s plus some pure junk. Not an awe inspiring collection!

My total sales that day amounted to almost $100. I didn't bank, it, of course, and the next Sunday took it with me to flea markets and bought more junk! Sound like I hadn't learned my lesson, you say? You're right.

On to the Flea Market!

My son-in-law, who had set up occasionally at a local flea market to sell his kids' outgrown toys and clothes, talked me into trying it. I loaded my cargo trailer (itself something of an "antique,") and drove to the market the next Sunday, arriving at 5:30 A.M. In total blackness, I searched for a spot that might be good for foot traffic, found one, and began to unload.

Nobody had prepared me for the predawn attack of junkie-monsters, some of them straight out of a horror tale! Dealers mostly, and collectors who descended like the hordes of Attila the Hun, flashlights instead of spears in hand. They began to do battle with boxes that hopeful sellers were beginning to unload from cars, vans, and station wagons.

These vultures (within a year I was one of them) hoped to find an unsuspecting beginner who didn't know values. I had a great Hires Root Beer barrel that I had tired of using as a lamp table. A fat bearded guy in a cowboy hat spotted it, actually lifted it out of my trailer and shouted, "Whatcha got on the barrel?" I looked at it carefully trying to see if there was something hanging on it, then realized he meant to ask the price.

Fig. 1-1 A large crowd means many potential buyers for your flea market business.

I hadn't the slightest idea what I should ask for the barrel. I had bought it a year earlier for $50 and figured that double would be fine, so I said "A hundred." He peeled off a C-note quickly, before I could change my mind, handed it to me and, shouldering the barrel, was on his way.

Gosh, I thought, I didn't price it high enough! But I had no chance to think about it as two disreputable characters started to lift things out of the trailer. One held my Krag-Jorgenson rifle that had been a gift to me from a neighbor when I was a child. My wife has never liked having guns in the house, so I had decided to sell it. Luckily I had given the gun a bit of thought the day before. "One-twenty-five," I told the man.

"Too much for me," he said, and left. The other one picked up the gun, pulled me aside and said, "Give you ninety-five." I was tempted to sell it, but realized that if this guy, who obviously knew what he was doing, offered me ninety-five it must be worth more.

So I stuck to my price. I reasoned that if two people were that interested the price was too low. "No," I replied. "I'm sticking to my price. Let's see what happens during the day." The second man left and I put a new sticker on the gun that read $175. I was learning.

It would be nice to end this part of my tale by saying that the gun sold at $175. Truth is it did not. I should have stuck to my price, even taken the gun home to bring back another day. But I didn't. I was in a selling mood. I got $110 for the Krag before the day was over, and that wasn't too bad, although probably $50 below top dollar.

Just think: *before dawn* I had learned three lessons:

LESSON #1: Research each item you want to sell at markets and in price guides to have an idea of the price range. If you know experts in the product line ask them. Decide on *asking price*, and *rock-bottom* price.

LESSON #2: Price and tag each item with your asking price *before* going to the market.

LESSON # 3: Don't be in too big a hurry to sell. Hold to a predetermined *rock-bottom* selling price just below your *asking price*. Take it home if the item doesn't bring *rock-bottom*.

LESSON # 4: It's worse to price too low than too high. Too high and you'll still own it. Too low and it's gone and you don't have a second chance.
    NOTE: Later we'll discuss what to do when you don't make rock-bottom after several attempts have been made to sell the item. That's time to bail out *at any price!*—well, *almost any price!*

From my amateur beginning just before 6:00 A.M. until about 8:00 A.M. (by which time I had begun to feel at least semiprofessional!), I dealt with dozens of people I learned later were dealers although many didn't have shops, nor did they set up at markets or follow any formal route of selling.

Flea Market Junkies

"Junkies" are people who come to the market early with their flashlights to wheedle, bargain, or intimidate—depending upon their personalities, experience, and the depth of their resident sadistic nature. They buy for as low as they can and sell for as high, often to other people in the same flea market. They're trying to "steal," (a phrase you'll often hear applied to a transaction that results in a super-bargain), then sell at a huge profit. All without spending a cent in rent or incurring any expense, other than coffee, as far as I can tell.
    The junkie doesn't collect state sales tax. He has a tax license to avoid paying sales tax, something he considers a sin worse than death. He doesn't say he has a tax license, he says he has a tax number. His accounting system is in his wallet or in her purse. No books are kept, no 1040s are filed with the IRS, and no federal taxes are paid. The flea market, at least for the junkie, is as perfect a tax-free grey market as can exist. It's moot whether there's enough in it for either state or federal tax departments to pay the enormous price that enforcement of tax laws would require.
    Some dealers object to the junkies' practices, but nobody interferes with their operations. You might expect flea-market proprietors to resent junkies for doing business without paying rent. But they don't seem to. Why?
    My theory is that the junkie provides a service: He becomes something of an expert in his field and through his buying and selling sets a kind of market price—sort of like a speculator in the stock market or commodity exchange. From the regular dealer's standpoint junkies know a lot about a lot of things and are often free with advice. Most of them are loquacious. To befriend a few

junkies is to have a veritable library of recently paid prices for collectibles. Finally, many are interesting, if slightly weird, personalities that the market would be a poorer place, character-wise, without.

8:00 A.M. was the time I had expected people to start entering the market, because a large sign painted on the front wall of the main building clearly named 8:00 A.M. as the opening hour. Before 8:00 I had sold more than $300 worth of stuff. There was a slight pause in the action, enough to permit me to get a container of black coffee. Then, the action picked up and I remember the rest of the day as an endless stream of people giving offers, making silly statements, bargaining, forcing money into my hands, until four in the afternoon. I was tired and happy to toss what was left into the trailer and drive home.

I sat down at the kitchen table and asked my wife for a glass of water. "You look terrible. Did you sell anything?" she asked.

"Yeah," I replied, "but I'm not sure how much." I extracted my bank from my front pocket and tossed it onto the kitchen table. It was a thick roll of bills, folded and secured with a heavy rubber band. "Go ahead," I said. "Count it."

She did. "Good Lord," she said, "I can't believe it." She passed the stack of bills to me. There were a couple of hundreds on top. I slowly and carefully counted the pile. It came to $880.

"Not bad," I said. "I think I made enough to buy us a box of Colonel Sanders tonight." That became the tradition. From that day on, every Sunday afternoon, on the way home, I bought a box of the Colonel's best.

I'd like to say that, since that beginning I've exceeded that first day's total every time I've done a flea market. That would not be truthful, although there have been days when the take amounted to several times the $880 I pulled in the first day. There have been days when I've sold furniture pieces to a total of four times that amount in a single day! There have been days when I've sold a twentieth of that amount by day's end. Even on those days, I bought the Colonel's chicken.

Pricing for the Flea Market

People go to a flea market with the intention of buying. Even if they don't *need* them, most people will buy things that seem like bargains. Every flea market buyer is avidly seeking to buy for 25 cents something that's worth $50. I know people who have whole garages full of junk they've bought at flea markets that they won't use and have no intention of selling or discarding!

Not every person who passes your stand is *your* buyer. If your prices are too low those who are not normally your buyers will buy—just with the idea of getting a bargain or because they think it's cheap and they can always resell it later. They'll be glad to pay you $25 for a $50 item that you bought for $10 whether they need it or not!

It's fair to say that during that first day at the market I had been bitten by the bug. Never again could I pass a flea market or a yard sale, even an antiques shop, without checking it out. My wife and I had been auction goers for many years, but, for the same reason we went to tag sales and markets, to furnish our home and collect things that interested us. Now I had the additional motivation: "I can resell that at a profit!"

Never again would I be able to look at a collectibles display and judge it simply on the basis of whether the things would look good in our home or how useful something would be. Now it was, "What's the price—what'll it sell for—whaddaya s'pose they'd take for it?" Later, as I began to get acquainted with a clientele for particular collectible lines, I began to ask, "who'll buy it?" And, finally, having built an inventory, "How will it look in my display?" Without thinking about all this at the time—without even knowing the right questions to ask—I was hooked!

After I had bought a few more things at flea markets, tag sales, and auctions, I went back to that first flea market. I was even able to get back into what I considered my "lucky spot." My take on the second experience went down to about $500, but I got better prices for most things I sold, and my *margin* (the difference between the total of what I had paid and the total sales figure for items sold) was much better. At this point, after paying for additional items to add to the inventory, I had almost as large an inventory as when I had started and was way ahead in cash—about $800 as I remember it.

It still did not occur to me that I had actually *started* a small business that would grow by giving parts of weekends and occasional evenings to it. My only plan was to wait until I thought I had enough stuff to sell and then drive off to the market for a pleasant Sunday of selling and greeting a lot of strange, interesting, screwy people, many of whom were beginning to become my friends.

At the point where I had put a thousand dollars into the bank, I began to think of taking a permanent, indoor space in the market, a space where I could store my inventory from Sunday to Sunday with a reasonable chance of its still being there the following market day. In short, I began to think of my flea market operation as a business. It was a part-time activity, but it was still a business that would lead, as you will see, to many other things.

Looking Ahead

The thought then occurred to me that in a few years I would be of retirement age. It seemed to me that it would be nice to have an antiques business going by the time I turned 65, with inventory, an established place of business, money in the bank, and a clientele that would provide continuing sales and an income to supplement social security benefits.

My wife's reaction to this idea stems from her brilliant perception and tolerance of my eccentricities, not the least of which is a confirmed tendency to be a pack rat.

"Great idea," she said, "but just think how you'll cut your options. If you own all those tons of stuff, you'll never want to leave it. You'll have everything invested in junk—you won't be able to buy a boat, travel, or live in the Virgin Islands. You'll have to stay home and enjoy your possessions even if it kills you."

So we thought up a scheme that would be aimed at my 65th birthday. It consisted of these two objectives: 1. Get rid of possessions. 2. Get started in a retirement business.

So I talked with the manager of a local flea market and rented indoor space. I didn't regret it in the years that followed.

Update: I am now 66 years old. We live on our yacht in the Caribbean (St. Thomas, U.S. Virgin Islands), and still own four 20-foot shipping containers full of junk. I guess she's right—people don't change. One of these days, I keep telling her, I'm going to sell all that junk.

CHAPTER TWO

Your First Day in the Market

Reading Guide. I promised that you can enter the antiques field and immediately make money. You're thinking, "So the old coot sold stuff his first day! Big deal. How can he prove it's worth it to read this semi-boring book." In this chapter you'll find out about:

- Selecting merchandise to sell.
- How to choose your market.
- How to price your items.
- What to take and how to arrange your space.

In this chapter I'll tell you things I've learned starting with the day I set up for the first time. I'll help you be better prepared on your first day than I was on mine, after which, if it's like mine, you'll know you've chosen an exciting avocation or lifetime career.

Getting Started

The only cash I had on my first morning was a couple of bucks for coffee. Within minutes the cash started to roll in! All the inventory I've bought since then plus props and fixtures have been paid for out of current cash income.

The "No cash" method involves selling items you already own. It's great to do it with antiques, but you needn't restrict yourself to antiques in the beginning. The main thing is to get going, learn how to sell, how to manage, and how to make your business grow.

Merchandise for Your First Day

Search every nook and cranny of attic, cellar, and closet. Don't forget the garage and barn. The average six- to eight-room house will yield a couple thousand dollars worth of "junk" which, converted to cash in the flea market, can give birth to an inventory of antiques that'll point you toward success!

Clear out old garden equipment, hardware, glass, and electronics junk. Hold back your antiques and make your mistakes with items you care little about. You'll learn how to deal with customers without risking good stuff. If you have collectibles, digest the next two chapters before offering them for sale.

Pricing Your Items

When you commit part of your antiques collection, you'll want to do a good job of pricing and know enough about the market to avoid the risk of selling too cheaply. The best way is to consult a friend who is an expert in your fields of interest.

If you've bought a lot from one dealer visit him or her and have a general discussion on pricing. You'll be amazed at how helpful dealers will be, particularly if they know you. Your friend might be delighted to have you enter the field professionally, since you'll be one more local person looking for the items he or she is interested in.

Visit every antiques shop and flea market you can find. Go to auctions. Read antiques magazines, although I admit magazines fall down when it comes to prices. That's because prices tend to be out of date as soon as an issue is published. Absorb price knowledge wherever you go.

Price Guides

A few words about price guides. Every dealer, auctioneer and appraiser I know has a library of them and consults them constantly. They do it to get all the input they can to make pricing decisions. They do not take one quote as gospel. The reason is that most price guide listings result from a single event—either a sale at retail, a sale at auction, or a price listed by a dealer in a show. All three processes yield different values. Prices also change through time. So in using the price guide one should take into account the method of pricing and the date of publication. There are vast geographic differences in prices from one region to another. Also, condition of the item is so important that in some fields of collecting an item in "excellent" condition can be worth five times the value of one in "poor" condition. Some price guides give little indication whether the item is in mint, excellent, very good, good, or fair condition.

The method of sale, geographic differences, and condition then, are the variables that cause prices to fluctuate wildly.

Many peope mistakenly assume that prices of all collectibles go up continuously. Although most prices have risen (sometimes more, sometimes less than the rate of inflation), a few items have decreased in value.

What no price guide ever tells you is what items your area is saturated with and which therefore won't sell except at give-away prices. The price guide is a *guide*. Don't expect it to be more. He who tells you, "The book value is . . ." tells fairy stories. Just finding a price in a book doesn't give you market value for that item in your market!

The best examples of wild price advances in recent years are in the art market. Even though few of us will ever deal in Picassos and Rembrandts, it's still important to realize that even lesser fine art can escalate in multiples, simply because of scarcity. This is far less true with more mundane collectibles.

Here's a rather homely example of a collectible that had a short life. At one time in my flea market booth, I could sell any large brass wall fire extinguisher (polished) for forty dollars. Even the unpolished ones went for twenty-five. I had trouble finding new ones to replace the ones I sold.

A friend who ran a wholesale drug business (the legal kind) asked me if I was interested in old fire extinguishers he had removed from his stores. Since I hadn't found any in months I bought eighteen of them for ten dollars each, convinced I had the world's best deal. I was the fire extinguisher king!

I learned that the sensational market of a few months earlier had dried up! Two years later I still had fifteen fire extinguishers left. I kept feeding them into my auctions, one or two per auction, until the audience's eyes glazed over: "Oh, oh," they'd say, "here comes another Miner fire extinguisher."

Try to remember what you paid for each item you're going to take to the flea market. If you can't find a comparable item to determine pricing, raise your original purchase price by an amount equal to inflation and double it.

If you paid full retail price ten years ago, you may have trouble selling at a profit after adjusting for inflation, unless you have a few things that were not too popular when you bought them and which have become collectibles during the time you've owned them. This has happened to some things from as late as the '70s and early '80s.

When you travel, remember to do comparison shopping in both antiques shops and in retail shops where modern counterparts of your items are sold. Gift shops and variety stores are good examples. Lots of antique items are bought as much for their use as to be collected and admired. Good examples are glass and kitchen implements like rolling pins, hand mixers, and bowls. New utilitarian items often sell at about the same prices as their antique counterparts.

Choosing Your Flea Market

If you live near a large population center you'll find places given over to flea market operation on weekends, usually on Sunday, but sometimes on both Saturday and Sunday.

Outdoor theaters, lumber yards, unused warehouses and other buildings, and outdoor areas that have space for parking and dealers' displays recycle their grounds on weekends as flea markets. Visit them all to decide which one seems best for you.

While you're checking markets with an eye toward choosing one, make a survey of current prices on items you're thinking of selling. You might even find a few things to buy that you can resell later at a profit.

Fig. 2-1 A typical flea market spread.

Here are some things to find out about markets in order to make your choice:

1. What's the earliest time you can enter to set up?
2. Can you reserve a space by paying in advance?
3. By what time is the best space taken if it can't be reserved?
4. Can one park the night before to reserve space?
5. Are tables furnished or must you bring your own?

Rental Fees

Ask about the rental fee for one day. It isn't going to be high enough to break your bank. In some markets you can pay in advance to reserve a good space, but don't expect a refund if for any reason you don't show up. In some you pay as you drive in, and in some you simply enter, set up, and start selling. The manager will collect later. For the better extravaganza markets, you must reserve and pay in advance even in markets where you can't reserve a particular space.

Choosing Your Location

What space to choose? Since dealers don't agree, it probably doesn't make much difference. Some dealers like to be near the entrance while some think people are moving so fast to get into the center of the action they fail to stop at the first booths they come to.

Near the refreshment stand? There's a lot of traffic near food, but not necessarily antique buying traffic. There's the disadvantage of being submerged in collections of cooking odors and litter that accompany hot dogs and soft drinks.

There's a lot to be said for setting up in the center of the market. You catch people going both ways if you're at midpoint. Shoppers aren't completely tired out by the time they reach you. It seems to me that most old-timers pick a spot near the middle in a line with the path from the parking lot.

You may have a choice of the end of a row or in the center. Corner space gives you the opportunity to set up tables on two sides. On the other hand, a center-aisle space with one front makes it easier to spot shoplifters.

Arranging Your Space

The most natural first choice is to set up tables along the front of your space so that you can stand behind them to deal with customers. However, it's possible your merchandise will look better in some other arrangement. If you have large items such as furniture plus small objects that belong on tables, it will probably be better to place tables along each side of your space with an open "room" in the center where your furniture will display well and people can examine it closely. Shoppers seem to open up and talk more when they are invited "into the store."

It's difficult to keep your eye on everything when you're waiting on customers. If you have valuables, you should have a glass-covered, lockable case. Shoplifters work in pairs. One engages the dealer in conversation and works to turn his head away from an accomplice who, moving out of the line of sight of the proprietor, fills his pocket or her purse without being detected. The locked case is the best way to prevent this.

Getting Attention

Consider how to display each large item as well as each group of small items to get attention focused on them. This won't mean much to the dealer who heads his station wagon into the space, lowers the tailgate and pulls stuff out onto the tailgate and the ground. No tables, no height, no thought at all. There's a better way. First, think about tables. If you're showing good glass and china, why not first lay a table cloth where these items will be displayed? A plain white tablecloth or even a clean bed sheet is fine for place settings, but sometimes individual items look better on black or navy blue velvet, the kind of coverings you are more likely to see in an antiques show. Such an underlining of quality adds value to your merchandise. How much? Ten percent? Twenty percent? Your guess is as good as mine, but it's certain that it does add value!

Tall Stuff

Quilts and wallhangings should be hung. If your vehicle is pulled into the back of your space, parallel to the front, why not drape it with quilts, spreads, and table cloths? They'll catch the eyes of shoppers who then will enter your space to ask questions about them.

Fig. 2-2 Consider arrangements for your wares other than a line of tables in front.

A hanging wall cupboard should hang—to give the viewer a better idea of how it will look in the kitchen. People who love to decorate their homes like to visualize items in use. Height in a space can be used to great advantage in displaying your items without great expense. Take three one-by-twos and join them at one end with a piece of rope or wire. Spread the other ends and you have a tripod. String a line between two tripods and you have a serviceable line on which to hang linens.

Try a Crowd-Stopper

Earlier I stated that the key to making a flea market sale is getting the customer to make an offer. True enough, but first you've got to stop him and get him to look at something in your display. The heart and soul of stopping traffic is buying the right items in the first place. If P.T. Barnum were a flea marketer, he'd pick items as much to stop the crowd as for their markup. Try to think the same way.

Curiosities, that's the idea. It might be a weird object such as a coffin (empty, I hope), or a stuffed condor, or something that piques the curiosity with the promise of hidden riches. It's not a bad idea to make the customer

Fig. 2-3 Another arrangement that shows items to good advantage.

think you don't know much. By the time the customer finds out how smart you are you've already made a sale!

Bargain Boxes

Before my first day in the market, I went through my workshop with a fine-toothed comb. I even found a fine-toothed comb, an old, Nineteenth-Century graining comb used by a painter to simulate the grain of natural wood. In addition I found tons of nuts and bolts, small hand tools, coils of wire, hinges, odd bits of metal (cut-offs—the ones you can't throw out of your shop but never seem to find a use for), electrical junk, storm window hinges (for windows nobody's used in years), plumbing supplies and parts, and . . . well, you get the idea. Like that *Good Stuff* you've been putting into boxes under the work-bench during twenty years of householding and workshopping.

I divided these wonderful items into boxes, each of which contained items I thought were of similar value. I had a nickel box (most of which I gave to kids who stared at it longingly), dime, quarter, half-dollar, dollar, and two buck boxes—six in all. I used beer-case flats—the kind that hold twenty-four cans each and have sides about three-inches tall. I put a rude but visible price sign on each box.

It's impossible to know exactly how much in sales came from these boxes during my first day, but I know I sold almost half of the stuff that was displayed, or I should say piled, in them. People love to "root," as my auctioneer friends say. Rooters included not only carpenters, plumbers, and electricians, but kids and housewives too. Especially attractive to men were the odds and ends of fishing equipment from a half dozen tackle boxes. I even found a couple of old tackle boxes to sell pretty cheap. I was introduced to the fact that old fishing tackle is a hot item. More about that later.

I believe the gross sale from my bargain boxes came to more than $50. It was truly "found" money because a lot of it was from items I had literally paid nothing for, stuff I had bought as box lots from auctions and yard sales. It helped me buy more stuff to sell later, and of course, cleared out some space in my overcrowded workshop.

One benefit of the bargain box is that most items from it are paid for in exact change. So my pocket soon began to bulge with coins, something I had completely forgotten to take to the market. All I had to start off with was the small amount one normally carries in his pocket. Ten or twenty bucks worth of nickels, dimes and quarters is essential, so important it has a name—the "bank"—and no store should be without it. Except for those who bought from my bargain table, it seemed nobody had anything smaller than a twenty, and, without those dime and quarter sales from my beer boxes I would have had a tough time making change.

In addition to stimulating brisk sales, the bargains stopped people who then looked at other things in my space, so I concluded that without the junk boxes I would have missed larger sales of items that may have gone unnoticed.

The bargain boxes also provided a bit of fun, and I firmly believe that flea marketing is the kind of activity in which fun should be as important as making sales! I couldn't help wondering what a well-dressed lady was going to do with a single roller caster for a dresser. I just hope it was the right length. But, maybe a wobbly dresser is better than a three-footed one. A young couple, who confided they'd been buying and refinishing second hand furniture, virtually cleaned me out of drawer pulls and cabinet hinges. And that old-fashioned storm-window hardware sold to a gentleman who was delighted with it. I suppose he had wooden windows that needed it.

Return on Investment

To emphasize the importance of those bargain boxes, let's follow what happened in a chain of events they started. In the next week, I spent fifty dollars on a large wooden tool chest that, after a bit of cleaning, sold for $125. The proceeds from that were invested in several pieces of sterling: a dresser mirror, a brush, a calling card case, and a couple of coasters. That sold for over $200. In a period of three weeks a few pounds of "worthless" shop junk had been converted into a couple of hundred dollar bills plus remaining inventory worth $50 or more.

Compare that with investing $50 in a savings account. In a month I'd be lucky to end up with 51 cents in interest income in my bank account. Match that with $250 (a 500% return) through the flea market!

You can see that you can do exactly what I did. Enter the flea market business with stuff you already own and very quickly generate enough cash income to start buying additional inventory plus supplies you need to expand your new venture.

Supplies and Equipment

Let's look at the things that will make your life in the flea market easier and your presentation more professional. Most folks start selling as I did with no equipment other than a chair to sit on and boards stretched on saw horses. If you're not sure you're going to like the business, skip this section and take only a thermos of coffee. However if you think flea marketing is for you, why not make it easy on yourself the first day?

Use this as a checklist and get these items a week before your first market. That'll give you plenty of time to do your pricing, labeling, and packing before the big day.

Labels and Tags.   The type depends on the kind of items you intend to sell. Some pieces of furniture can be priced with a selfstick label, either a small or large one. But people are used to looking for hang tags on furniture, so they're probably best. If you have pieces that need description (date of manufacture, style, etc.) use large labels.

Small stickons are good for pricing items like glass, china, and tools. Get several sizes so you can choose the one that gives room for whatever you wish to write.

Jewelry tags with string loops for attachment are good for small items. Hand-assembled, they're more expensive than plain labels, but are worth the extra money. There are little dumbbell-shaped selfsticking labels that wrap around the clasp of a brooch or the leg of a toy soldier and self-stick. They're great for many other small items in addition to jewelry.

Cardboard Boxes.   You'll use a lot of boxes for carrying small items. Cut handholds in the sides to make them easy to carry. Banana or melon boxes with handholds already cut are the most useful and among the strongest you can find. They're almost as good as the boxes sold especially for transporting antiques and they're free at the supermarket. Try to get the manager to hold some for you. Liquor boxes are strong, and you've read how handy beer flats can be for display, carrying, and sorting. Small fragile things can be wrapped in tissue and packed in egg cartons.

Newspaper and Other Packing.   Wrap breakables for transport. Don't make an exception! You think you're going to drive very carefully, and you can't remember any holes or ruts in the road. Things will get broken anyway. Wrap everything in gobs of newspapers. Styrofoam packing peanuts aren't good. They blow around and make a mess. Special surgical pads, available from a hospital supply house are best.

Paper Bags. Not for packing, but for packaging. Once someone's bought something from you, pack the purchase in a sack or plastic bag. Many people won't ask for a bag, but it's professional to bag every purchase. Save all bags from purchases you make at stores. Or buy them from a wholesale paper house. They're not expensive. At first you might ask friends, relatives and neighbors to save bags for you. I find it useful to divide them into three piles—small, medium, and large—then pack them in three separate boxes by size. This makes it much easier to grab the right size when you want to pack a purchase.

Folding Tables. Few markets furnish tables, so count on taking your own. Aluminum picnic tables are light and easy to carry, but they won't stand up to flea market punishment. Eventually some three-hundred pounder will sit on your table, and that's when the light one ends in the dumpster! Folding banquet tables at a hundred dollars are the choice for long service and stability even though they're heavy to carry.

You can make a fair substitute by using a six or eight foot length of plywood that's 24- to 30-inches wide with 1- × 2-inch-lumber under the outer edges for apron support. Folding legs from a hardware store are easily bolted under the plywood top. These tables will be lighter than banquet tables, almost as sturdy, and the total cost for materials will be $40 to $50 per table.

Three or four card tables should get you started. They're a pretty cheap item at country auctions as are longer folding tables. Watch for them.

You can make temporary tables by suspending a sheet of plywood or a hollow door over saw horses. If you want elevation, cardboard boxes on top of a table will support boards that can be draped to form an attractive raised shelf for glassware, lamps, or books.

The main thing is to think through all the stuff you're going to sell and find the display devices you'll need to show it off to good advantage.

Chairs. Excitement won't keep you from getting tired a couple of times during the day. When things slow down as they do once in a while, you'll be happy to sit down and have a cup of coffee or a soft drink. Light folding chairs are easiest to pack and carry, and they'll do double duty later as seating for you at country auctions where chairs are not provided.

Coverings. Your ground level display will show off better if it's on a ground cover. It'll keep cleaner too. Tarpaulins, burlap, or bed sheets are fine. Hold down the corners with stones to keep them from blowing. The cleaner these cloths are the better. Avoid the ones with big grease spots.

Tape. Pressure-sensitive tape, masking tape, duct tape—you'll find dozens of uses for them.

Sun Shades. In summer, a large umbrella will be useful. Even better is a plastic tarp supported by metal poles.

Rain Cover. This is mainly to protect merchandise, not you. Take a roll of plastic sheeting. When it starts to rain, unroll it over your tables and cut off lengths to fit. Make special provisions for any items that will suffer from being wet such as electric and electronic equipment. Have a supply of plastic zip-lock bags into which you can quickly put these items in the event of a downpour.

Tool Kit. Handy items to have along are: a coil of wire, wire cutters, hammer and nails, pliers, screwdrivers, utility knife (drywall knife), nails.

Sign Material. , Take along sheets of cardboard, such as the old shirt-front cardboard, a pad of paper, pencils, magic markers, and selfstick tape.

Cleanup Materials. Best for cleaning hands is heavy duty hand cleaner from the hardware store. It contains lanolin, has a pleasant odor, and feels cool after a few hours in the hot sun. Paper towels and foil-wrapped moist towelettes are nice too.

Helpers. At some time during the day you'll want to walk around and see what other people are selling, and you'll have to leave to go to the restroom and get refreshments. If you can't get a volunteer for full-time service, at least make arrangements for a friend to spell you for a half hour both morning and afternoon. If this isn't possible, a neighboring dealer will usually watch the next stand while its owner goes for coffee, especially when the coffee-runner offers to buy.

Miscellaneous. You'll want sun glasses, a large clean towel if you tend to perspire a lot, and an ice chest with cokes, orange juice, or whatever you like to drink. Most markets have refreshment stands, but it's nice to be able to reach down for a cold one!

Your Bank and Making Change
Plan to take a minimum of $25 in coins plus small bills. Most people will try to give you correct change, but it's more professional not to ask them to do so. Have a good supply of quarters if you're selling less expensive items, plus bills in one, five, and ten dollar denominations. The 20s will mostly take care of themselves as the money rolls in during the day.

Count your bank, and *all* of the money you take to the market. Write down or remember how much you spend on refreshments or anything else. Subtract those purchases from what you end up with and that's your sales figure for the day. Now, isn't that a simple accounting system?

How to Set Up
Most spaces in outdoor flea markets are wide enough to allow you to park your car across the back line from left to right. You should have a clear area between the car and the front of the space about ten feet deep and twenty or so feet wide. That's close to two hundred square feet in which to make your

display. It seems like plenty of room for everything, but you'll sell better if you make every square foot pay its own way!

Start with your car that's parked across the back of the space. Put some stuff on the roof, and if you're driving a station wagon, consider parking it so the tailgate faces the aisle where people will be walking. Use the tailgate for display in addition to the roof.

Keep spare boxes, bags and other not-for-sale junk in the car. If you have too much stuff for a single space, rent two spaces. I know guys who rent four or five adjacent spaces at every market they attend. Of course they have lots of help to watch all that stuff, but the extra space pays off.

More Space = More Profit!

My first indoor space in a flea market was ten-feet across and only six feet from front to rear. There was room for one eight-foot table leaving a two-foot passage and a three-foot deep walkway behind the table. I made good use of the wall in back of the space by hanging things as high as I could on a sheet of plywood affixed to the wall. Then I made a second level on top of the front table with boards resting on cement blocks.

When a neighbor moved out of my area of the market I took over his ten-foot space, filled it with inventory and my sales more than doubled! Soon I was able to rent an *island space* (three sides), had to take on help to assist me, and once more increased sales by more than the amount of the additional rent.

If you go into a market with a friend, take two spaces side-by-side, set up as though it were one space. You can each take care of your own customers, but the *effect* of the larger space is to produce sales more than double what they would have been with a single space. Don't ask why, but it works—as long as you pack the space with good merchandise.

After a couple of outdoor markets, I found I could make an eye-catching display on top of my station wagon by anchoring the top edge of an antique quilt under the rockers of an old rocking chair on top of the car and letting the quilt cascade down the side facing the front of my stand.

Holding down the center of the quilt's top edge was a well-shined solid brass fireplace fender and an antique rocking horse. It was a beautiful display and really stopped people. I must add that, unfortunately, the quality of the quilt was not great so, although it stopped ladies who were interested in quilts, it only sold for $25. The New England fireplace fender seemed to astound Pennsylvania people. One man asked what it was. When I told him it was a fender he replied, "What kinda car?" The rocking horse sold quickly at a good price.

The main thing is to have an attractive display high at the rear of your stand that will cause people to walk into your "store." While they're there they'll see other things they might like.

Setting up tables across the front of their spaces is as far as most dealers go in providing display elevation. That's okay if your inventory is limited. But you'll make the whole area work for you if you use all of the 150- to 200-square feet it contains. The way to do that is to place tables along the sides of your space from front to rear. Then either leave the front open, or place only a small table there and leave an entry aisle on either side of it to indicate you'd like people to come inside. You can also place a table from side to side in the rear if you don't use your car as part of the display.

With such U-shaped space, people usually walk in and circle your stand, looking at many of your displayed items before exiting. Remember, you can't sell your merchandise unless somebody sees it and gets interested in it! You've got to encourage shoppers to see everything you have! Sometimes it takes hundreds of people going past before that one person sees something you always knew was a winner. Don't take a chance on having that prospect go by without seeing the item of her dreams!

There's an additional risk of shoplifting in the "open store," and your best answer to that threat is to have a helper. Usually only one of you is working with a prospect, and at that time the other is keeping an eye on the entire space.

Some items that are for sale, like tables, chairs, and baby carriages, can become display devices in themselves. Fill them with items that relate to their main purpose—a blanket slung over a doll bed, a parasol clamped to the baby buggy, or candlesticks on a table. Silverplate place settings can decorate a dining table. Always keep sterling in a glasstopped case under lock and key.

Under the Tables

Don't forget the space under the tables. That's the area that can attract your "rooters" like nothing else. I've noticed that some people seem to be convinced that the real bargains are always under tables, because they seem to spend most of their lives there, looking for good deals. I guess they believe the dealer carelessly throws things of unknown value under tables, so that's where they look.

Put good items under tables, along with junkier pieces. Let the customer have his little triumph! Back to our friend, the beer flat. Line them up under your tables and fill them with tools and kitchenware. Under-table boxes might be an exception to my injunction to price everything on labels or tags. If the stuff you put under the table consists of items priced at a dollar or less, just throw them in the flats and boxes and be prepared to sound off the price or mark the box "$1 any item in this box!"

Name Your Own Price

I've tried a lot of things over the years, and one of my screwiest ideas that sometimes works has been my "Name Your Own Price" box. Even when it didn't sell much it was lots of fun. I used it for items that had literally cost me nothing. It has held door knobs, old screws, door plates, worn out stuff of all kinds. "Nothin' into it, nothin' out of it" is OK, I reasoned.

I had come to the conclusion that invariably if a customer makes an offer and you accept it, she's bought it. I could not remember ever having someone walk away after I had said—"OK, I'll take your offer."

Well, the "Name Your Own Price" box proved the exception. A lady picked up a door knob and asked me what I wanted for it. Pointing to the sign behind the box I said, "See, Ma'am, it's a 'Name Your Own Price' box. You tell me what you'll pay for it."

"This isn't worth anything," she said.

"OK," I replied, holding out a bag for her to put it in, "You got it for nothing."

Confused, she carefully replaced the knob in its display and walked away, literally leaving me holding the bag.

Young Customers

I've enjoyed kids like the ten-year old who asked if he could go through my "Name Your Own Price" box. I said sure he could. He searched intently for several minutes, piled some items in a heap and said, "Give you ten cents for 'em."

I accepted his generous offer and watched him bound away toward a beaming parent who had obviously coached the young man in how to buy at the flea market. I think of him sometimes, imagining him striding through the market as one of the new generation of confirmed Flea Market Junkies!

At the end of your first day, you'll pack up, drive home and count your take. My prediction is that you'll be amazed.

One piece of advice—if you decide to keep doing the market, put the day's profit, plus your bank for next Sunday, away in a safe place—safe from being spent for anything other than merchandise for the market or maybe supplies for your new business. If you do that, you'll be on your way to becoming a successful antiques entrepreneur.

A Line of Credit

There's an exception to my statement that I built a flea market business without the investment of money or borrowing anything. Several years after starting, my bank extended a "line of credit" to help me expand inventory. This helped after I started my mail order business which required much larger purchases for inventory. My bank's branch manager asked if I thought my business could profit from expanded inventory! Wow! I was surprised at his volunteering this idea, but after remembering that bankers are in business to let other people use their money, I decided to take advantage of his offer.

One point to be made here is that I probably couldn't have borrowed from a bank, unsecured, without first proving I could run a small business on a cash basis. The "No cash" method made it easy to get started, but more important, it got me into the habit of operating within the supply of cash produced by sales and demonstrated to the banker that I could handle money, make it grow and produce a profit.

You may wish, after you've demonstrated you can make your business grow, to arrange for a line of credit; then use that money to make your business grow even faster.

You'll have to demonstrate you know how to handle money. The terrible truth about loans, unsecured or secured, is that they have to be paid back and cost money (interest) every day you hold the bank's capital. I wouldn't advise operating on borrowed capital—your bank's, your spouse's, or that of Aunt Suzy—until you've been in the business for a while, probably five years. By operating within current revenue, you'll have a glorious feeling of independence.

CHAPTER THREE

ollectibles and Antiques You Can Sell

Reading Guide. In this chapter you'll read about antiques and collectibles to consider buying and selling in your business. WARNING: Evaluations are based mostly on the author's experience in New England and Pennsylvania. Read this for ideas, but check carefully in your area before making substantial investments.

If you find products in this chapter you believe you would enjoy buying and selling write their names here, and use this as a reminder of items you wish to study later:

- _____
- _____
- _____
- _____
- _____

I've known few people who stick with a single line of antiques or collectibles. The temptation is too strong to try something "new." Interests change and one's tastes broaden. There are so many things one might get into that within a year after entering the field you'll probably broaden your line. This is exactly what happened to me.

Antiques people have a passion for *things*! I've thought many times that as antiques dealers we look at things with the same emotional reactions normal folks lavish on people or sometimes on animals. We meet a thing, we fall in love with it ("Courtship?"), we buy it ("Marry?"), live with it, perhaps develop a desire to collect other things like it ("Polygamy?"), and eventually, when our ardor cools, sell it ("Divorce?"). Thus goes the cycle of Life with Antiques!

Getting Started

Looking for antique furniture for my own home brought me into contact with such items as tools and primitives. Antique furniture dealers often have old tools hanging around, and they're most attractive. I thought of my first few wooden molding planes as decorative objects. But I've always been interested in cabinetmaking, so I used them and found my old tools to be more than just decorations—they proved helpful in repairing and restoring antique furniture.

Another staple of the antique furniture dealer is the "primitive"—usually items of hand-wrought iron, tin, or brass. Decorators are fond of using such objects. The list would include candlesticks, fire tongs, andirons, waffle irons, peels, grills, pots and kettles, hinges, locks and other door and window hardware. I collected these to hang around our kitchen fireplace and give atmosphere to our early Nineteenth-century Pennsylvania home.

And of course, there was the pure junk I've mentioned in earlier chapters—stuff bought, for the most part at flea markets and auctions in New England and Pennsylvania. Those were the things I took to my first flea market. Fortunately, Pennsylvania, in which we were living at the time, is a good source of material, so it was not too difficult to replace what I had sold in order to keep my new part-time business going.

The Candle Shop

Very early in my new career, I discovered that certain items go together. My wife loves brass candlesticks and has a nice collection of them, a collection, by the way, that has increased in both quantity and value.

The candles we used in our own home were the beautiful hand-dipped ones sold by the Williamsburg Soap and Candle Company in Williamsburg, Virginia. I got in touch with the company and arranged to buy them at wholesale in order to start a small candle display. It eventually grew to cover a ten-foot table, and was my steadiest seller of any one line of merchandise. It was also the only new item in my display.

Precious Metals

There's something about solid gold and sterling silver that's always intrigued me. I found I could buy beautiful things made of precious metals, especially sterling silver, very reasonably at local auctions, apparently because most people could not be sure whether an older item was plated or solid. I soon learned how to tell the difference and always bid on items made of precious metals.

I developed several buying principles. For example, I found I could pay $6.00 for a sterling teaspoon and always resell at a profit. For sets of six or more, I could charge a higher price per spoon. Through experience, I developed buying rules for knives, forks, hollow ware, and of course, complete sets. Within a year, I was selling complete sets of six or eight place settings for $1,000 to $2,000. I bought them for about half that. I practiced estimating weight (it's kind of inconvenient to haul jeweler's scales to a farm auction!), learned how to test both silver and gold for purity, and studied the popularity of various patterns.

I did well in precious metals. It's accurate to say I was self-taught, but my knowledge came from a combination of talking with other, more experienced, dealers and collectors and taking chances by buying things I would then put up for sale. I seldom lost on a short-term silver investment.

Pocket knives, marbles, prints, and advertising "ephemera" were of interest to me, so I studied and dealt in them. Such items led me to an interest in antique toys (defined as anything played with before 1940!).

On to the Big Parade

By the time I left the flea market to help start an antiques co-op (more about that later) my inventory of toys was in the hundreds. Having a military background, I was particularly attracted to antique military playthings, so it was inevitable that my toy interests would center on toy soldiers, cannons, and military vehicles. It was not too long before I had amassed an inventory of thousands of toy soldiers. I undertook a study of Britains (English soldiers) and the popular American dimestore soldiers of the 1930s, 1940s and 1950s.

Later when I took up auctioneering, my auction specialty became toys and dolls, and within another year I started a mail-order business selling toy soldiers to collectors all over the country. Some of these experiences will be discussed later in chapters on auctioneering and mail-order selling.

My point here is *no matter what you start selling in antiques, the field is wide open for your interests to develop and your knowledge to increase as long as you keep studying and learn everything there is to know about your specialties*. As you learn, you'll be exposed to the broad expanse of human history that underlies the objects you study. The bonus is, in addition to having all this fun, you can make money at it!

For the sake of completeness, I should mention that my inventories and interests also expanded to stereo views, photographic items, musical instruments, sheet music, coins and banks, and dozens of other categories. My prediction is that yours will do the same.

"I Don't Promise You A Rose Garden!"

One thing I must explain is that not every pathway led to success. I won a few and I lost a few. Winners more than made up for losers both in numbers and dollars. Diversifications that succeeded did so mostly because they were categories that were in good demand. Most losers were things I thought beautiful or interesting but which were not in demand in my area. I erred in trusting my own judgement to the exclusion of making observations about what was selling all around me!

An outstanding example of how far off personal tastes can be was my collection of glass boots. I had been collecting them for years and decided, long after I started in the flea market, to see whether they would sell. I found that I was the only boot collector in Pennsylvania!

The really successful category of antiques has a combination of attributes that includes elements of scarcity, age, workmanship, condition, and (that which is most difficult to describe) desirability.

But, Do They Want It?

What is desirability? Simply stated, it means that enough people want something to create a demand. Some very scarce old things, even when in good condition, are for some reason not desirable while a more readily available item may be avidly sought. Character collectibles provide a good example. Billions of Shirley Temple collectibles have been manufactured since Shirley was on the silver screen. They're highly collectible even though most are not scarce. If you came up with a Jane Withers mug it would be very scarce, but I would bet it wouldn't sell nearly as well as a Shirley item.

Laurel & Hardy sells. But if there's a Wheeler & Woolsey (Movie comedy team contemporary with Laurel & Hardy in the thirties) collectible around I'd let someone else purchase it. It would be scarce as hell, but nobody'd buy it! It's a good example of the kind of thing I've been stuck with. You can tell a customer that something is the rarest thing on earth, (and maybe it is) but if she hasn't *heard of it* she won't buy it.

A Lucky Strike Flat Fifties cigarette tin sells for more than a Zaphirio Tin that's ten times as scarce. People know Lucky Strike, they don't know Zaphirio.

Zez Confrey and Paul Whiteman are legendary jazz giants, but their records won't sell as well as those of Bing Crosby or Billie Holliday. Elgin sells watches. Coke sells trays. Stanley sells tools. People want to collect the *scarce* examples of collectibles with *familiar* names of persons, performers, celebrities, and companies. Swing with the winners. Otherwise you'll be stuck with a lot of losers.

On Top of the Market

Current experience is what keeps you on top of the market in choosing products to sell. At any given time you'll have a few dogs that used to be hot but that you can't give away now. Sometimes, after a period of dormancy, an item will come to life again, stimulated by an article in a leading antiques or home magazine, and take off. Then, just as quickly as it rose in sales, it may fall.

One summer Sunday I set up in an outdoor market next to a man who was selling mace (tear gas) packaged in a spray can to be used for self-protection. That was his only item, but he sold several hundred dollars worth. At day's end I asked him if I could buy some at a wholesale price. He told me he was the distributor and would give me a wholesale price if I bought 12 cans. They only cost three bucks a piece, so I didn't take a big risk. A year later I still had seven of them. For a long time my only customer was a man who came back for three successive weeks and bought a new can every time! I shuddered to think what he might be doing with them. There's still one in my car's glove compartment! Hold onto your tear gas guns! Some day the market will come alive!

One good thing about selling antiques is that, if anything just plain refuses to sell, it'll always look nice at home. Or, you can give it to Aunt Suzy for Christmas. Except for mace.

Selling on Consignment

If you don't want to invest in stuff you know nothing about, consider consignment selling. Consignment means the owner gives you custody of goods without money changing hands until sales are made. You're responsible for holding the consignment in good condition. If it's stolen or damaged, you're legally liable to the owner. However, if it sells you earn a commission smaller than the markup you'd earn if you'd bought the items outright.

If you *buy* an item and sell it for twice what you paid for it you've earned a margin of 50%. If you take the item on consignment your commission will be much less than 50%. The normal consignment percentage is from 20% to 30%. What you lose in markup you gain in taking less risk. With consignments you risk only your time.

I have accepted consignments, but I generally prefer purchasing outright. The main reason is that the margin is better. Another thing to consider is that items in a display booth suffer the effects of wear and tear. If they belong to me, I don't have to explain damage to anybody except the purchaser. I've taken consignments mostly when the item has a high value and is something I know little about. Thus I accepted $6,000 worth of period furniture from a retired dealer and did very well in selling it at a commission of 20%. It took several months to sell the fine pieces, and my consignor was very happy with the results. The experience took place in an antiques mall where there was only a slight risk of damage. The consignor and I discussed the value of each piece and agreed on an asking price and a rock-bottom price for each one. Most of them sold for a price in between.

Another offer of consignment was on a collection of fine English china. I knew very little about china, but I had time to make a bit of a study and so after learning something about the set I decided to buy the collection instead of accepting consignment. I paid $700 for it, thinking, after my research, that it would sell for close to the $2,000 price I hung on it. After holding it for a couple of months, I reduced the price to $1,500. Still no action, although a few people wanted to buy individual pieces.

I reduced the price to under a thousand and began to worry. It was displayed in a gorgeous pine china cabinet that was priced at $3,000 and about which I had also begun to worry! That was a very worrisome period!

A dealer from another city happened by and told me he had a client who loved that pattern. I worried more as I helped him remove each piece for inspection. He sat on the carpet in the floor of my booth and carefully ran his fingers around each rim, inspected the front and back of each piece for cracks, and finally offered me about $200 more than I had paid. I tried to get the price up a bit, but he assured me his customer knew his prices, and his offer was as much as he could possibly pay me and make a small markup for delivering the set to his client. Of course I agreed. On the following Sunday I sold the cabinet in which the set had been displayed!

Another consignment experience got me into selling art. I agreed with a friend who operates an art gallery and framing shop to try a few of his fine art prints on consignment, mostly as a favor to him. They sold and I've been in prints ever since. He sold me his discarded picture frames which could be perked up with a little cleaning and paint. I found I could make about 400% on used frames, and it turned out to be a good business for a year. Then frames stopped selling. I wasn't stuck with many, and I framed a lot of prints for my own home during this period. The net result of the entire frame experience was a good profit.

It's Up to You!

You can guess from all of this that most flea market and antique market success is the result of experimenting and that I'm not going to try to talk you into or out of any of the items I'll discuss below. I won't be able to make you an expert in any of these lines because only experience can do that for you. All I can do is give you the benefit of my observations on selling as a result of my experiences in the flea market, antiques mall, and auction room. The value and marketability of all of these things will vary from time to time and from place to place. This chapter can only be a very general guide on what to sell. You've got to take your own chances, make your own waves, and do your own learning! That's the fun of it!

Agricultural Items

This is a field in which the supply of objects must be short. Farms are failing all over the country, and as much as I hate to see it go, I'm afraid the good ol' farm auction, with the country auctioneer selling from the back of the honey wagon and from the front porch, are going the way of the dodo. Watch for them though in the papers. You may find one or two a year, depending upon where you live.

I hit the rural scene as an antiques dealer at the end of "the good ol' days." In Central Pennsylvania where we lived, I could attend two or three farm auctions a week and I bought a large supply of harnesses, sleigh bells, horse hames, corn huskers, Mason jars, hand tools, and beautiful handmade wooden objects. People loved to use them, and still do, to decorate their country homes. Dealers have cleaned out most of the single-family farms and the decorators have cleaned out the country antiques shops of most of these items.

The craze continues, hyped by magazines like *Country Living*, whose editors and writers try to make us think that American farm and small town families once lived among stacks of handpainted watermelon plaques and folk art alligators. Many antiques dealers have decided to join 'em rather than fight 'em, and have stocked up on newly made craft items that are poor replicas of anything that ever came from the country.

A good example, almost as prevalent in present-day decorator circles as

the ubiquitous watermelon slice, is the checkerboard. You can take a 12- ×
12-inch piece of weathered lumber, beat it up a bit, then paint a checkerboard
on it, scruff it some more, and get $35 for it. It ain't antique, but if that's how
you want to supplement the dwindling supply of rural items, go ahead. You'll
make money.

I had some cut-off ends of 100- to 150-year old boards that came from my
old house and wondered what to do with them. I made cutting boards and
sold them to a couple of arts and crafts retailers at $5 to $10 each. The best
sellers were in the shape of a heart or had a little heart as a handle. Worthless
wood into "folk art!" They sold quickly and dealers wanted more. After a dozen
or so I got tired of it and never did it again. Just didn't have the heart.

Animals

People who love animals collect things that relate to them. Always buy according to subject matter. Art objects that relate to poodles, boxers, Lhasa Apsos,
or any other dog that's a hot seller, will probably do well for you. Cat lovers
are legion. One problem—most collectors of things like cat stuff have just
about everything.

There are animal related objects, of course, other than art. For example,

Fig. 3-1 Originally made for use
as a lawn ornament, this
handsome deer provided a
ride to a young visitor to the
antiques market before it sold
to a decorator who bought it
for a client.

collars, licenses and toys in animal form, are good sellers. It hasn't been one of my specialties, so I can't give any red-hot examples.

Bears are a current fad. How long it will go on I don't know, but with old Teddies selling up in the thousands, and with special shows devoted to bears, I've got to believe it will last a long while. There's something so irresistable about the idea of a threadbare stuffed animal that some kid played with for three or four years, that it almost makes grown men cry! I'll cover the Teddy Bear later in this chapter.

Architectural Products

Restoration and preservation have become important movements in almost every community. Led by The National Trust, state and local governments have set up historic districts and worked to achieve placement of buildings and entire districts on the National Register of Historic Places. Even though the official designation is given to few places and buildings, individuals and families who own old houses have responded to the publicity attendant upon Historic Register programs and begun to restore and preserve their properties.

Until twenty years ago, the most popular feature in home magazines was on the theme of remodeling. The trendy writer of that day, assisted by an architect, would show how one could absolutely ruin a beautiful example of Victorian architecture by modernizing it! They knocked off third floors, installed floor-to-ceiling windows, and thoroughly bastardized beautiful original designs. All to the horror of preservationists whose voices in protest were not loud enough to be heard.

During the last two decades we've come to our senses, and everybody's interested in replacing rotten shutters, rusty Nineteenth-century hardware and deteriorated siding with authentic materials. Purists eschew the reproduction route and look for the real thing in materials for their restorations. If you can remove a load of old lumber that's been extracted from a building being demolished to make way for a shopping center, you'll probably find a willing buyer with little trouble.

Hinges, locks, plumbing fixtures, even clawfooted bathtubs, are good sellers. Marble-top sinks are much in demand. This is one area of antiques distribution where it pays to fix, polish, and restore. I've sold hundreds, maybe thousands of cabinet and house parts that I've polished with my trusty cloth wheel and jeweler's rouge. I've compared what they've sold for fixed up with the prices I got when I didn't restore them. I can say that your time spent in reworking such objects will be repaid at the rate of at least $20 an hour.

Once in a while you can hit a real bonanza. Consider that original 8-inch wrought H-L hinges can go for a $100 a pair, and a fancy door lock for upwards of $700! I haven't been lucky enough to enter that league very often (and it's just pure luck even if you know what you're looking for).

Don't forget fireplace nuts, prospects for fenders, kitchen implements, cranes and hanging kettles, clockwork spits, and skewers. Sometimes I wonder if anybody ever hung all that stuff around a fireplace. I don't think they did, but the things sell well now, so who cares!

One problem this area shares with furniture as an antique product line to go into is the space it requires—both vertical and horizontal—for display. If you go into it seriously, progressing from a few pieces of hardware to 20-foot lengths of antique lumber, you'll need a barn or warehouse. In the beginning, buy smaller hardware to give it a try.

Sources? Until you begin to look, you won't be aware of any of this material. You have to know where to look for it. Watch auction ads for lumber yards or cabinetmaker shops going out of business. Wrecking companies sell you their castoffs or even give them to you for the hauling. You need to learn how to recognize wood varieties and what's in demand in your area, as well as the items of hardware that were used in old buildings. Prospects are homeowners who are restoring, cabinetmakers, historical society members, and restaurant owners. Decorators are also prime buyers.

Art

This is a broad field covering the entire range of every artist whose work could conceivably be displayed in a flea market or antiques co-op. Much art is sold at auction, and most of the truly great art is sold by famous galleries and important auction houses. What I'll talk about here is art that is a practical item of inventory for a flea market or middle-class antiques co-op, definitely the lower end of the market.

We hear occasionally of a collector or dealer finding a famous work in a farm house or tenement, but believe me, the chance of that is so slim I'd forget about it. A more realistic opportunity comes when you buy an old book (not a particularly valuable one) that has color lithos in it, detach the pages with illustrations, frame them, and if they're attractive enough, sell them for $5 to $15 each as decorative items.

Some book people object to this, and I agree with them when it comes to destroying good books. I wandered into a rare book dealer's place in New York looking for a nautical print to frame. The dealer tore out three pages from an Eighteenth-Century "Cyclopaedia" and sold them to me for $15! I couldn't believe my luck! He had *destroyed* most of the value of a rare book.

The best kind of print to sell at a flea market is an inexpensive litho or old advertising piece, framed or unframed. Often the frame is more valuable than the paper it holds. Most people attending flea markets don't expect to see really good art, and most don't know how to judge it. They're interested either in buying something to hang on their wall or adding to a collection of objects that may or may not be art.

For example, there are collectors of Titanic memorabilia. There are books, paintings, prints, magazine stories, and other works to remind us of the sinking of the ill-fated nonsinkable ship. A print, nicely framed, of the Titanic will sell. One thing that should be said here and repeated later is that highly specific collectibles like Titanic memorabilia have a very *thin* market, which is to say very few people among thousands that pass your stand will be interested. However, what a thin market lacks in numbers it makes up in avidity. Collectors are *hungry* for items in their fields of interest.

Make friends of such customers. Get names and phone numbers. You don't know when you'll run across a new Titanic item, and when you do, why wait for 10,000 people to pass before you sell it? Buy it, go to your phone file, and call the lady who loves Titanic stuff.

There are similar collectors of President McKinley, Teddy Roosevelt, the Dionne Quints, and practically anybody who's been in the news for the last 200 years, including Red Ryder and Elvis. Know your collectors, cultivate them and buy for them!

In the beginning, you don't know who the specialized collectors of art are. You can make a good guess when you see a well-dressed executive-type running the stem of his pipe across his teeth as he looks longingly at your newest Wallace Nutting print. (Nutting was a furniture maker, antiques writer, and photographer of the early Twentieth-Century whose handcolored photographic prints are in demand only among specialized Wallace Nutting collectors and dealers who know that to have one is to have a sure sale to such a client.)

Your target should be as much to get a name and phone number as it is to make a sale! If the print is a Nutting your prospect doesn't have, you'll probably make the sale with little trouble. Tell him, before money changes hands, that you very often find Nutting prints and ask if he wants you to call him when you get the next one. He'll probably be glad to give you the information. Otherwise, you'll have to take a chance that he'll come back every week or two to see what you have that's new in his field.

You'll find people with primary collecting interests involving art only as it depicts something else that is their main passion. Examples are art objects that portray Indians, Civil War, World War I, Depression, Great Plains, or world fairs. Any time you can take a chance for a small amount of money, buy the art *for its unusual subject matter*, and put it on display. It's your bait to catch collectors of other things. Unless you know the art market very well, avoid buying the picture, print, painting, photograph, or sculpture, just because it's pretty. Buy for subject material.

There's a semifamous painting that's hung in the Louvre called "The Balloonist." I had a chance to buy what seemed to be a well-done copy at a country auction and counted it a bargain at $160. The damned thing was seven feet tall—too big to display well in my indoor stand at the antiques co-op. I consigned it to a friend who owned an art gallery. After he sold it, my check for the sale price, less commission was $160. As I say, win a few, lose a few— I'd love to know where the balloon is flying today!

Art Nouveau, Art Deco

Twentieth century furniture, jewelry, and decorative items have come into their own as collectibles. It's time to get into these fields, learn about them, and profit from them.

I sold a pair of bronze art deco elevator doors at auction for $700. The same doors were resold for over $2,000, just a few months later.

Several ladies I know have made a specialty of selling jewelry and clothing

Fig. 3-2 Art Deco and Art Nouveau are heavy sellers in some areas.

made in the early Twentieth-Century. Both are in great demand with young women.

At one of my Pennsylvania estate auctions, there was an ugly oak library table, about 30 × 48-inches, with a shelf underneath and a leather top that was held fast by brass tacks. I hate to tell these stories on myself, but a fellow can't be expected to know *everything*, now can he? Anyway, the table started off with bids in the $20 range, as is usual for fairly recent, undistinguished second hand furniture, and I was soon calling bids in the $200 to $300 range. I almost fell over! Obviously it was from the Stickley school, a type of furniture I personally never have cared for. Whether it was real Stickley I don't know. I haven't studied the genre. A dealer walked off with it for about $400, and Lord knows what it's sold for since.

As an auctioneer I try hard to know what everything I sell should bring, but I missed on that one! If you'd been there with the knowledge you're going to amass as a result of reading this book, you'd probably have bought a $2,000 table for less than $500.

Banks

Banks are divided into two types: mechanical and still. The former has a mechanism that causes the bank to do something (a horse to kick, a dentist to pull a tooth, etc.) when the coin is inserted. Still banks have no moving parts and are cheaper.

·   It's hard not to get interested in these beautiful examples of factory-made playthings. As sculpture, they caricature America's attitudes over the years toward animals, blacks, occupations, places, and institutions. Anyone with an interest in American social history is fascinated with banks. The scarce ones are valuable, especially if their condition is near perfect. Other points to look for: mechanism that works, lack of repairs and replacement parts.

One major drawback to dealing in banks: there are fakes, and most fakes are pretty good. I've made money on banks, but I've also fallen for reproductions. So, it's important to learn how to tell the original from the repro. There are price and identification guides on banks, and articles on them are constantly appearing in the antiques magazines. The most definitive and reliable writing on banks appears as a series of monthly articles in the magazine, *Antique Toy World*.

It pays to get the feel of old iron and the ability to recognize a repaint. It's impossible to do more here than advise you to consult the literature and develop a friendship with dealers and collectors who specialize in banks. They'll all be happy to share their knowledge with you in return for your keeping them in mind when you find something they're interested in. I worked very early at learning how to recognize old cast iron because of my interest in kitchen equipment, tools, and toys. That has helped me a great deal in the occasional dealings I've had in banks.

Bars and Bar Equipment

Novelty bar items continue to be good sellers for both antiques dealers and gift shops. One of the best bar items is the bar itself. I once used solid mahogany, raised-panel soda fountain furniture from a Nineteenth-century apothecary to build a home bar. I sunk twin stainless sinks into a laminated maple cutting surface under the front counter and lighted this work area with fluorescent tubes. On the corners were the old mahogany Corinthian columns. The bar turned out to be very usable and quite beautiful. It even had an antique brass rail (actually from an ocean liner!) for drinking friends to put their tired feet on.

I put a lot of labor into building my perfect home bar and it was absolutely gorgeous. A picture of me posing behind it appeared in the December, 1981 issue of *Early American Life* (I was the editor and publisher, so why not?), after which my wife and I began to feel that the bar made the library look too much like a bar room so we tore it out. The bar (in piles of mahogany, pine framing and maple, plus plumbing fixtures, and the brass rail), carefully disassembled, sold for over $1,000. The new owner put it together all over again, and he was delighted with it.

Architectural components auctions sell complete (large—like 40 feet) bars for prices between $10,000 and $50,000. So there's obviously money in bars. Combine the collection of old wood and architectural parts with a knowledge of how a bar should be designed (here's one field where doing the research is very relaxing!), and you have the beginning of a good business.

Baskets

Nothing's a more sure sale! Your only problem in buying baskets is terrific competition. There are so many female dealers and lady collectors of baskets that you'll never attend an auction where you'll be the only bidder or even close to it! It makes it hard to buy baskets at a decent price. At any auction at which there's a collection of baskets to be sold you'll find a dozen dealers hanging around until the baskets are sold, after which they leave. That's all they came for.

Basket ladies who haunt flea markets and garage sales arrive early to beat the competition. All you can do is keep your eyes open for basket buys and buy all you can at decent prices. Prices have been going up wildly of late. And you can just about forget ever finding the rare Nantucket Lightship basket or genuine Shaker basket. Whoa—why do I say that? The last thing I want to do is discourage you. Learn what these valuable designs look like and how to identify them. There are plenty of good books on the subject—the latest and best by Martha Wetherbee of New England. Buy the books, study, and keep your eyes open.

Resist the temptation to clutter your counter with broken, frazzled, and frayed baskets. They don't bring enough to be worth hauling. Go for the best ones. And study! Know what a Pennsylvania rye straw basket is, and learn the names for the various shapes and styles. The time spent will pay off.

Bells

Cow bells, ship's bells, sleigh bells (not too many good ones left), dinner bells, glass bells—all kinds of bells are good. Bells sell!

Black Memorabilia

Until the 1950s Black Americans were portrayed in images that range from unflattering to dehumanizing. Toys, books, games, dolls, posters, doorstops, signs, tins, and postcards are just a sampling of the forms used by a callous commercial world to take advantage of the prevailing bigotry of the period and turn it into profit.

The more scurrilous items command the highest prices. However, even gently humorous portrayals ("Gold Dust Twins" soap packages, for example) command a good dollar.

Some outstanding collectors are black people who see the objects as representative of an historical period that, although in a sense best forgotten, is interestingly preserved in these rather recent artifacts. There is a collector club, books on the subject, and museums. There is still, in my experience, a fairly good supply of Black items.

Blacksmith Items

There are a couple of possibilities here. First, look for products of the smith wherever you go, particularly in country outlets. You can occasionally luck into some nice material from the early twentieth century or even further back.

We've already touched upon values for architectural hardware. There are, in addition, kitchen items such as sugar nippers and ladles that command good prices. Hand-etched and inlaid spoons, ladles, and strainers can go into the hundreds of dollars at retail. Learn how to tell handforged antique ware from repros before you commit to large purchases. Repros abound.

However, don't turn up your nose too quickly at the better products of modern blacksmiths. There are a number of smiths working at forges today who are making objects in exactly the same way as their predecessors of two hundred years ago. Such a line could be a worthy addition to your antiques inventory.

If you handle new merchandise, you should clearly label each piece with the statement that it is a new, not antique, product. That's only fair to your buyer who will appreciate your honesty. Never try to foist off a new object as an old one. There's lots of repeat business in this kind of merchandise.

Blanket Chests

In addition to collectibles and antiques, people go to flea markets and antiques malls for objects they can *use*. If they also appreciate antiques, they're liable to pick your antique household item as their first choice. If they can't find it at the flea market, then they'll go to Sears or K-Mart.

The blanket chest is a good example. No doubt a new chest will be more serviceable than an old one. Hinges are a lot better on new ones. As a matter of fact, I've seen few antique blanket chests with good hinges. It's the nature of the beast that the hinges bend and wear out and the lid closes sloppily. However, many women who want a box to store blankets and linens in prefer an antique chest to a new one.

The blanket chest is more than a storage place. It's also a piece of furniture that can serve as a coffee or end table, and, if it's strong enough, as a piece of sitting furniture—a chair or love seat—depending upon its size.

The carpenter's tool chest is a good example of a utilitarian object that people buy both to use and admire. In recent years, they've been in more demand than chests originally built to hold blankets. One dealer I know turns over eight or ten tool chests a month. He buys one for $50, repairs and refinishes it, and resells it for $100 to $500.

Books, Magazines, Newspapers, Catalogs

The first part of this essay on books will be on what I call the second-hand book business. Skip to the last part if you're interested in books that are themselves antique.

My natural inclination as a new antiques dealer was to sell old books and magazines because my main business career for thirty years was in publishing.

I've edited and published both books and magazines. So you can see why, as a lover of the printed word, I would naturally want to deal in these objects.

It's possible that items you know a great deal about and love may not be great to sell in your market. Books—second hand books—sell in flea markets. But to make a big thing of them, you should have protected indoor space where you can arrange books on shelves—thousands and thousands of books on hundreds and hundreds of shelves!

You'll have to buy thousands of books in which you personally have no interest in order to give the buyer a chance to browse, because that's what book buyers like to do! And you're going to look for deals where you can buy a hundred books for fifty cents apiece hoping that one book in the lot will sell for a couple of bucks to make a profit. The other 99 books stay on the shelves so people can spend interminable hours looking through but not buying them. It's a little like the postcard business but requires more space.

Then, it seems to me, you're going to have to develop a way to rid your shelves of books that won't sell after you've had them fifty years or so. You must make room for the hundred and three boxes of books you bought at last week's auction.

If after my somewhat exaggerated description of the problems of the second-hand book business, you still want to go into it, my advice is that you go to auctions and yard sales. There you'll find your books at the right price, an average of a dime eacn. So much for second-hand books.

If you know antique book prices or can learn, it's a fine business. Sometimes recent books escalate rapidly in value when there's a scarcity due to a low print run and a continuing high demand. If you can pick up these books, somebody will come along who wants them. A good example within my own experience is a book called *The Golden Age of Toys*, a magnificently illustrated oversize book published in the 1960s. It has been out of print since then. I think the original price for this art book was around $40. I bought it "in remainder" (bargain table) at Scribner's in New York City for less than half that. Today it's worth $250.

Another good example are the original books about Teddy Bears and Teddy Roosevelt, written during the lifetime of President Roosevelt and detailing the travels of the bears themselves, during which they meet the President. They're worth over $50 per copy. Note that in both cases the subject matter, not just age, determines value.

My main advice on books: assign a value *only* when you have a market example of a price already received for that book. Don't assume it's valuable because it is old or scarce. The subject matter and whether or not it's a first edition are all-important.

If you happen to buy boxes of books cheap at an auction or tag sale, take out any valuable ones and price the rest cheap at 50 cents to a couple of bucks and try to turn them over fast. If you're seriously interested in selling books as a specialty, go for it and become your market's number one expert source. You'll probably do well.

Bottles

Genuine old bottles and flasks command good prices. However, common nineteenth and early twentieth century machine-made glass that's been dug out of privy pits and dumps over the last twenty years doesn't sell for much. Most of it is ugly and it will just clutter your display and crowd out more profitable items. Don't fall for old bottles unless you know them to be authentic and of superior quality.

The bloom is off 1910 bitters bottles and dirt-filled root beers, in my opinion. I had a friend who, in the '60s filled bushel baskets with old bottles every time he saw them for sale during his travels. They're worth exactly the same today as when he began to stuff his commodious barn with them. It'll take a great many barnsful to corner the crummy bottle market.

Brass

Lots of brass items at flea markets these days are cast in foundries in Formosa, Taiwan, or India—all new. I believe U.S. brass foundries were forced out of business because it cost so much to adhere to our higher air purity standards and our foundries could not compete with those of countries where there is little control over air pollution.

Fine brass castings are still being made. An excellent example is the line of Colonial Williamsburg products available at the restoration and by mail through their catalog as well as in selected retail outlets. It's beautiful stuff, but for the real antique buff it doesn't have the appeal of a true antique.

What makes the surface of any metal object have that soft, aged look is its collection of microscopic scratches that have come to its surface over the 50, 100, or 200 years since it was cast. Look at the surface of a 200-year-old candlestick under a strong magnifying glass and you'll see what I mean. Brass is a relatively soft metal and just handling it imparts tiny scratches to its surface. You'll see the tiny random marks, thousands to the inch, running every which way absolutely at random. This is the best way to determine if a piece is a true antique. It's not possible to duplicate accurately the aged patina with any technique I know of. There are supposed to be chemicals that will give a simulation of the aged look, but I haven't tried any, and I'm sure the magnifying glass will reveal the difference between a chemically aged piece and a true antique.

Neither dealers nor collectors are interested in newly made brass items. So, don't get stuck! It's easy to make a misjudgement.

There are lots of solid brass antique items that can still be bought reasonably. Tools, spring scales, and candlesticks are all examples. There are two good ways to learn the price range. One is to shop other antiques shops in your area. The other is to shop gift shops that sell *new* brass items of good quality. You'll be amazed at how close the new items are to antique ones in price. Even though they're collectible, antique value has not yet *quite* come to many of these kinds of items. Learn the local price range and buy right!

One warning: In polishing your old brass, *do not* use steel wool or sandpaper. A soft cotton cloth with polish or jeweler's rouge on a cotton wheel chucked to your electric motor or drill press is what you should use.

Boxes

This may seem to be unnecessary or over-specialized, but I've sold so many little boxes that I've come to think of them as a collectible. Time and again I've had proof of the fact that ladies want boxes for their treasures, men want boxes for tools, and kids need them for toys even if they seldom seem to put them away! If one collects jewelry, coins, or stamps, it's nice to have a box suited to the dignity of the collection.

Stationery boxes and lap desks are good examples. I've never seen anyone using a lap desk to write on, but I've been told they were carried in carriages so the traveler could write letters home at day's end (probably not during the bouncing of the horsedrawn carriage). They look pretty in the living room or bedroom and ladies like to put jewelry in them if they don't use them for stationery.

Grocery boxes with colorful lithographed labels go well in a country kitchen, or stacked as bookcases. It would be well to display such items in your selling space as if they're in use. Stack several and fill them with books or kitchen utensils. Your customers will get good ideas from that kind of display.

I've refinished old solid mahogany or walnut flatware boxes, relined them with green or red felt, and sold them for a 100% to 400% markup over orignal cost.

Type drawers make excellent wallhanging display racks for collections of miniatures. The authentic nineteenth-century ones have virtually disappeared, so you might be limited to those you can buy through the antiques magazines. Their sellers try to make you think they're genuine, but at the prices at which they're advertised I don't see how they can be. Anyway, it's an example of a new item that will sell well with your antiques.

A box's value increases with the right kind of corners. This also applies to corners of furniture drawers and other objects made in the form of boxes. There are four kinds of corner joints: butted, grooved, box-jointed, and dovetail-jointed, in order of easy to difficult to make and weakest to strongest. The simple butted joint is easy to make and the weakest. The dovetail is both difficult to make and strongest. The price for a box or other case-like object varies according to the type of its joints. You'll pay top price for dovetailed objects, but they'll sell at a higher price and much faster than if their joints are simpler.

Any wood can be made into a salable box. Lately, people have come to love the soft, warm look of old pine although it's a soft wood, scratches easily, and is not a superior cabinet wood. Walnut, cherry, and mahogany are the strongest and best woods for boxes as they are for furniture. Lots of boxes have been made of oak which is a favorite wood of some people. Learn your woods and their relative values.

One final idea on boxes: Any kind of slant-lid shop desk (a large box with no legs, meant to sit on a table), of pine or oak seems to be a good seller.

Women like to put them in living rooms on top of tables and in dining rooms where they might use them as a sterling chest.

If you can find a box for a reasonable price, buy it, refinish it, and add it to inventory. It'll soon sell.

Buttons

There's a highly developed collecting hobby surrounding antique buttons. Affi-cianados belong to local chapters called button clubs that are affiliated with The National Button Society. A favorite activity of collectors (mostly women) is to mount collections of buttons on glass-covered trays that hang on the wall. They enter trays in competitions sponsored by local clubs and the national organization. Rare buttons of exotic materials and artistic design are the most sought after.

Chances are you won't find many collectible buttons in the button box you buy at a country auction for a dollar. But it's always possible that you might find a good button or two, perhaps old military or Scout insignia. When I buy such a box at an auction or garage sale, I go to a friend who's a button collector and can advise me on the probable value of what I've bought. Of course, if there's anything really good, she wants to buy it if she doesn't already have it. Prices range from $1.00 to a $100 or more for historical buttons.

Candles

Early American rooms with authentic furniture (either antique or repro) and furnishings, demand candlelight. One good friend of mine lights her home exclusively with candles. Her husband once threatened to get a seeing-eye dog, claiming he couldn't find his way around the house at night. He was allowed to place *one* electric lamp in his den for serious reading. That's extreme, but it's true that candle light goes well with antiques. There's no such thing as antique candles. The best you can do is to buy hand-dipped tapers, available from such suppliers as Colonial Candles of Cape Cod and Williamsburg Soap and Candle Company. They sell tapers at wholesale prices with discounts that escalate with the size of your purchase.

It wasn't long after I opened my indoor flea market stand that I bought a modest supply of candles from Williamsburg Soap and Candle Company. I started with several of the more subdued, "colonial" colors. They sold pretty well, and I discovered an interesting thing—as I increased the size of my display and the number of boxes of candles (12 to the box) on display, I not only sold more in units (boxes) but also more per square foot of space devoted to the display.

Thus I learned through experience that displaying ten of something sells more than ten times the number you'd sell if you only displayed one and kept replacing it instantly as it was sold. That explains in turn why supermarkets pile up a whole bunch of cans of grapefruit juice in a giant stack! The display of 1,000 will sell more than ten times the number of cans they'd sell if they displayed 100 cans.

Don't ask me why bulk displays work. They just do. Take my word for it, and the word of every mass merchandiser. Of course, I'll admit it's kind of hard to make a mass display out of antiques! But you can apply this principle when you sell nonantique items. The other general rule I learned is that a "department" will help related things sell better. Keep your eyes open, if you put in candles, for such items as candle molds, candlesticks and candle-making supplies. They'll sell well in your "candle department."

To price your candles, start by doubling the price you pay at wholesale. Then look at three different retail displays of candles in your area. One should be a gift shop, one a department store, and one can be an arts and crafts shop. Write down the price per dozen and per candle by each of the sizes (six-, eight-, ten-, and twelve-inch lengths are the most popular) you find in each store, then compare these prices with those you calculated by doubling your wholesale cost. After you've added a per-candle cost for freight, you can adjust your price schedule to give you whatever competitive position you think you need to get the candle crowd coming to you for their future needs.

You'll be able to sell at 20% less than other outlets and have a markup of close to 100%, giving you a huge competitive advantage. I found it important to use a classy sign giving the source, method of manufacture, and discount. It reads, "Genuine Williamsburg Candles—Hand dipped—20% OFF!" That's merchandising!

The competitive *disadvantage* you have is that giftware outlets are classier than flea markets. Some people may find it hard to believe you're selling quality candles and not seconds. That's why it's important to have a good sign and to keep your display clean and well-arranged, a cut above the usual image of the flea market.

Candy Containers
The first figural candy container was made in 1876. They've been popular ever since, first as promotional product packaging, then as toys after the candy was gone, and finally, in recent years, as highly desired collectibles. Their retail value as collectibles is from $10 to $300 with most in the $25 to $100 range. Beware of reproductions and try to buy complete containers with closures. You'll have less trouble selling them than finding them to buy!

Canes
People will buy walking sticks, either to use or to display in their cane and umbrella stand inside the front door. Look for hardwood canes with brass, gold, or ivory trim.

Carnival Glass
Carnival is an example of a fairly recent product (1905–1930) that's become an instant antique. The rare types and colors are priced in the thousands of dollars. Use a price guide and beware of reproductions.

Fig. 3-3 This display case in a Pennsylvania antiques mall contains over 40 early glass and tin candy containers.

Carvings

Handcarved or whittled items enjoy a good response. This is separate from the market for true artistic sculpture and could well be included in arts and crafts. Occasionally a good folk carving will sell in the hundreds of dollars range.

The best examples of outrageous value are the works of an itinerant Pennsylvania whittler, Wilhelm Schimmel, of Carlisle, Pennsylvania. Some of his incredibly ugly eagles and turkeys, which he traded for meals or a night in a barn, have sold for $20,000 to $30,000. A disciple named Mount carved similar monstrosities worth a quarter of the amount paid today for a Schimmel. Such figures are not difficult to fake, and one piece in a museum is thought by some to be a forgery.

In my own collection of miscellany is a pair of handcarved wooden pliers in perfect full-size replica. There doesn't seem to be any way the sculpture could have been carved from one piece of wood and have both halves joined as they are. They work perfectly, but, although they are carved of one piece of wood, there is no obvious way the two handles can be separated. The two halves are fully articulated and work exactly as a pair of pliers should! It's an amazing piece. What's it worth? I haven't the slightest idea. And that's the problem with an unique piece. It's difficult to predict market value.

Chairs

You don't need to know much about chairs to make money buying and selling them. Experience will soon tell you what will sell and what won't. Most sell—it's just a matter of price. Bums (Country Windsors) go from $20 to $40. Fine Chippendales can sell for thousands.

Almost every old chair will have loose parts. Hardware stores and catalogs sell materials for tightening them. You can install new parts, refinish, and resell them quickly. Buy sets of four or six. That's what most people look for.

China and Glass

China and glass comprise the mainstay of half the antiques dealers I know. I'm always disappointed when, driving on a country road, I turn where the sign says "Antiques," only to find the whole store consists of piles of glass and china, along with clever signs that say you'll have to buy it if you break it. Most dealers like glass and china more than I do, which is fortunate for collectors of glass and china. These items are not my bag. I don't care if I never see another piece of glass, except maybe to hold my beer after a long day in the market.

The field is immense in products, makers, blowers, patterns, books, price guides, dealers, and collectors. If you're not into these items as a fairly advanced collector, I suggest you stay away until you can do a lot of research and perhaps befriend a collector or dealer who can help. Or, take a short course, if one is available in your area. They often are.

Glass collectors will find what they search for no matter how you display your glass. You won't have to take lessons in display. Just put 'em out on the table and they'll find 'em!

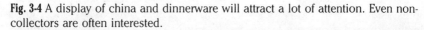

Fig. 3-4 A display of china and dinnerware will attract a lot of attention. Even non-collectors are often interested.

My glass friends advise me on pricing the glass and china I buy by accident. So through the years I've learned a little about it in spite of myself. In return for their help I help them with tools and toys about which I know something. Very often I'll buy their toys and they'll buy my glass—or we work out a trade.

Christmas Items

In my first book about antiques, I wrote that you shouldn't expect to sell Christmas-related items in months other than November and December. This seemingly logical advice was from my limited experience in an indoor flea market. Since then I have had more experience with auctions of Christmas items and in an antiques mart where they sold well the year round. My revised opinion is that the seasonal problem hardly exists. There are Christmas shops in Myrtle Beach, North Carolina, and Rockport, Massachusetts that do enormous business in summer!

Huge increases have taken place in the prices of Christmas collectibles. Any kind of Santa or Kris Kringle (better still, Der Belschnickel—he's the guy with the bundle of sticks in his pack!) sells well.

In my toy soldier business, I found that Santas made by the old toy soldier companies are much in demand. I sold one Barclay sitting Santa (with pack at his *side*) for $200. This is a little 2-inch-high fellow made to sit on a sleigh.

If you can develop sources of supply, you can specialize in Christmas collectibles. It's a perfect companion line for toys, dolls, and circus figures. Believe me, Christmas for you will be all year round!

Civil War Collectibles

Hundreds of thousands of Americans and people in foreign lands are conscientious students of our nation's Civil War. There are a number of collecting hobbies related to this very deep interest. Weapons obviously form a core collecting interest. Common sabers today are $200 to $300 each. Rare carbines go to five or six times that in excellent condition. Autographed photographs and stereo views are sought after.

Signed letters—and they don't have to be signed by Lincoln—are valuable, as are insignia, medical equipment, and books that pertain to the period. The value of magazines such as *Leslie's Illustrated Weekly* (the "news weekly" of that day) has been rising.

Clocks and Watches

What a field! Of all areas of antique interest, clocks may be the most historically important and interesting. Beginning with the clock-makers of New England, clock-making soon was pursued in New York, Pennsylvania and New Jersey, then by people in all sections of the country. One could make a life's career out of any one of several parts of the clock and watch fancy—horology as it's correctly known. Just to look at a fine tall case clock ("Grandfather's clock" as some say) or an Eli Terry or a twentieth-century Stennis is to view both a mechanical marvel and a work of art. Prices have been escalating, and many companies manufacture and import time pieces that imitate the products of the nineteenth century and earlier masters.

There are many sources of clock and watch information. The National Watch and Clock Collector's Association in Columbia, Pennsylvania publishes a fine monthly magazine plus a newsletter that specializes in clocks, clock parts, and clock literature for sale. There are schools of clock-making, and no end of professionals specializing in clock and watch repair. What I'm saying is there's an opportunity for anyone who has enthusiasm and patience to study and become an expert. The study will produce great rewards. I've found that trading in clocks can be quite profitable, and they add interest to my antiques display. But it's hard to make a killing because of severe competition on the buying end.

A young friend of mine in the indoor flea market assembled clocks that he bought as kits through mail order, then sold them in the market. He claimed he got a pretty good return on his investment. One day I displayed a nineteenth-century Connecticut ogee clock. It was in rough condition and I hadn't paid much for it, so the price was only $100. My friend was shocked that "that old mess" could command such a price when people only had to walk across the aisle and buy perfectly good *new* clocks from him!

He was even more amazed when I sold not only that one, but a second one, a little cottage clock for $75. A few weeks later he bought his first antique clock, and within a year he quit the new clock business and completely devoted

Fig. 3-5 A display of clocks will attract buyers. They are a popular item because they are both useful and decorative.

his time to the antique clock market. He began to buy old clocks, do repair work on the cases himself, and take them to an expert repair man for work on the mechanisms. His business is far ahead of where it was with new clocks, and he has much more fun at it.

Even if you don't specialize in old clocks, one or two in your display will enliven it and stop traffic. Everybody loves to look at clocks!

Clothing

The practical approach to selling used clothing is to deal in items of feminine apparel from the 20s and 30s. It's a specialty that demands careful and artistic display in a more or less permanent location where afficianados know they can go when the spirit moves them. It doesn't seem to work as well for transient dealers who set up in a different market each Sunday.

Women usually buy vintage clothing to wear, not just collect. They may wear an item as is (after a cleaning) or combine parts of it with other pieces or garments as a costume. There are ladies whose formal attire consists 100% of antique clothing or items made from parts of such garments.

Men's antique items, except for accessories, are not in as great demand. Stick-pins, cuff links and even formal shirt studs will sell but not at big prices.

A good companion to a twentieth century clothing line is jewelry from the same period plus small antiques that reflect the same design concepts, i.e. nouveau and deco. Dress stands, display dummies, hand mirrors, boudoir boxes, deco or nouveau furniture and dresser sets all go with the clothing.

Women who dress in vintage clothing are obviously your best prospects for these other items and can be developed into regular clientele. In addition to buying for themselves, they'll buy gifts for their male friends or relatives.

The number one markets for antique clothing and related items have been metropolitan areas and suburbs. Los Angeles, New York City and Boston are first class markets.

A related market exists for military clothing. It's been fashionable for young people of both sexes to dress in surplus, discarded, or antique uniforms. Add canteens and disarmed hand grenades, bullet belts, and helmets, and you have a military specialty, one that used to be called, "War Surplus," but which now mostly sells to those who march for peace.

Coins

The philatelic hobby (coins) is probably second only to the numismatic fancy (stamps). Many of us began in our youths to save old or interesting coins from change, and like removing stamps from envelopes or amassing vast numbers of match books, the activity is one that often continues into adulthood.

There's a fixed supply of each coin minted. Rarity is the main determinant of value and, after that, condition is all important. A mint-grade coin can be worth a hundred times what a fair specimen is worth.

Most true collectors are interested only in coins that are in mint condition or close to it. Flea market commerce in coins is in the hands of specialists, usually one or two per market, who seem to monopolize the local trade. Other dealers occasionally sell "junk silver"—"solid silver" coins in denominations of 10 cents to $1.00 made prior to 1966.

Coins aren't silver any more except for an occasional commemorative. The value of old "junk silver" coins depends on the spot (market) price of silver and the amount of silver in each coin. The unit of exchange that's quoted daily in the *Wall Street Journal* is the $1,000 "bag," and that means a quantity of any combination of dimes, quarters, and halves made before 1966 whose "face" value adds up to $1,000.

Unless you're a long-time collector this is a field to avoid until you give it a lot of study.

Coca-Cola Items

This is the largest of the collecting hobbies that have to do with commercially produced beverages. It's infested with reproductions. Items range in price from $1.00 to $1,000, with such specialties as advertisements, ashtrays, banks, radios, bookends, bottles, fans, and trays.

A collecting hobby as well as a fine business can be built if one studies, buys, and sells the promotional items of bottlers including Coke, Nehi, Dr. Pepper, Moxie and others.

Comic Books

What was written earlier about books applies to some extent to comics, but modern comic books have a mystique all their own. They're nostalgia to those who loved them as young people. Comic book collectors come in all shapes, sizes, and ages. The market is supported by specialized dealers and auctioneers.

If you're a collector of comic books you already have a pretty good idea of prices and are familiar with the price guides. If not, and if you happen to buy a load of comic books, you'd better get a price guide pronto, plus a friend who can advise you. Don't offer them until you've done your research.

Copper

Like brass and tin, copper is collected although usually in different forms than the other two. One good example in recent years has been solid copper, tin-lined cooking vessels. At one time every good restaurant, hotel, and ocean going ship had its collection of copper cookware.

Ships put into the port of New York and chefs took their pots and pans to the International Retinning Company on the west side. Until recently this company continued to serve owners by retinning pots and pans, but I'm told they're no longer in business. It's unsafe to cook in nontinned pots, so buyers of copper cooking vessels simply display them on kitchen shelves or hang them from pot racks as decorative items. Do not cook in solid copper without the tin lining. Acids in foods react with the copper to produce poisonous chemicals.

Retail prices run from $60 to $200 for a single pot. American pieces are most desired in this country and the maker's mark enhances value. Sometimes the initials or symbol of an estate in New England or New York will be found, and this increases the value.

"Country" Items

There's been a craze for a couple of decades called American Country. It started off like a cyclone at about the time The Waltons became popular, was accompanied by the increasing popularity of country music, then was abetted by promoters of newsstand magazines that specialize in what their editors call folk art and country decorating.

Anything, old or new, that's reflective of a romantic vision of earlier American rural life seems to be called folk art. It plucks a string in the hearts of folks who decorate their homes in simple style but who haven't the slightest idea what the American countryside was or is like. They've been talked into buying phony country pieces to go with their folk art by editors of the home magazines, who may or may not ever have seen authentic country design or real folk art. Their magazines' circulations have increased enormously with the trend.

Lots of wood and tin are being formed, some by hand, some by machine, into products that any self-respecting farm family would have rejected and any country store proprietor would have laughed at. Flour bins, ludicrous lamps, and miles of calico are ringing up huge sales, and apparently people love it. Books and magazines are devoted to it. It's practically all new material. Antique objects that truly can be called folk art are enormously valuable, most of them in museums.

If you want to join in the perpetration of nouveau American Country into the American home, get in touch with people who can supply you with ersatz antiques. For a discussion of real folk art, see Folk Art, later in this chapter.

Cowboy Heroes

Collectible products that were manufactured to exploit the popularity of Western movie heroes have been steady sellers. Best bets are: Gene Autry (e.g., one toy holster and belt: $80), Hopalong Cassidy (black hat: $150), Lone Ranger (Plastic radio: $400), Tom Mix (Blow gun kit: $200), Roy Rogers (Advertising sign with flashlight: $85), Cisco Kid, Davy Crockett, Red Ryder, Wyatt Earp, and any Hartland plastic figures. Marx cowboy plastic play sets command prices in the hundreds of dollars.

Cracker Jack

With some preplastic Cracker Jack prizes being sold at $5 to $50 each, Cracker Jack items are a number one collectible in the smalls category. A 1939 box with Jack and his dog, Bingo, is worth around $50 in excellent condition. More than 10,000 different examples of prizes were produced, and billions of boxes have been sold. Production today is around 400,000,000 a year.

Decoys and Carved Shore Birds

Working birds are true folk art. I exclude new birds that have been made (some machine carved) to capitalize on the interest of the antique and art worlds in the real thing. Stay away from the ones that are produced just for decoration. Go for the old, working birds. The really expensive ones are by known carvers who have come to have reputations among collectors.

Depression Glass

I don't much care for cheap glass, most of which was manufactured to be sold for next to nothing or to be given away during the great Depression of the thirties. Some of it was given as a premium with a 25-cent movie ticket. More of it was sold in five and dime stores for upwards of ten cents each. Now it's collected with some pieces going for a hundred dollars or more.

Disneyana

Mickey and his friends are known throughout the world, and products based on their images command good money. "Cels" (the original animated celluloid art from actual films) sell up to $5,000 each, but it's easy to enter the game with a five dollar purchase. Join the national collectors' club and get some books on the subject. Almost every broadly based collectibles price guide will give you ideas on current prices of some items.

Dolls

Because of my interest in toys and toy soldiers, I became exposed to dolls at auctions and in shops, and couldn't help noticing the fervent collector interest in them. After I became an auctioneer, I was fortunate to have toy auctions in which there were a few dolls. Then I conducted a couple of specialized doll auctions. I can truthfully say that these auctions were among the most pleasurable I have ever done. The doll collectors and dealers I have met are fine people and certainly devoted to their hobby.

If you have any bent toward the doll field, by all means get into it. You'll never regret it.

Doorstops

Cast-iron doorstops, mostly produced in the nineteenth- and early twentieth-centuries, are avidly collected. They're generally 6- to 12-inches in height and were originally painted in bright colors with a hard enamel finish. Girls, boys, animals, fish, houses, characters, and flowers are typical subjects. Present retail prices run from $45 to $400, with some even higher. Beware of reproductions since many are being cast now, some from the old original molds.

Ephemera

These are objects manufactured of flimsy materials and meant to be discarded after brief use. Ephemera includes posters, packages, trade cards, cigar bands,

Fig. 3-6 A display of antique dolls that's sure to catch the eye of every little (and big) girl who passes by.

punch boards, anything of paper, tissue, or plastic, often intended to wrap, advertise or accompany another product. There is a national association of collectors and there are many specialized dealers.

Fabrics

This can be a darned good specialty. It wasn't too many years ago that a box of fine linens would sell at a country auction for a dollar. No more! Auctioneers have learned to separate the better pieces and sell them one by one. A baby's dress can bring $50, and a stack of linen towels might hit $25 or $30.

Fabrics has become a fine specialty for an indoor stand in an antiques co-op. Auctions provide your best buying source. Sometimes you can even find goods in yard sales. This is another category on which my opinion has become much more bullish since my last book as I've seen prices escalate.

Farm Toys

This category covers the beautiful scale machinery models distributed by tractor manufacturers to publicize their lines, as well as tinplate toys by such producers as Marx and diecast models by Lesney and others. There has been an enormous surge of interest in value in all farm toys but especially in the promotional toys sold by farm machinery manufacturers. These are highly detailed scale models of tractors, binders, plows, and wagons. The leading manufacturer was Ertl. In my recent experience these finely made toys sell from $50 to $200, and I imagine some have gone even higher.

Firehouse Collectibles
Alarms, axes, bells, belts and buckles, helmets, lanterns, and trumpets are all collected plus badges and medals that were given out at conventions and parades. There is a limited number of collectors but the ones who are looking for this material are very anxious to buy.

Fireplace Equipment
I happen to love fireplaces, so I thought this would be a red hot "used" item based on the fact that I've bought a lot of stuff for my own fireplaces. Just shows how your own taste should not dictate a business decision. After purchasing fireplace stuff at auction and then having it hang around for months, I concluded that very few people love their fireplaces as I do! This is not an exciting market. A modern fireplace set in pristine condition with roller screen, andirons and three implements in a stand (originally sold new in a fireplace shop for $40) will sell at the flea market for $5.00—if you're lucky! Antique cranes and pots are a different story. See under *Blacksmith Items*.

Fishing Tackle
Having been a fishing nut all my life, I took naturally to collecting fishing equipment. In fact, I was collecting it (not for resale—just to have it) long before it became a red hot collectible. There are areas of the country, like Northern Indiana, where reels and wooden bass plugs were made, where every Saturday and Sunday collectors scour antique shops and markets looking for old plugs.

I read recently of a single bass plug that sold for several thousand dollars! There are split bamboo fly rods by such masters as Hardy, and Thomas and Thomas that go for similar prices. Those are the two big items: plugs and bamboo fly rods. Colorful bobbers, tackle boxes, and creels are sought but the prices are not nearly as high.

Look particularly for brass reels, "Kentucky" reels made by Meek and Milum, and early products of still existing companies like Shakespeare, Winchester, and Pflueger—they're the winners. I see lots of cheap Japanese bamboo fly rods from the 1960s and '70s being offered at flea markets for $50 and up. I don't think they sell. They shouldn't at those prices. Their owners confuse them with the good ones made in the U.S.A.

Folk Art
The word, "folk," according to traditional definition, is the majority of a people which delineates group character and tends to preserve the form of its civilization in custom, art, craft, legend, and tradition for its own use and pleasure. "Folk art" is the art and craft production of such a majority in objects for

decoration or for use by the folk. These objects have come to have considerable value as collectibles.

Folk art is not created to be sold, not made to be marketed, but is produced in forms that evolved through the history of the folk for the cultural use of the folk. Most of it is in museums and in the hands of collectors who discovered it early in this century. Even at huge prices it is hard to find.

By now you know my opinion of modern mass produced folk art, made today to mimic genuine folk art. It can be quite decorative, but I doubt there's much lasting merit in any of it. Now, in the real world of marketing, phony folk art sells, and one can make a business of it in a flea market. You may even like it yourself. Just because I do not care for it is no reason for you to avoid it.

Frames (Picture)

My friend who owns an art gallery had a stack of old frames that had been taken off pictures brought to his shop for reframing. I think he gave me my first batch, then I paid him something like $10 per stack (maybe 50 cents per frame) after that. It was well worth it to him to get rid of the old junk.

I took the frames to my shop, tightened them, stripped them of their paint or varnish and refinished the surface by sanding and either varnishing, oiling, or painting them.

Frames generally sell better with something in them, so I searched magazines for printed art with which to fill the frames. Large, fancy ones I left blank. Small, simple ones brought from $2.00 to $5.00 each and larger ones yielded prices of $4.00 to $8.00. Huge gold ones with ornate decorations (which I soon learned to repair with modeling paste and gold paint), sold for upwards of $50.00.

Set up a wall of chicken wire in your space and hang frames and framed pictures on it. Your art department should bring in a steady profit.

Furniture

It doesn't seem respectful to devote a few paragraphs to a subject as important as antique furniture. But there are lots of good books, any one of which will give you a hundred times the information in this limited space. They'll help you learn to identify periods, woods, and styles. From the many price guides that are available you'll get some idea of what various kinds of furniture are worth.

In the flea market you'll sell pre-owned furniture such as tables and chairs as well as chests of drawers and bookcases, partly because they're old and partly because they're serviceable furniture the buyer intends to use at home. People tell you they're looking for "something old," but that's because they yearn for antiques and can really only afford *used furniture*.

It's rare that a collector will find a fine antique piece in the flea market, but it's a common occurrence for young people trying to outfit their first home to find furniture with which to start housekeeping. They're your customers, and you should buy for them with true antiques as a secondary quest.

If you go on to display in an antiques co-op or mall, you can get into better examples of period furniture, the kind sought by antiques collectors.

Most dealers in antique furniture have gone through the progression from used to antique. I bought a lot of used chairs and tables for $3.00 each in the beginning of my antiques career. My last buys carried price tags of over $3,000. You learn as you go up the scale about styles, construction, finishes, woods, periods, and value. Once you're in the groove in correctly estimating value, you'll make a higher profit with the more expensive items.

Appraisal is the key. Your first step is to identify the period during which the piece was in fashion. For example, the most frequent example in the market now is Victorian, 1840 to 1900. It isn't necessary to know the exact year or even decade.

Then, after you know generally the age of the piece, look for signs of what's happened to it during its lifetime. Have parts been replaced? Has it been refinished? Is the hardware original? One must carefully examine every square inch of a piece of furniture, inside and out, before a pattern emerges and a true estimate of value can be made.

Classes in identification and evaluation of antique furniture given by museums and adult education departments of local schools can be of great help in the initial learning. But hands-on experience is what will make you an expert furniture buyer. You'll want to learn what sells best in your own area so as to devote your efforts to the most profitable lines.

Fig. 3-7 A dining room set, assembled from country chairs, bench and table with original paint. Cabinet in rear is a pie safe with pierced tin panels in the doors.

Fig. 3-8 An "antique" that's bought because it's both attractive and functional: the Hoosier cabinet, named for the state where it was made. Just as useful today as when it was first introduced.

One of the best academies of advanced education is the auction house, and, unless you get carried away and buy something, it's a professional school that doesn't cost a penny! At first, treat the furniture auction strictly as schooling. Take a notebook and pencil. If you arrive early you can write a brief description of each piece along with your guess of what the selling price will be.

If you arrive after the auction has started, write down a quick guess (instant appraisal) as to what each piece will sell for. This is a terrific way to practice making quick estimates. In estimating from a distance, you'll often go wrong because you haven't made the close inspection that makes for a thorough appraisal. The process will prove to you how important it is to make a thorough inspection.

Beside each of your appraisals, when the piece is sold, record the hammer price (the selling price). As you attend auctions and practice appraising, you'll be amazed how your guess will begin to approach the hammer price. When you consistently come within 20%, you're ready to stop studying and start buying. On second thought don't stop studying, just start buying!

The use of the auction as an educational tool should not be confined to furniture. What you've done with furniture can be repeated with any other field of antique interest.

Gambling Devices

The pinnacle of collecting interest in this field is the slot machine, with values into the thousands of dollars per machine. Retired casino games and sophisticated machines can go even higher. But there are lesser collectibles that sell briskly. These include poker chips (clay ones, not cheaper paper ones), dice, and punch boards. Old roulette wheels and big six wheels sell best to people who use them to decorate their game rooms.

Games

Board games have been popular as family entertainment for more than a hundred years. There is a devoted group of collectors who are choosy in terms of quality, condition, and completeness. The prices are not fantastic—most sell for under $30 at retail. Almost any board game from the 1930s to the 1950s is probably worth your investment of $8.00 or $10 to see how it will sell in your area. But, first, make sure *all the pieces are there*. (There have been instances where games have sold in the thousands, but this is rare.)

The only interest a collector will have in individual playing pieces or partial sets will be to replace pieces missing from a set he owns. He'll not pay much for such parts. He knows you can't sell them except at a small price to a collector, and since there are so few collectors and so many broken sets, prices stay low. Until you know what a game should contain in parts and playing pieces, it's best not to take too deep a plunge.

Jigsaw puzzles should be mentioned under games. I haven't done much with them, but I know a man who makes a specialty of selling them in an area where there are a lot of retired people. The problem of how to make sure all pieces are there in an unassembled puzzle is not easily solved unless you love to do jigsaw puzzles and are willing to spend a lot of time testing the merchandise.

Glass

It's a wonderful and profitable line for anyone who wants to take the time to learn it. There are specialties within the general field—Heisey, Sandwich, Imperial and Fenton, to name just a few that are all worth concentrating on.

Those who succeed in glass, in my opinion, make a deep study of the subject and maintain an extensive library of books and price guides for identification and establishment of value. To research a piece you need the name of the maker and pattern. It's well to have a knowledgeable friend who can help.

Guns

You don't need a license or permit to own, buy, or sell an antique firearm. It's obvious that an eighteenth century flintlock, say a Kentucky Rifle, is an antique.

But what about a World War I revolver in shooting condition? Would you be breaking the law if you sold it without having the buyer register it?

As an auctioneer in a state with gun control laws that covered all but sporting weapons, I made sure that every gun sold as a nonsporting and nonantique weapon was delivered from the auction to a registered dealer who then registered the weapon to its new owner before he could take possession of it.

Firearms with historical connections (Revolutionary, Civil, or World War, for example) are in demand. World War II weapons command good prices. Old sporting arms like shotguns by famous makers, depending upon condition, sell well. It's possible to pick up guns at auctions and resell them at a good profit.

WARNING: At an auction where guns are regularly sold, you'll find a platoon of gun guys who hang around and watch the sale. For each gun there always seems to be a different, single, strong bidder among the gang! That's your tip-off. When one of the gang bids, you can bet he's bidding on his own gun. If it doesn't sell for what he thinks is enough, he buys it back. In other words, he protects his price. I've seen the same gun come up in as many as four of five successive auctions.

Most of these birds haunt flea markets and buy from private homes. They put the guns they buy into an auction where the auctioneer lets them get away with this sleazy, if not dishonest, buy-back practice. He may or may not charge them a reduced commission for guns bought back.

Price protection by the consignor is not a rare thing in auctions of any expensive items. Watch for it at auctions of Oriental rugs, coins, and furniture as well as guns. In some states it's illegal, and always unethical, but I don't know what can be done about it.

Usually when I see price protection I don't bid. Once I bought a Winchester 94 I thought I'd make money on (although the owner was protecting), kept it for ages and finally sold it for $10 more than I'd paid. You'll pay retail at a gun auction, because owners protecting their guns will beat you every time!

Handcrafts

I don't like crafts as items for resale. Macrame, wooden toys, ceramics, and other hobby goods don't seem to go with a solid business in antiques and collectibles. Truly old weathervanes, quilts, and such items qualify as folk art and if you can find authentic ones, you'll do very well with them. The problem is a continuous supply. You'll probably be limited to buying a piece here and there.

I've seen would-be dealers who've tried to turn their home workshops into folk art factories. They display their little wooden toys and whirligigs for a few weeks, but never seem to last even when their products are well made and priced low. I can only conclude they have not made a profit from their efforts.

If you try, you'll probably build doll houses, toys, and cutting boards. Except for the cutting boards, which I found to sell well, I'd skip the whole thing.

Hardware

As indicated earlier, there's a lively market for building hardware for people restoring their homes. If you can luck into a quantity of building hardware, either new or old, you can make money on it if you buy it right. Hardware is a perfect example of what many people go to flea markets to buy. They know they can save money by buying there.

There are wholesalers of new hardware who supply flea market dealers at such low prices that flea market people can compete successfully with local hardware outlets. Many of the brands distributed this way are suspicious. I doubt the quality equals that of the offerings of the hardware store. But, the interest is there, and a display of used tools can be profitable.

Hatpins

Hatpins and their vase-like holders are in demand. Ladies display them on dressers and, even in these hatless days, wear them as hairholders. Value, depending on the period, materials, and design, can vary from $2 to $200. Some holders are valued in the hundreds of dollars.

Horse Collectibles

Bells, brasses, leather goods and horsecare equipment sell well and are a most attractive addition to any display. Of course the market is a specialized one. If your business will be in a horsy area, this is one specialty you should consider.

Indian Collectibles

You'll need good books on identification to help you tell authentic old work from pieces being made today. Hands-on experience is indispensable. I once saw some dolls said to be genuine Hopi go at a Pennsylvania auction for $500 each. I could have sworn they were brand new! Maybe they just hadn't been dragged around in the Western dust. I only know I wouldn't have bought them, no matter what the auctioneer said about their origin. I could have been wrong, because this isn't in my area of expertise, but I wouldn't touch them.

Portraits, paintings, jewelry, beadwork blankets, and trinkets are hot items, but you'd better know a lot more than I do about them! It's one study I'd like to undertake some day! Ah, if one just had the years for everything!

Iron

There are iron collectors just as there are collectors of brass, tin, and pewter. Learn to identify old iron if you want to deal in kitchen and workshop equipment. There's a thriving industry of present-day blacksmiths who are making excellent objects of wrought iron. Nothing wrong with it, but it isn't antique and should be labeled as newly made.

Irons, Hand

Not too many years ago it was impossible to walk through a flea market without seeing a few steam or hand stove-heated (sad) irons for sale. Not so true today, but there are still a few around. There are collectors, but prices haven't risen much for the most common irons. People seem to buy them for doorstops. Watch out for reproductions, especially in miniatures. Collectors want perfect examples of the fancier kinds without rust and pitting and with all parts present.

Jewelry

It's possible to buy and sell jewelry without being an expert in the field, if you take some precautions for self-protection. At a minimum, get a gold and silver testing kit, and learn how to use it. Get a gram weight scale, and follow the prices of spot gold and silver in the daily paper. Learn how to convert weights into values and develop proficiency in using the test kit and scale.

Examples of items you can buy at bargain prices in auctions and make money reselling are watches, rings, brooches, Victorian costume jewelry, and stickpins.

Learning about gems and their values is a tough one. Gemologists are made, not born. It takes schooling, study, and practice. Your best move is to get acquainted with a qualified gemologist in your area and be able to call upon him or her for an appraisal when you're in doubt about a purchase or about pricing something you've bought.

Test everything you buy, even if the seller tells you it's not precious metal. The seller might be wrong, and the piece could be platinum. (One was that I once bought for junk!)

The safe way to calculate what to pay for a gold or silver piece is to estimate the value of metal in the piece based on the latest spot price, the weight of the piece, and the percentage of pure metal it contains. Then offer that amount or a little less. Your markup will be equal to the antique value plus manufactured utility value.

Kitchen Items

Lots of women buy rolling pins, egg beaters, and coffee grinders—some to use, some to decorate the kitchen. They're prime box lot items in auctions, and usually can be marked up by a multiple of three or four to one (sale price to cost). This is a line that will sell at a good profit if you take time to display it right. Make little folders to use as price tags and tie each one to the piece with red yarn. Get somebody with good handwriting to do the price writing (if your handwriting is as bad as mine). You will sell more, sell faster, and probably deal with fewer discount requests by using such professional techniques.

Knives

There are fine ID and price guides to Remington, Buck, Winchester, and other knife lines. These books will show you how to identify more desirable models and makers and give you an idea as to how to price your finds.

An advanced knife dealer will be happy to pay plenty for examples of good pocket knives in mint condition, but he'll also buy old beatup knives for parts.

For kitchen and butcher knives, there's a somewhat less active market. They're usually bought for use in the kitchen, but collected when they bear such a name as Remington, Winchester, or Keen Kutter. Name and condition are what count.

Lighting

Lamps and lanterns will sell well if they're of good quality and if they have good names. Aladdin is an example of a brand name that sells well even if it's not very old. Tiffany is another example. Railroad and ship's lanterns sell, not so much because they're light fixtures as for the romance of their transportation background.

Regular household lamps and fixtures are at the low end of the collecting interest scale. Miniature lamps that burn kerosene are an exception. If you can put together a selection of living room and table lamps at really low prices, I think you'll do all right with it. Try to buy low and sell as a utilitarian item unless the lamp is an Aladdin, has B & O or another railroad on it, or is a ship's lantern.

Of course, old gone-with-the-wind lamps, Dresden lamps, and others of that ilk are good sellers.

Limited Edition Collectibles

I believe that things made with the express intention of being sold as collectibles are not collectible. Lots of people agree with me, but obviously dozens of firms that advertise modern collector plates every week in the *Antique Trader* do not. The *Trader* heads the section, "Collector's Items For Sale." One thing I've never understood is why *Antique Trader*, undoubtedly the nation's leading weekly paper on antiques which caters mostly to dealers and super-collectors of every imaginable kind of antique, devotes several pages each week to ads that sell modern collectibles—plates, porcelain bells, and statues. They are not antique and in my opinion will lead to heartbreak for many people who are deluded into thinking they're building a retirement cache when they invest in this material.

It may be that an exception to my rule must be made for some modern collectibles such as wildlife art. I've sold state duck stamp prints and limited editions of wildlife art at auction and have seen their prices continually rise. It's a collectible that men seem comfortable with. Only time will tell.

Medallions and other commemoratives produced in precious metals in limited quantities do not seem to have developed an aftermarket. So far most list at far less than their issue prices except in the advertising literature of dealers who specialize in them. The fact that production was limited doesn't seem to have elevated their value beyond the worth of their precious metal content. I do not think plates and medallions are good bets for future appreciation and I would not choose to deal in them.

Locks

Here's another man's collectible like knives and marbles. This reminds me of an antique dealer—I've forgotten his name—who had a great idea when he opened a tiny shop on the east side of Manhattan with a name something like, "For Men Only." In it he specialized in things like locks, pocket knives, scrimshaw, soldiers and other military merchandise, and marbles—items that have been used by men or played with by boys through history. I believe he did very well—at least he seemed to be every time I visited his tiny, crowded shop which I understand is no longer in existence.

There are door locks, padlocks, and handcuffs, to mention just a few types. Railroad locks are collectible. Look for better metals such as brass and very old, highly engraved, iron locks from Germany. There are books and price guides.

Marbles

Fanciers of collectible marbles have a society all their own. Swirls, sulphides, figurals, every type of marble, is collected. The larger the better, the more complicated the pattern the more valuable, and of course, those in better condition command premium prices.

There's a national marble collector's club and both ID and price guides on the subject. They go well in an inventory display with toys, knives, and other men's collectibles, although there are a great many women who appreciate their decorative possibilities and enjoy collecting them.

Miniatures

Furnishings for doll houses and shadow-box rooms are known as miniatures, but so are tiny scale replicas of furniture, animals, and houses, just to give a few examples. The companies who made toy soldiers also cast miniatures of people, animals, gardens, and vehicles. They make interesting displays and are often assembled as collections in type trays and shadow boxes to be hung on walls. If you deal in valuable miniatures, as I did in toy soldiers, you will want to protect them in locked cases

A wonderful way to display miniatures is to have a broad rack of lighted shelves with sliding glass doors in front. Be sure to install lighting under each shelf to light the figures below.

One dealer I know has handled inexpensive ceramic and porcelain miniatures as a sideline to a general antiques business, mostly furniture. It's her rent-payer, producing enough margin each month to pay the rent, usually more.

Movie Items

Anything that has to do with The Wizard of Oz, Judy Garland, Mickey Rooney, Mickey and Minnie, or Shirley Temple will be a winner. Even Harold Lloyd sells—and few young people today could even tell you who he was! Steer clear of lesser names, and watch out for reproductions such as the Shirley Temple cobalt tumblers that now seem to be appearing on the market by the millions.

Musical

If you've been tuned to music all your life you'll want to include some musical items in your flea market or antiques co-op display. While not wanting to actually specialize in musical items, I've always kept my eyes open for musical instruments, sheet music, records, and other musical merchandise.

I've bought some rather rare instruments at auctions which nobody (occasionally including myself!) in the audience could identify. Thus I became the owner of a *tiple* (kind of a cross between a guitar and ukelele), handmade guitars, banjos, and some freak instruments such as ocarinas and a paper-roll-fed sax. How's that for a weirdo? I made money on every one of these!

Sheet music is good too. Get a price guide. I love music, and I've enjoyed dealing in musical items, but I do not rate it high as a specialty.

Needlework

Old samplers sell well but are nearly impossible to find. When they come up in New England or Pennsylvania auctions, they sell for such high prices they scare away all but the truly brave. Common examples of embroidered table cloths sell for cheaper and are less of a risk to buy. Jacquard coverlets are good bets, particularly if they have signature squares in which the maker's name and place of origin appear. Books on needlework are in demand by people who still wield the needle.

Oriental Items

There are enough collectors of Orientalia to make this a fine specialty. Cloisonne, Occupied Japan, and oriental rugs are all in demand. The craze for "mud men" now seems over. Orientalia is a study all in itself—an interesting one—and potentially profitable. Get books and price guides as a starter, even if you have collected for years.

Pens and Pencils

Most automatic pens and pencils that you'll find were made from the 1920s to the 1950s. In excellent condition (just about all the collector is interested in) they will sell from $25 to $75 with a few higher. Prime names are Conklin, Eagle, Eversharp, Parker, Reynolds (the first ballpoint in 1945), Schaefer, and Waterman. Most people do not know the mechanical pencil has been with us since early in the 19th century. A prime example is an early 19th-century automatic in a 15-karat gold barrel. It opens with slide-type action rather than the later click type.

Pewter

Anything stamped "Pewter" will definitely be pewter but just as surely not old. That designation was not inscribed on pewter pieces before the twentieth century. Look for American pieces you can identify by the maker's "touchmark" on the bottom of plates and inside mugs. Be prepared to pay *lots* for good pieces. Some pieces in my collection are worth from $60 to $400 retail, and mine is a modest collection. The great New England pieces go for thousands and none is now coming from barns or attics. They're mostly in museums.

The pewter market is in a state of *maturity*. The price of admission to the game is high, and there's little room for the beginner to make mistakes! Watch out for Britannia hollow ware pieces like sugar bowls or teapots that were originally silverplated but which, with the silver now worn off, look like pewter. They're often sold as pewter and indeed the metal is very similar. But they have little collector value.

Expect to pay $100 for a fine plate, $400 for a charger in early pewter.

Plates, chargers, spoons, and mugs, are being cast at the present time by master craftsmen who are honest in applying their touchmarks. Even honesty does not protect the unwary and overly hopeful beginner! The author of a recent and mostly authoritative book on antique pewter attributed a mark shown in a pictured piece to "an as yet unidentified eighteenth-century pewterer," when in fact the piece was cast by Tom Stauffer of Lititz, Pennsylvania in the 1970's! The mark of this superb craftsman shows clearly in the picture! I know because I own a dozen of Tom's plates which are indistinguishable from the originals except for Tom's touchmark.

Photography

This has been an interesting specialty to me, because I've always been interested in photography and have owned state-of-the-art cameras until fairly recently. The automatic ones have gotten beyond me with features I don't need and for which I am overtrained!

Fig. 3-9 Old (and not-so-old) cameras and photographic equipment are sought by many collectors.

Old cameras, tripods, enlargers, developing equipment, and other photo machinery have always sold well for me. In addition, I can keep any cameras I want from a large buy and sell what's left at a nice profit, in effect adding to my own camera collection without cost. What could be nicer? In my experience price guides in this field tend to be far behind the steady rise in market value but useful—particularly in identification.

As for photographs, look for leather-encased (or gutta-percha) ambrotypes and daguerrotypes which sell for from $5.00 (condition: poor) to $50.00 (condition: excellent). Subject matter means a lot.

Political Memorabilia

There are collectors for every politician and every campaign, even local ones. People collect material that has to do with past mayors and sheriffs as well as national figures. However, the most popular items are connected with U.S. presidents. Get to know collectors who come by your stand. Search for what they collect. They'll help you learn values. There are price guides, mail order auctions, and specialized dealers.

Look for books, pins and medals, glass, buttons, jugs, mirrors, trays, watch fobs, bells, toys, cigars, and other historical artifacts connected with famous politicos. One friend of mine owns a towel purported to be stained with presidential blood. It supposedly was discarded shortly after President McKinley met his fate. Amazing how far collectors will go!

Postcards and Trade Cards

One devotes huge table space to postcard inventory and much time to arranging cards by subject matter. Customers spend hours searching, so you should have chairs for at least three people to search at one time. When they finish, another three take over. After an hour a customer buys two fifty cent cards.

Sometimes he buys a $10 card. Wow! It's a specialty in which a lot of table space produces small sales, not a good yield in margin per square foot of space. I think post card dealers are collectors who enjoy sorting cards and discussing them with other collectors.

Trade cards (see separate listing) go well with postcards but are seldom seen in such large piles. There's a market for all cards and they're historically fascinating.

Posters

Some posters are collected as objects of art, others because of subject matter. For many years, the poster was a principal form of communication. Propaganda campaigns in World War I and to a lesser extent in World War II were conducted by poster. Movies were promoted, political campaigns advanced, and products touted on colorful boards attached to fences, buildings, and streetcars. Movie, transportation, product, travel, and sports posters are particularly desirable. Peter Max and other psychedelic posters have become collectible. Learn how to detect reproductions.

Portraits

These are pretty good sellers, even old unidentified Grandpa and Grandma photos which people like to hang in game rooms to be "instant ancestors."

Tintypes and ambrotypes in gutta percha case frames are the best sellers. Cabinet cards sell well and are pretty cheap.

Printing Paraphernalia

Presses, type cases, metal type and engravings, and even old presses—huge ones—are all collected. Much of it is difficult to transport and may hang around like the man who came to dinner.

Prints

Realize that you're dealing with the marketability of an artist, printer, or lithographer; the condition and subject of the print and frame; and the intricacies of adapting the subject and colors of the whole thing to somebody's decorating scheme. Then you know what the considerations are when somebody contemplates buying a print.

Prints can be sold raw, matted, or framed at much higher prices. You'll learn which is best for your market as you go along, and the price per print when you buy it is never so high that you take a big risk. You can often find a book from which you can cut lithographs or stone-engraved prints. Framed, they'll sell at a good markup.

I once bought a book for $5 and sold prints out of it for a total of more than $400. Not a bad markup. Doesn't happen every day, but if you get into prints it will happen occasionally.

Good subjects? It depends upon what *your* market wants, of course, but try Western (cowboys, Indians), blacks, arts deco and nouveau. The works of artists like Parish and Nutting as well as lithographers such as Prang and Currier sell well, even as repros far removed from the original art print.

Quilts

Top seller. Deal in the best handstitched quality you can find. Learn to identify *hand*stitching (quilting), since most collectors do not want machine-quilted examples. However, *nonquilted* quilttops are often bought by people who like handwork and either stitch it themselves or have it done.

Before you buy a finished quilt, check for wear on both front and back. Learn something about patterns that are in demand so that you can converse knowledgeably.

A quilting frame, on which material is quilted, can be used as a display rack and is a valuable antique to sell. Another display idea is a rack made of dowels stretched between A-frames. Good quilts are scarce. Even recent good ones go for big bucks.

Radio Personalities

Most kids' radio programs offered product premiums in the '30s and '40s that are now highly collectible. In addition, cards, figures, games, and toys were offered as "tie-ins" to the popularity of such leading characters as Little Orphan Annie, Jack Armstrong, and Charlie McCarthy. Amos 'n' Andy's Fresh Air Taxi (Marx toy) has sold in mint condition for over $1,000. Most premiums are in the $10 to $30 range.

Radios

In my experience most radios of the 1920s, 1930s and 1940s do not sell for much more and sometimes less than their original prices raised by inflation. Because the market is fairly thin you can buy them at auctions and in junk shops for very little, and they are a reasonably good flea market item.

Exceptions occur, and some very rare sets go into the hundreds of dollars in retail value. Remember to dust your radios because they'll hang around long enough to gather a good coating. The largest buy I ever made was a half dozen old battery models. Not having paid much for them I wasn't disturbed when they sat for months. Then a man bought all six at twice what I had paid.

Railroadiana

Objects once aboard the railroad in your area are the ones that sell best in your market. The list of things is large: lanterns, dining car china and flatware, schedules, switch locks, timetables, prints—no end to the stuff railroad buffs look for. Collectors who find you occasionally have their specialty will make a regular jaunt through your market every week.

Razors

Razors, particularly straight-edgers, have been highly collectible for years, along with shaving mugs, brushes, and other equipment—including barber chairs. Mugs and blades of unusual design with illustrated panels go particularly high.

Early brass safety razors are sought after. Don't ever throw them away if you get them in a box lot. Your best bet on highly specialized collectibles such as these, items of which you'll probably never amass a large inventory, is to sell to a dealer who specializes in them. Let him know you'll take a low markup for an immediate sale. It's better than hanging onto specialized items for months waiting for a collector.

Records

A record that cannot be played has no value. Check carefully for cracks and scratches. Play it if possible. The big collecting activity is in 78-RPM records made from the 1920s through the 1940s. Rare ones in excellent condition in original jackets can go from $5 to $50 each. But that stack of records from the shelves of an old Victrola you bought at auction will yield an average sale of 25 cents per record if you're lucky, and some of them will still be around after a year! A few people collect 45s and 33⅓s, but they pay low prices. Compact discs will probably someday become collectibles, so hang onto them! If you buy records look for top condition and star names people recognize, like Goodman, Crosby, Holiday, and Darin, for example.

Robots

Tin and plastic robot toys are being collected with astounding fervor. Collectors advertise their wants in robot toys as people used to in mechanical banks. It's amazing when you realize that these ugly little monsters are quite recent. The first ones made their debuts in the late '40s! Prices in the hundreds and thousands of dollars are not rare. My advice is to buy them and hang on for a little while. Their prices might go through the roof in the next ten years.

Rose O'Neill

It all began with a young woman named Rose O'Neill who drew her first Kewpie doll when she was 14 years old. Promoters seized the opportunity and, beginning with the first doll in 1913, the sale of Kewpies took off. At peak production, 28 factories turned out the dolls. Originals sell for up to $800, common ones less than $100. There are reproductions, and current limited editions may or may not rise in value.

Scientific Apparatus

I've had success selling surveyor's tripods, compasses, weather, medical, and other instruments, despite the fact that I don't know a darned thing about any of the basic disciplines associated with them. Telescopes, binoculars, just about anything with shiny brass parts and bound in good leather cases is a sure seller. Try to buy cheap if you're not an expert in these things. You'll learn as you go along, just as I did.

Scouting

Scouting material, particularly Boy Scout related, has been collected for years. Handbooks, paperweights, neckerchiefs and slides, jamboree patches, uniforms, and equipment appear in flea markets and antiques malls. Beware of reproductions.

Scrimshaw

Scrimshaw is the product of eighteenth- and nineteenth-century whalers and walrus hunters who cut and decorated pieces of whale or walrus bone. They are supposed to have worked on these pieces to relieve the tedium of days and nights at sea with little to do. The beautiful, sometimes artistic, always interesting designs were inscribed on bone with needles and knives and then filled with lamp-black or ink. The real scrimshaw (whose creators are called *scrimshanders*) qualifies as one of our most desirable and *romantic* collectibles from the era of sail.

You'll see pieces that look remarkably like authentic scrimshaw for sale at flea markets or yard sales. That's because reproductions are being manufactured and distributed to the flea market trade by the folks that gave us the "Wells Fargo Belt Buckle," (an object which existed in real life only after a canny Englishman about twenty years ago decided to change history).

The same intrepid fakers are now perpetrating a similar scam on their

American friends by casting polymer plastics in unbelievable detail to simulate 100-year-old scrimshaw tusks, teeth, and bones.

Before you decide to invest in one of these miracles, get a book on the subject and visit a few museum collections until you understand what the real stuff looks and *feels* like. There are plastic pieces being sold in gift shops in the form of cuff links and tie tacs decorated in scrimshaw technique, but they're clearly labeled as newly made.

Any of these pieces is realistic, so much so that a friend of mine—an experienced dealer but a novice to scrimshaw—was taken to the tune of a couple hundred dollars on two pieces that turned out to be virtually worthless. Beware!

Silver

Seven years ago, in the first edition of this book, I wrote: "For at least the next ten years I believe [owning] silver is like having money in the bank." I went on to point out that silver will probably increase more than the rate of inflation.

I was dead wrong. During that 7-year period my silver was indeed "money in the bank," in safe deposit boxes where it languishes today at about the same value in inflated dollars it held 7 years ago! It's had a couple of spurts but its value, after rising, has always settled back to about the price at which I bought it from five to ten years ago.

If I had put the money I spent on silver into a savings account I would be several thousand dollars ahead! If I'd put it into antique inventory I would be many times that much ahead!

Now I feel like I'm holding onto Confederate money waiting for the South to rise again. Framed on my wall is a form letter from an investment company specializing in silver (they've since disappeared, I think) with a headline in 90-point type proclaiming: "Within eighteen months, if you hold silver, you'll be rolling in profits." That was written in 1983. Maybe the clipping is worth money to a collector. I just know my silver hasn't moved off dead center. Moral of the story: Do *not* believe people who make lavish predictions on any kind of investment. Second moral: Don't make predictions.

However, don't be afraid to deal in silver items if you want to buy and sell in the short term. If you wish to trade in silver items, watch the spot prices and try to turn your silver inventory over as quickly as possible.

Smoking Material

Tobacco accessories sell, usually not for fantastic sums, but steadily. The appeal of ashtrays, humidors, smoking stands, and other impedimenta associated with the noxious weed have slackened a bit due to the decrease in tobacco usage and the stigma attached to the habit, but the old collectors remain.

Tobacco collectibles may become even more valuable if no-smoke compaigns reduce the number of users further and fewer accessories are manufactured.

Don't ignore other attributes of tobacco-related materials. For example, I have a smoking stand with three handcarved bears and a music box carved on top of a Black Forest tree trunk! It's so ugly it's beautiful, and it's a neat conversation piece in our library at home.

Soda Fountain Collectibles

The soda fountain virtually disappeared in the mid-twentieth-century. Earlier, beginning in the 1880's, the retail ice cream counter was a social center for both young and old. Nostalgia insures a high level of interest among people whose early social life began with dates made at the soda fountain.

Trade cards, fans, buttons, and postcards are examples of advertising-related fountain items. Equipment, such as scoops, spoons, tulip-shaped sundae cups, and twisted wire chairs and tables are all collected—along with dozens of other items. Counters and dispensers, malted milk powder jars, and signs are sought by eager collectors. A Beech-Nut Chewing Gum display rack from the 1920s can sell for $300, and a Borden's Malted Milk jar with label should fetch close to $200. Ice cream scoops go for $20 to $50 depending upon quality.

Sports Collectibles

Here's a fine specialty, and an ideal business if you're a follower of baseball and football, around each of which is built enormous collecting interest. My apologies to basketball buffs (of which I'm one) but few people are interested in old basketballs and sneakers.

Baseball cards are the number one interest, followed by autographs, and anything printed in the old days of Babe Ruth, Hank Wilson, and Red Grange. Several dealers and two auctioneers I know have made a specialty of sports and do very well indeed.

There are lots of little known possibilities. For example, the makers of toy soldiers cast little baseball and football players in action poses back in the '30s and '40s. Auburn Rubber Company's footballers sell for a high price. Autographed bats and footballs sell fast.

Stained Glass

Leaded, stained glass is sought by decorators for use as an architectural accent in today's homes and commercial buildings. Until you become known for this sort of specialty, it may take quite a while to sell even your very good pieces. But you'll get high prices when you sell, and after a time, the people who can use leaded glass will remember you have it and come to you when they need some for a new project.

Leaded glass is heavy, fragile, and hard to move, but it seems to be well worth the effort. It will enrich the atmosphere of your display area and give notice to decorators that you can supply them with nice things for their clients. If your space has an outside window, be sure to hang pieces of leaded glass in the window where passers-by can see it.

Stamps
Like coins, stamps require lots of knowledge and experience. I don't recommend them to a new dealer without philatelic experience. Put in your time as a collector (one of the nation's largest hobbies) before you try to deal in them.

Stereopticans
I had always been interested in stereo views, those old 3-D photo cards that give a realistic 3-dimensional effect when looked at through a viewer. Everyone who's ever attended an antiques show has peeked through one of them. I had even sold a few, but I had never thought I would invest heavily in them. Then one of my ads for "Antiques Wanted" in the local newspaper was answered by a lady whose late husband had been a collector of stereo cards, viewers, even oak cabinets built to hold cards. I examined the collection and found it contained several thousand cards, twelve viewers, spare parts, and some rare items I'd never before seen.

I was sorely tempted to make an immediate offer, but decided first to consult a dealer whom I had known to trade in the stuff more than I had and a friend who had been a semi-serious collector of stereo. Both these people warned me that, from what they had been able to learn, I would have the collection around for an awfully long time before I liquidated it. They gave me the impression that I would get picked to death by other dealers, and my investment would be far better spent on other items.

Being an ornery cuss fascinated by an opportunity to add a bit of spice to life, I decided to make a quick and dirty study of the stereo field. I got advice from price guides, visited shops of dealers, spending all of three days making my survey. I wasn't convinced that money spent on the collection would be a good investment. I found no excitement in anything I read or in the conversations I had with people about it. However, the subject matter appealed to me, and I had a strong hunch I would do better than break even and that I'd learn a lot along the way. I thought, this may be my last chance to get into stereo views in a big way and learn something about them.

So, in spite of the negatives, I made an offer, received a counteroffer to which I agreed, and found myself the owner of a trailer-load of stuff I knew next to nothing about.

It took a week's full-time work to reorganize the collection by subject, photographer, and publisher and to divide it into logical sub-collections upon each of which I put a price of between $15 and $150. Thousands of individual cards were filed in alphabetical order, by subject, for example—Airships, Civil War, Dogs, Sears Roebuck.

I decided to market the collection at a Renninger's Flea Market Extravaganza in Adamstown, Pennsylvania—an event for which I had made a reservation months earlier. Things now seemed destined to fall into place, despite the looks I kept getting from my wife who wondered when our dining room table would be freed of the boxes full of strange-looking cards it had held for weeks. She wondered aloud whether I'd ever get compensated for what must have seemed to her to be a horrendous waste of time.

A week before the show, a local collector learned of my treasure, visited my home, and relieved me of more than a hundred cards, an oak cabinet, and several viewers. In that one sale, I made back the investment originally put into the collection. At the Extravaganza I sold an amount equal to three times the purchase price of the collection. For the next year it produced a steady sale of pure profit.

I began to look for cards and viewers in my travels. I passed on lots that were priced too high (particularly viewers), but there was an occasional buy that, with my new experience, resulted in a profit. At a toy show in Allentown, Pennsylvania, I was able to buy an original set of 150 cards with two viewers packed in their fitted wooden traveling case. I made another gem of a buy during a trip my wife and I made to North Carolina. I would never have given either of those a second look if it hadn't been for my earlier experience. That's the point I'm trying to make in this book. Get in, get your feet wet, and take some chances to come up with winners!

My stereo experience is always my answer to anyone who tells me "Don't risk money in collectibles you know nothing about." What it proves is that you can always take a crash course, as I did, if you're interested enough to find out how to turn an opportunity into a bonanza.

Store Items

Posters, cases, cabinets, high button shoes, cash registers, and other country store items are dandy props for decorators, restaurant owners, and proprietors who wish to create an "antique" atmosphere. There are still things available from old retail outlets. You can only make a rare find if you're out looking!

A few years ago I bought half the interior of an old drugstore. It cost a $100 and so far I've taken in more than $5,000 from sales of items from it. In addition it provided beautiful wood and hardware for my own projects in my home, including my mahogany office desk made from the old cash register counter. You may think there are no deals like that one lying in wait, but how will you know if you aren't on the alert?

These artifacts not only sell but dress up your display space. An old brass cash register and a shop desk make your space look like a country store. Unusual old fixtures like these *stop people* and have benefits far beyond inventory value.

Teddy Bears

The bear craze has been going for about 20 years with no sign of abating. Old bears, new bears, beautiful bears, ugly bears. Special bear shows are held and people love it. If you can find antique bears by all means buy them.

Tin

Many things were made in the eighteenth, nineteenth and early twentieth centuries of "tin," actually sheet iron covered with a thin layer of tin to keep it from rusting. The proper name is tinplate. Old tinplate was made by dipping the iron sheet in molten tin, the same way copper pots are tinned on the inside except that the sheet of iron was totally submerged so that both sides received a coating of the protective metal. You'll know old tinplate from new by careful inspection. Hold it so that light reflects from an unpainted surface. You'll see "waves" in the surface of old, handdipped tin much like waves in paint that's been brush applied.

Modern tinplate is plated by electroplating and the coating is perfectly smooth without the wavy imperfections older tin shows. Either product is satisfactory as a metal to be worked into all kinds of household gadgets, and these are mostly what's collected. Boxes, trays, cups, and cookie cutters all sell for relatively low prices. Ladies love to hang them in their kitchens. Men go for lamps and tools made of tin. It's an easy metal to cut, bend and form into almost any shape.

Tools

My antique tool collection provided the inventory with which I started in the business of selling antiques. There's great demand for old tools, although they're getting scarce and prices are increasing rapidly.

In addition to antique tools you can do a good trade in used tools that are still serviceable. You can buy them at auctions, clean them, polish and sharpen them and make a good profit reselling them to craftsmen. This is an ideal business for an itinerant dealer who sets up at different markets.

Toy Soldiers

The two major categories among American collectors are American Dimestore soldiers and Britains. Dimestores are so named because F. W. Woolworth, Kresge, and Kress were the prime outlets from their introduction around 1930 until the 1960s. At that time, beset by increasing costs, fear of allowing children to play with objects partially made of lead, and the general fall in popularity of military subjects companies that had survived World War II went out of business.

During more than three decades of production, Barclay of New Jersey, Manoil of New York, and Grey Iron of Pennsylvania produced hundreds of action and parade poses, vehicles, and accessories for young collectors. The ones that were well taken care of and have come down in pristine condition are the most valuable. Collectors buy individual figures. A few sell for upwards of $300 each.

In addition to military figures, these companies all produced civilian figures which are also collected, particularly the farm and ranch figures.

The British firm of Wm. Britains, Ltd. was, and still is, the prime producer of smaller, 54mm figures of British and worldwide military forces. Britains figures are collected mostly in boxed sets, generally retailing to collectors for $100 to $500 per set of six to twenty figures tied in their original boxes.

As mentioned in another chapter, toy soldiers have provided me with a wonderful specialty. I have sold soldiers in a flea market, an antiques co-op, at auction, and by mail order. The number of collectors is small, probably no

Fig. 3-10 A display of tools like this will attract males to your booth.

more than 2,000 top collectors in the whole country, but they are most anxious to buy.

Richard O'Brien's excellent book, *Collecting Toy Soldiers*, is the bible of the field, although there are other books, magazines, price guides, and reprints of old catalogs that are also helpful.

uying for Resale

Reading Guide. If you've started your business and sold for a Sunday or two, you know you must replace the inventory you're selling or you'll soon be out of business! It's time to buy! Actually, you should have started buying weeks ago, but don't panic! If you follow the advice in this chapter, you'll soon have a veritable warehouse of goodies to sell at a handsome profit. Make sure you read here and understand:

- Buying in your flea market and from "pickers."
- Strategies for buying from homes.
- Opportunities in auction buying.
- Mail order buying.
- How the estate sale works.

We'll try to help you in dealing with sellers with words on:

- Setting your purchase price.
- How to make the offer.
- Joint ventures.
- The "big bills close."
- Bank line of credit for financing purchases.

The most important single part of your business is the few hours each week you spend in homes, at auctions, or elsewhere making purchases. The experts will tell you, "The profit's in the buying!" It's not easy, but you've got to learn to do it or go out of business. I've seen new dealers fold after a few months in the market. They started with family heirlooms, sold them, and ended their careers with early retirement because they had nothing left to sell!

At some time during the first six months, a dealer who hasn't yet started to buy realizes there isn't enough inventory to sell. So the dealer runs an ad, but is timid when it comes to making the house call and also reluctant to deal with anyone who tries to sell something at the flea market.

Some people are frightened by the idea of buying. They like to sell but are afraid to buy—afraid, perhaps, that they'll get taken or spend too much. They may be worried they'll offer too little and offend the seller. Those dealers who come to grips with their fear of buying are the survivors.

Buying in the Flea Market

People will stop at your stand to offer merchandise. Some new dealers are so concerned with using every minute of flea market time to make sales they take offense when somebody comes to them who wants to *sell*!

Don't get angry—Rejoice! You've got to buy in order to sell! Fortunately, the flea market seems to produce almost as many sellers as it does buyers. They're looking for someone who might be interested in buying stuff that's overflowing their attics, or playrooms. When they see your glassware or furniture or see your sign that says, "We BUY Antiques!" (if it isn't up yet, do it NOW!), they'll want to show you their things.

Flea market contacts are usually not as productive as leads produced by newspaper advertising. However, some will pay off, and your best bet is to follow each lead quickly.

Ask if the seller has the items with him. If they're in the car trunk, turn your stand over to your helper, and go to the parking lot to take a look. Make your offer firmly and positively—then wait for a counter-offer. Don't be afraid to offer a bit low, then increase your offer. Anybody who brings something to the market to sell can sell it to somebody. If it's a good buy you want the purchaser to be you. If you buy early enough in the day, you've even got a chance to sell some of your buy that very day and recover part or even all of your purchase price!

If the person doesn't have the merchandise handy, take the name, address, and phone number and make a date to call. If you let the lead get cold the seller might have a change of mind, or another dealer will beat you out. Contact the seller the same day after you've left the market and make a date to see the items.

Early Morning Buying

Visit your market's transient dealers early, before everybody else gets around. They'll be driving from as far away as 100 miles or more each Sunday, loaded with household goods, food, collectibles, and antiques. They hope to get rid of everything and may not come again for months. Most of the buys I've made from dealers in my flea market were from those who had traveled a long distance.

You'll find an occasional specialist who sells in different areas of the country and retired couples who do the markets the way boaters take off on a cruise. There's always the chance of meeting a collector who's tired of his collection or who needs the money, or who, like you and I, decides to try the market to see if he wants to make a business of it.

Any of these could have something you can resell, mostly single units or small quantities. You're not going to buy a ton from one person. But if you spend an hour and buy items that make $100 profit, you've invested time wisely.

The time to make that investment is early in the day. Just as I described my own early A.M. experience in Chapter 1, there will be predawn buyers circling your market looking for good deals. If yours is a popular market with an opening time of 8:00 A.M., dealers will be setting up beginning at 5:00 or 6:00 A.M.

Dealers may drive in the night before and sleep in their vans and cars to get first crack at the dealer trade—that's you! To take no chances on missing buying or selling opportunities, show up then.

A flashlight is a necessity, obviously, for buying in the dark. You'll be circulating while sellers are unloading and setting up. If you're looking for a specialty, ask each dealer who seems to be a likely prospect if he has it. As you walk around, you'll hear people asking, "Any bayonets, any military?" or "Fishing tackle—any old rods and reels?" Soon you'll be doing the same.

You should have your analytical tools with you—a gram scale to weigh gold or silver, a silver and gold test kit, ultra-violet light if you want to check china for covered cracks, a magnet for testing brass (plated iron pulls the magnet, solid brass does not), and a hand calculator if you need it for computations. A carrying bag such as the yachtsman's ice bag is a handy way to carry things you might buy.

Some people won't be in a pleasant mood this early, particularly if they've spent the night in the cab of a truck. Some react with pain when you ask questions. Some snap back. Some walk away. It's all part of the game. If you're going to buy, you'll have to put up with it.

It's considered bad form to interrupt another's talk with a dealer. Competition being what it is, there's a need for some rules of conduct, and this is the first one. You'll expect that when you have the dealer's ear no one else will interrupt.

Since it's a competitive situation, make your buy quickly to get the deal. One good technique that fends off competition while you make up your mind is to hold the item until you make an offer and get the seller's reaction. Nobody will make an offer on something you're holding (if they follow Good Conduct Rule #2). This is not easy with a large chair—but not impossible. If you can't pick it up, tilt it back and hold it at an angle. Get the seller's attention and hold on until you've decided whether to make the deal.

If you meet a dealer who has the stuff you want to buy, cultivate a friendship. Make it clear you'll be interested in anything he comes up with in your line if the price is right. By developing a friendship with a person who finds your thing, you'll have set up a dependable source of supply.

If that person continues to find your merchandise, he'll bring it to you first since he knows he can sell it quickly and at a decent profit. He'll learn you're an expert in buying that type of merchandise, so even if it's a new specialty he's never bought before, he'll begin to understand the value of your advice. That guides him in buying items for resale to you.

I made up a one-page flyer on "How to Buy Toy Soldiers for Resale to Minertoy." In it I described in a few words the types of soldiers I wanted and gave a general idea of the prices I would pay. As pickers, I had several local people and a couple of dealers hundreds of miles away. I tried to line up antiques shop owners when I traveled by talking with them about soldiers and giving them my brochure, but I had less success with them than with people who lived closer by.

The Picker

The people just described are called "pickers." They buy (pick) merchandise with one buyer's wants in mind. They spend full time attending auctions, calling on houses, and visiting markets constantly looking for material to resell to dealer/clients. They are the true wholesalers of the antiques field. The friendship of a couple of pickers will result in a steady stream of merchandise. Once the picker thinks of you first, try to buy *everything* he brings you and, if possible, at the price at which he offers it.

Don't put him through unnecessary haggling. It's better to treat your picker as a professional and buy at *his price*. If he follows your guidelines and buys right, you won't overpay. The flood of merchandise your picker brings will more than make up for an occasional overpayment.

I tell the picker when I think I'm paying too much for something, but pay his price anyway. What I'm doing is warning him that if his price goes higher I may not be able to buy from him. He gets the idea. It's better than arguing over price.

House Calls

Doctors don't make house calls—antiques dealers do. It's the most productive technique for buying anything from pots and pans to high-style antiques. It's like pulling the handle on a slot machine—the suspense makes it fun! House calls occasionally result from having friends who know you're in the business. They might quiz you at work or during a poker game, or they may visit you at the flea market to say hello. They're probably checking out how you do business. If they like what they see, they'll tell you about stuff they'd like to get rid of and invite you to their homes to see it.

Most of us hate to deal with a friend who asks us to clean out his basement playroom. You worry about his visiting your stand after you've paid him $100 for a basementful and discovering the price you've put on one item will recoup $75 of the $100 you paid him for the whole thing! Or you might imagine his thinking, "Look at those books—he's got 'em priced at a $1 each! He only paid me $2 for the whole lot! He's gonna make a fortune and all I got outta it was a lousy hundred bucks!"

The truth is your seller probably won't visit the flea market. (If he were one to do so he'd have set up and sold the stuff there himself!) If he does, he won't remember the individual items and take time to add up prices!

In many years of buying for resale, I've never had a seller check up on how I've priced items I bought from him. I try to make the point that my expenses are such that I have to buy at a much lower price than I will resell his items. I tell him that in buying a lot of items I'll lose on some and make a profit on others. Buyers understand and appreciate being let in on the secrets of the business. It even helps close the deal.

A houseful of junk takes a long time to sell. To do an outdoor market you must load and unload each day. Your costs include losses to rain or shoplifters, plus rent, advertising, and money tied up in inventory. To double your purchase price should be a *bare* minimum. *Tripling* the purchase price is the rule that most dealers follow.

A Case History: The Junk Pile

A man I played tennis with but had not known off-court, asked me if I would be interested in clearing his cellar of its accumulation. I was glad to help him even though it didn't sound great when he told me the family had not collected antiques.

At 10:00 A.M. the next Saturday, in the man's basement, I found a mountain of "junk, almost all of it in original boxes, neatly stacked on a huge island of metal shelving. There were souvenirs from family travels—the things you buy on trips but never use. In addition there were books and records, radios, golf clubs, kitchen appliances, boxes of greeting cards, tape recorders, sweaters, T-shirts, and other gift-type clothing that had never been worn, glass and china, a thousand items that represented 30 years of Christmas and birthday presents, souvenirs from European and American travel, purchases that seemed like a good idea at the time but that never got used.

There wasn't an antique or collectible in the pile, but it was super-clean stuff that would sell. Since there was no collector interest, to move it I would have to price it to my customers at 10% of retail value. That meant I had to buy it at a nickel on the original retail dollar. The value to the seller of getting the piles out meant more to him than the money he would receive for it.

I explained to my friend how I would handle it and added, "I know you're going to think my offer is low and that I'm trying to make a fortune on this, but. . ."

"Nonsense," he replied, not wanting to listen to my explanation of the bid that was to follow, "You know what you have to do to dispose of this stuff. I've got to get rid of it. I'd probably give it to you free for hauling it."

I figured a thousand items at 10 cents each would come to a $100. It just didn't seem like enough so I threw caution to the winds and offered $150. After a quick conference with his wife, my friend returned to the cellar and said, "When can you get it out of here?" I paid the $150 and returned that afternoon with help to do the loading.

It took two trips to haul it all to my garage. Our automobile stayed outside until I got it sold. I priced it at 10 cents on the retail dollar, except of course for things like the tape recorder, radios, and golf clubs which went a bit higher.

On that buy it's hard to know exactly what the final sales figure turned out to be, but I know I took in at least $500 for that pile.

If any feeling remains that I earned too big a markup, look at the facts beginning with the purchase price of $150 and final sales of about $500. That's a gross margin of $350. I spent five hours of my time and $45 for help in hauling the stuff. I put wear and tear on my car and trailer, hauled, loaded, and unloaded for several weeks and baby-sat the merchandise at the flea market. Finally, there's my expertise which I used when I appraised, priced, and marketed the pile. The service rendered to the seller was well worth the markup. That's the way a house buy should go.

Buy it All

The advantage of buying the pile and not picking through it is that you acquire a quantity of material you can work on for a while. If there's stuff you think might hang around too long, convert some of it to instant cash.

One way is to be a picker and take things to people who will buy them for resale. There are several dealers who do the same thing with me when they run into my specialties. One dealer gets my glass, another dolls, another my antique tools (now that I'm out of that business), and another the military items I sometimes find along with toy soldiers.

Another way to dispose of stuff for almost instant cash is to consign it to an auction. That usually results in getting your money in a few weeks.

An Estate Dispersal

Here's a typical dispersal of an estate that came to me through the recommendation of a friend of the executor. The executor called me and asked me to take a look. Prior to my call he had brought in a long-established antiques dealer. The dealer told him that the lot was worth between $10,000 and $12,000, but he didn't have the ready cash to buy it all. He offered to take it into his shop on consignment, a proposition which the executor believed wasn't in the best interest of the estate since he wanted to dispose of the stuff quickly.

The dealer then offered an estate sale, a method of dispersal described later, in which everything is price-tagged and sold on location by the dealer who acts as sale manager. This was rejected by the executor who realized that after the glorified tag sale there would still be stuff to dispose of.

That's when I was called in. I wasn't sure I could handle it, but I always like to look at estates if they might contain things I specialize in. I was glad to see carpenter's and cabinetmaker's tools—most of them common but in nice condition. There were collector-quality toys and 30 still and mechanical coin banks.

There were guns, small furniture (the larger pieces having already been sold to a furniture dealer), odds and ends including sterling, silverplate, and linens.

How To Appraise

To figure this kind of bid, list everything along with your estimate of retail price. Add the prices and divide the total by the factor you use in your pricing formula.

In the junk pile case I used a higher factor, but in this one, with items of more predictable retail value, I used a factor of three. I calculate that some things will sell lower, some higher than my estimates, but I'll average out okay. Allowing for selling expense and a mistake or two in judgment, the margin should work out to be no less than 50% of gross sales.

I am conservative in my appraisals. For example, say I'm buying a kid's sled. It's similar to one I sold a year ago for $125 but not quite as good. I'll appraise the sled now at $90. That value gets added to all the other *retail values* in the collection, so that when I divide by three I'm including the sled at a wholesale value of about $30.

If I think the item will sell quickly it gets a higher appraisal. If it's something I'm picking for somebody else and will sell instantly, I'll appraise it even higher. If it's something that'll hang around for a year before it sells, I'll appraise it lower. You should consider each item individually, except when there are lots of things of small value that can be grouped as in the case of the junk pile described earlier.

In the case under consideration, my final figure came to a retail total of a bit under $12,000. I bid $4,000.

The executor said, "What about the offer of $12,000 from the other dealer?" I knew the deal was about to be made or broken according to my answer to the question on the table. "It wasn't an offer," I answered, "but an estimate of $10,000 to $12,000. If he offered $10,000 you should have taken it. If he offered $5,000 I think you should have taken that. You've got to realize that he was talking about a consignment sale in which he would have no risk."

I didn't want to bad-mouth the other dealer by accusing him of high-balling to get the estate for a tag sale. But I wanted to set the executor straight. I said, "We're talking about my *buying*, not doing a yard sale. With markdowns, the $10,000 to $12,000 could come to $5,000 or $6,000. Then the dealer would take his commission of 25% or 30%, and the estate would end up with maybe $3,000 clear with stuff left over that would still have to be disposed of. I'm offering to *buy* the whole thing for $4,000. It's off your hands—the estate has its money, and I worry what to do with it."

"Why would he have offered $10,000 or $12,000?"

"He didn't," I replied, "he estimated a retail value. That's not an offer. I don't know who he is, and it wouldn't be proper for me to criticize his methods. Of course, it's possible he wants this deal badly enough to stretch things." I added, "If you don't take my offer I believe you should call in other dealers to get competitive bids. Or, consign it to an auction house where you'd have a chance for a net equal to my offer, certainly more than you'd get in a tag sale, and you wouldn't have anything left over. My appraisal is based on experience, and my $4,000 is a firm offer."

He thought for a minute and replied, "When can you get it out of here?" I told him, and we shook hands.

Here's what happened to the merchandise:

I consigned to an auction items that would take a long time for me to sell. Income from that was about $2,000 after commission. Being in the business I got a better deal from the auctioneer than somebody coming in off the street. I paid 15% compared to 25% others who aren't in the business would pay.

An additional $1,000 was realized in sales to flea market and antiques dealers who are people I "pick" for.

The better remaining collectibles brought another $1,600 from collectors I contacted by phone or letter.

The remainder, a fifth of the total, went into inventory and took three months to sell, netting $2,800. The total came to $7,400. My investment was $4,000 in merchandise. The gross return was 84%, even after selling expenses.

From the standpoint of the executor the deal made great sense. He wanted to move the material quickly and didn't wish to take a chance on consigning it to a dealer or to an auction. I gave him the agreed-upon amount immediately. If he had chosen the auction route (not a bad alternative as I pointed out), he would have paid 25% and needed to gross $5,000 to come out even with my bid of $4,000. He had the immense advantage of solving his problem in one quick sale without waiting for results.

What this example illustrates is how, once you're in the field of dealing in antiques you can easily broaden and become an expert in dispersal of estates. The key is in defining your role—you're not just a dealer, but a specialist in dispersal.

Buying from Homes

When I first made house calls, I didn't expect people to answer "Wanted to Buy" ads when they had no intention of selling. I was amazed when I found both men and women who would invite me into their homes and then refuse to sell or even negotiate when I made a decent offer. Why?

I believe the person simply wants an appraisal, has no intention of selling, and doesn't stop to think that this behavior is even slightly inconsiderate! A relative or neighbor saw the person's collectible or collection and said, "Susie, you ought to find out what that's worth! People advertise in the paper who'll come to your house and tell you." Susie wants to know if she's rich, so when she sees your ad she calls you.

Another reason, I believe, is just plain devilment. An older person who's lonesome gets a half hour of entertainment from your struggle to buy her precious item. It needn't take you long to make an offer if she has only one or two items. The real problem is when there's a whole houseful.

If early conversation makes you think you're dealing with a nonseller, end the call as quickly as possible. Out of pure frustration the first few times this happened to me I hung on, trying desperately to make the purchase. It didn't take long to realize the so-called seller was laughing inside.

To qualify the person's interest early in the meeting, I've learned to say something like, "I'm interested in your furniture and I'd like to help you by buying it all. Let's save a lot of time—you tell me what you want for everything." The answer can be revealing. If she has no intention of selling, she'll say, "I want to know what it's worth."

My answer: "Ma'am, it'll take me two hours to do a professional appraisal, item by item, and certify the values. I'm a certified member of Appraisal Committee of the Pennsylvania Antiques Association (here I show my appraiser's card), and my standard rate for an appraisal is $35 per hour plus travel time." Chances are she has no interest in paying for an appraisal.

"I'm sorry I misunderstood," I add, "I thought you said you wanted to know what your furniture is worth. That calls for an appraisal. On the other hand, if you wish to sell it, I'll be happy to negotiate a price. Do you want to sell it?"

Now she must answer yes or no. If she hedges with "It depends on what it's worth," she's not ready to sell and it's time to leave. Whatever you do, don't do a free appraisal!

If it's one or two items, a quick estimate can be made. If your offer's rejected, ask, "If my offer of $750 isn't enough, what would make you happy?" She's doing the selling. She should know what will satisfy her.

I've often said something like, "Well, $750 won't make you happy. I'll bet if I offered you $2,000 you'd take it. "Oh yes," she'll reply, "that'll be fine."

"I said I'd *bet* you'd accept it, What I've *offered* is $750 and we seem to be headed for somewhere between $750 and $2,000. It isn't going to be $2,000. I'll go $800. How about it?" Maybe that will get a counterproposal. If it doesn't, that's it. Don't beg. She's proved she won't sell.

A friend of mine, a dealer who's an expert in house call technique, told me that when the person asks him what he'll offer, he says, "Ma'am, you're the seller. You've got to tell me. If I like your price I'll buy it."

If she says, "What'll you give?" he answers, "Ma'am, I won't *give* anything. I'll *pay* you if you'll tell me the amount and I agree to it." He keeps trying to get the seller to name a price. He says it works for him, that people who want to sell will come up with a price. Those who want a free appraisal aren't going to sell anyway, so why waste time?

Seller's Worry Meets Buyer's Remorse

I bought six toy soldiers from a lady for $35. They were not great, and when I got home I had buyer's remorse–I was darned sure I had paid ten bucks too much. But a deal's a deal, and she seemed a nice lady.

She also rethought the deal. I had left my card in case she found anything else to sell me. She called to say a neighbor told her I robbed her on the soldier deal. "What should I have paid you?" I asked.

"Why, my neighbor told me they're worth a hundred dollars at least."

"Ma'am, I don't want to see you dissatisfied. I'll return the soldiers, and you just give me my $35 dollars back."

"Well, he said he would have given me $50."

"Good," I replied. "Give me his name and phone number. I'll arrange to get the soldiers to him. He can give me $35 and pay you the $15. I don't want either of you to be unhappy."

"Well, that's not what I want. I want you to give me $15 more."

"No Ma'am," I said, effectively putting an end to the nonsense. "I'll cancel the deal, but I won't make a new one." She said goodbye, and I kept the soldiers. It was a case where both seller and buyer were unhappy. That's the way it goes sometimes, fortunately not often.

Happy Sellers

It's better to have satisfied sellers. They may be more important to the success of your business than happy buyers. They'll recommend you to friends who will call when they have things to sell. Sometimes a seller will test you by showing you things, sell them to you, then call you in a couple of weeks to "see some things I didn't remember I had."

This happened to me with a man who had a collection of tin toys and soldiers to sell, a much larger collection than he revealed after answering my ad. On that first visit, I bought everything he showed me—about ten pieces.

A month later he called again and I went back a second time. Then, after another month came a third call. At the end of the third and final visit, he told me he had checked with a friend of his in the antiques business who, although not involved in toys, has an idea of their value and has price guides which he shared with my seller.

After each of the first two visits, he consulted his friend and they looked up prices in the guides. His friend had explained how dealers have to buy at wholesale prices and advised him that my prices were fair. The man thanked me for giving him decent prices because he had no idea of the value of his things.

I had included $50 each for two character toys on my first visit. I sensed at the time I could have bought them for much less, but if I had, there would not have been a second, much less a third, call.

Strategy

Your best lessons on handling house calls are learned through experience. Start by being courteous and understanding with regard to the quality of the items. Since you have no idea to whom the collection may have belonged, it's dangerous to criticize the items in an effort to buy them cheaply.

If they had been prized possessions of a widow or deceased mother, you can appreciate the seller's opinion of you if you say "This is junk—not worth anything." You're not just looking at costume jewelry or kitchen items. Your looking at the possessions of a loved one! Anything you say about them is a reflection on that loved one. Just make your offer.

Don't go overboard in the other direction! I've made house calls with one man who trips through rooms exclaiming "Oh, wonderful! Just lovely! Bee-you-ti-ful!" By the time we get to the kitchen the seller thinks she's going to get rich! She looks shocked when my friend is willing to pay only $200. Her expression says: "If they're so damned wonderful, why're you offering me so little?"

In place of either denigration or extravagant praise, you might say something like, "Your mother certainly took good care of these things." That makes the seller feel good but doesn't promise anything.

When It's Old

Some sellers have read just enough about big values in antiques to expect a fortune for anything that's old. You may even have to tell a seller that not everything old is valuable. Age is, after all, only one factor in determining value. Give the seller confidence that you are a professional and sincerely interested in paying a fair price.

If there's a large quantity of items, don't share item-by-item estimates with the seller. I carry a notebook in which I write down and add up my estimates. Then I make my offer but refuse to discuss values of single items, except when the person is paying for an appraisal. Even then, there may be items that need further research. If this is the case, I make notes and do the pricing later. An appraisal is always written and bound in professional form, with a rationale for the value of each item. That's what the client pays for. A *buying* estimate is your private property.

If you need to explain your refusal to discuss each item, say, "Ma'am, I can only estimate. Sometimes I guess high, sometimes low. The value I place on any one item doesn't mean much, I'm going to give you my offer for the whole lot."

Occasionally you'll find a seller has only a few items that interest you. Ask, "Would you be interested in selling some of these? They're nice, but some are just not in my line."

More often than not the seller will accommodate you. I found a valuable toy in a pile of junk that had been lined up for inspection on a back porch. It was such a great one that I was afraid that if I offered what I *should* pay for it the seller might hold it back thinking she should get a second opinion. So, I selected the toy and four pieces of junk and made an offer for the armful. The seller didn't realize that the toy was worth more than the other items put together and then some! She probably divided my offer by five and figured she was being overpaid at the rate of $35 per piece. I believe she thought she got the better of me when I had actually paid her a fair price for one good piece and zero for the ones that were worth exactly that!

I make a firm offer and won't bargain when I'm indifferent about whether I want the stuff. If the collection is a good one however, and my first offer is rejected I ask for a counter offer, saying, "Well, what *would* you take for these things?" If this produces a price that's in my ball park I have something to deal with. If the counter offer is acceptable, I've got the deal. I say "yes" fast, peel off the money, say thanks, and leave with the treasure. My advice is don't talk too much, don't oversell, don't hang around. Pay and get out.

The "Big Bills" Close

Always carry plenty of hundreds and fifties to close the buy. There's nothing as convincing as big bills being peeled off. It's too bad we don't have $1,000 bills any more.

According to dealers who use it, a "Big Bills Close" can be very effective. What you're after, as you get into bargaining on a purchase, is to have the seller take your money.

When the "Big Bills Closer" thinks agreement is near, he peels off C-notes to the amount he's offered, pauses, then plunks down one more. He pockets the remainder. The seller says "yes" by picking up the bills.

The solution to the problem in closing is to get the other person to perform an act that's symbolic of giving assent to your proposition. The salesman can get a buyer to give assent by signing a contract. You as buyer get assent by getting the seller to take your money.

Let's say you've made an offer of $500 and the seller counters with $800. To use "Big Bills," don't say another word. Just start plunking down bills on the dining room table. The choice of how many bills is yours. Your positive attitude makes it apparent that it's your firm and final offer.

"One, two, three . . ." on to the point where you want to stop. With your original offer of $500 and the seller's counteroffer of $800, you continue counting: "four, five, six . . ." and stop. Look the seller in the eye and say "There you are—$600."

If she picks up the money the deal is made. It's a lot easier for her than saying "Yes."

Emotional Strings

Sometimes a seller has an emotional attachment to a piece or a collection and finds it difficult to face the fact that it's about to be sold and moved out. If it's sterling silver tableware, imagine how such a person will feel if she thinks you'll sell the family heirlooms to be melted down!

Head off emotional reactions when you enter the home and meet the seller. Don't rave about her things, just show consideration of her feelings. She wants to think you "love" her things. Such sellers feel much happier if they believe you're going to keep the item or collection for your own use—they're comfortable to know it will have a "Happy Home." If it is going to be for your own home, by all means say so. I would not lie about this, however. Nor would I pretend that I'm a collector, not a dealer. If the opportunity comes up in negotiating with such a person, I make it clear I'm buying for resale. If they don't want to sell to me, that's okay. Handing a business card to the person when you first enter reinforces your reason for the call and heads off emotional overtones.

Reward the Seller

One dealer friend makes it a practice to reward the seller with a later bonus payment after he's sold a number of items from the purchase. He calls on the seller at her home and gives her a bonus of 10% to 20% of the original purchase price. It cements relations and if that person has anything else to sell, you can bet she'll call him. She'll tell her friends about him too!

Not long after my friend told me of that practice, I had occasion to purchase a substantial quantity of rare toys from a lady whose brother had owned them as a child. I researched values because I had never dealt in these items before that day. I talked with other dealers who had handled them and consulted price guides. Based on that research, I offered a sum that was accepted. My purchase price assumed I could sell them for between $1,000 and $1,500.

The price guide was four years old and I wasn't totally confident of the advice I'd received, so I priced the toys higher than my investment would dictate. Instead of $1,500 the toys sold for almost $2,000. I visited the lady and shared the additional margin with her. My act was simply keeping faith with a very nice person, enhanced by a bit of guilt for not knowing the value of her things when I made the purchase.

She regarded it as a sign of professional integrity. It was truly "Bread cast upon the waters," since after that day she called me back at least ten times to buy more, finally resulting in my handling the auction of the entire household when she and her husband moved into a retirement home.

In "Over Your Head"

Sometimes you're behind the eight ball if you don't have expertise to evaluate a buy, or if you don't have cash to float the deal, or worse, both. If you're used to dealing in flea market items, what do you do when a friend offers to sell a few pieces of fine art? What if the apparent value is in the tens of thousands and you have only enough cash to float a purchase of a thousand or two? In addition you haven't dealt enough in art to be sure of your ability to evaluate it. What a pickle!

First, let's examine a solution to the financing part. If you can make an accurate market appraisal and your credit is good, you may be able to borrow money from your bank. This will be easy if you've been a customer of the bank for years and have met your obligations to them completely and on time. Let's say you've borrowed money on an installment contract to buy an automobile, and they carry a $60,000 mortgage on your home.

Getting a Line of Credit

Go see the president of the bank or the branch manager and inquire about a line of credit. He'll ask for a financial statement showing your assets, liabilities, and net worth. It's like a balance sheet that a company issues to show its financial condition, except that it's a financial description of your personal financial status.

The bank will also want an income and expense statement. Don't wory about the form of these things. Your banker will have blank forms on which you can make the statements. Make sure your information is truthful and complete.

He may have to submit the papers to a loan committee, but that won't take long, and in a few days he'll phone to tell you how much of a credit line you've been given. Generally he'll have asked you in the initial discussion how much credit you need and what it will be used for. You might say that $30,000 will be your maximum need at any one time and that you'll use it to finance inventory purchases for your antiques business. You should make it clear that you'll repay each withdrawal as quickly as you can make sales that bring in the gross income to do so. He may ask questions about your business that have to do with margins, expenses, rate of turnover, whether you give credit, and so forth.

What a line of credit means is that you have borrowing power equal to the credit line of the $30,000 that was extended to you by the bank. You can borrow any part of it at any time simply by phoning the bank and naming a sum of money to be put as a deposit into your checking account. You are not asked to give the purpose of the loan. The agreement will stipulate that your loan account must be cleared (paid up) for at least one full month during each year. Then, at the end of the year the bank will renew your credit line, or even increase it, for another year.

The amount of interest you will pay is usually a point or two higher than the prime rate and will change with the prime during the year. It will be far cheaper than the interest you would have paid if you had taken an installment loan, since it's computed on a "simple interest" basis. The size of your repayment is up to you, and you must pay interest due each month. The loan must be cleared by the end of the contract year.

Joint Venture

The other solution is to find a business partner, preferably one with experience in the type of merchandise you're buying *and* an outlet to share in selling the material once you've bought it. Your partner should be someone you trust and get along with. If there's a shadow of doubt on either of these questions, forget the whole deal. While the bank won't try to run you business, a joint venture partner might!

The partner should be one who, in addition to providing some financing, can lend other advantages to the deal such as supplying a large truck or providing a store location where part of the stuff can be sold. If he's a specialist in the merchandise you're thinking of buying, so much the better. His expertise will be helpful in figuring the offer. Each partner makes an evaluation of each item or group of items, then the estimates are compared and talked through to a price decision.

Here's the way a joint venture can work: You each put up half the money for the buy and share in the expense and work of buying and hauling it to your location and that of your partner. Together you go through the items and agree on prices for each one. You agree on a rock-bottom discount (usually a percentage to be applied to any items). You decide which items to liquidate immediately through an auction house or to some other dealer or collector— the partnership acts as "picker." The income from those immediate sales is immediately divided fifty-fifty.

The remainder of the merchandise is divided between your two locations. Perhaps his antiques shop is the place for higher-priced items and your flea market location will serve ideally for lower-priced ones. Maybe each of you has a mailing list of collectors who might buy some of the items. You might put an ad in a collector paper if that seems warranted, the expenses of such a promotion being split evenly. All decisions are made jointly and expenses shared equally.

The strength of the joint venture comes from taking advantage of the strong points of each member. It doesn't make any difference where or by which of you the items are sold, you split the cash expenses and the income evenly.

If after an agreed upon period, say six months, items remain, they should be liquidated and the results split evenly. You might divide items—"One for you, one for me"—or you might consign them to an auction house and split the proceeds. The point is to write an equitable ending to the partnership. The voyage of many partnerships ends on the rocks of despair because no provision was made for equitable termination.

In such a joint venture, you have laid off half the risk, half the work, and of course, you've given up half the profit to do it. But think of the alternative. There wouldn't have been a chance that you could make the deal at all!

Buying from Antiques Shops

To make your antiques business grow you should be on the alert for good buys wherever they can be made. My travels have often taken me to many sections of this country and Europe. I've bought for resale in thrift shops, junk yards, building materials yards, salvage yards, "jumbles" (in England) and high-style European and American antiques shops.

Many of us have learned the following truism about the antiques business:

    The antiques business is really a transportation business. It consists
of relocating things from where they can be bought cheaply to where
they will sell for more.

It's why we have pickers and haulers who find furniture and primitives in Pennsylvania and haul them to North Carolina. Then, a few years later, when supplies in Pennsylvania are depleted, pickers and haulers will be filling their trucks in North Carolina and hauling back to Pennsylvania!

You can be your own picker when you travel. Remember that as a dealer you almost always have the advantage of buying at an automatic discount from another dealer. This seem to be a traditional 10% to 15% off when you show your tax license, business card, or other means of identification. Many dealers will give more and once they know you're a dealer bargain to a lower price, if it's an item they've had around for a while. They are less reluctant to discount deeply to a dealer than they are to a nondealer. To the public, a deep (40% or more) discount is a sign of weakness. To a dealer who understands the business, it's simply a matter of an item that won't sell *where it is*. The dealer buys it because he knows he can sell it in his area.

It might be well to summarize the whole subject of dealers buying from dealers by saying:

   A conservative estimate holds that 80% of *all* selling by antiques dealers is made to *other dealers*.

The antiques business is like a giant pyramid game—the antique moves from dealer to dealer (through dealers, auction houses, pickers, and haulers) until the last one in the chain gets stuck! It is sort of the "Peter Principle" of antiques dealing.

   The antique gets sold at increasing markups until it reaches its ultimate level of overpriced unsaleability.

That's not *quite* true of course, because usually somewhere along the line a collector or a museum buys it or it gets broken and thrown away.

Many dealers I know say they can make a call on any antiques shop in the country, and buy *something* they can sell at a profit. This is probably true of most advanced dealers who have clients waiting for them to come up with something special.

It may be that the higher you go in the trade the more of a picker you become. You graduate from the crap-shooting pose of a new dealer who's guessing what will sell to the position of rendering a "buying service" to select clients. In a sense you're taking a commission for procuring items and turning them over to collectors or other dealers.

It's easy to make mistakes. I've bought beautiful duck decoys in New England that I thought would sell fast to the duck hunters of Pennsylvania. No, I quickly learned that the Pennsylvania boys want Pennsylvania birds! The only way to prevent that kind of disaster is to know the wants in your area and look for items that satisfy them. When you find the right deal, buy and buy fast!

I've bougtht rye straw baskets in New England for a $1 that resold for $40 in Pennsylvania. Cast-iron hardware that's plentiful in Pennsylvania goes well in New England. The Southwest has been a fine market for oak furniture when it's been a drag in the Northeast.

Some items that are wanted in a given area just won't sell any place else. I own four paintings by a New England artist that are worth pretty good money in New Hampshire, but the artist is virtually unknown in Pennsylvania. I wouldn't think of trying to sell them there!

Generally speaking, don't drive by an antiques shop without making a call. You'll find something to buy, and at the very least it can be fun to compare notes. Once in a while you'll establish a relationship that can result in good business for both of you. You might each supply the other person with stuff for his specialty. I've left 50 business cards for every one that's paid off, but that one makes it worthwhile. And you'll meet a lot of interesting, nutty people— with a sprinkling of curmudgeons. That's the business!

Yard Sales, Tag Sales, Thrift Shops

My own experience shows that once you're an established dealer spending time at amateur outlets is mostly wasted. Others violently disagree with me, and it's certainly worth the effort to try in your area. Who knows, you might dig up some good sources. At one time my wife and I were able to buy silver, lamps, furniture, primitives, and rare books in New England tag sales and at a local Fairfield County thrift shop.

The Estate Sale

In the last few years a professional element has entered the tag sale market. It's called the "Estate Sale," run by dealers as a consignment sale. They sign up the home owner, organize the sale, price everything, and generally do a good job of managing all aspects of a tag sale. They've transferred a large part of the markup in second hand treasure from the dealer, who used to shop tag sales, into their own pockets.

As has been said before, if you can't beat 'em, join 'em. Many antiques dealers have started organizing estate sales as part of their own services. It's a new, and apparently, profitable, way to conduct business and worth looking into as something you might try after you've had general antiques selling experience, especially if there's no one in your area offering the service.

You, as an antiques dealer, offer the Estate Sale service on either a straight commission basis or on a commission plus fee basis. If it's straight commission you bear all expenses and charge a commission of about 50%. On commission plus fee, your commission would be lower—say 35%—but the client pays for advertising and labor to use in the sale (clerks, cashier).

You set up the house, price and tag all items, and brief your help. You arrange the house so that people enter only through the front door and exit past a cashier at the kitchen door. A clerk is positioned to give help in each two or three rooms. Each item to be bought is carried to the kitchen where the cashier takes money and issues receipts. Larger items, of course, can be marked "Sold" and removed later. There should be nothing visible in the house that's not for sale. Nonsale items are removed to the basement or another location. Basically, you're setting up a store that's intended to sell out in two days.

On day one (usually Saturday) the door opens at 8 A.M. The opening time is strictly adhered to. Potential buyers line up at the front door awaiting opening time, and at eight o'clock you admit as many people as you can handle at one time. The cashier in the kitchen keeps track of how many leave through the back door. When five leave, five more are admitted through the front door.

On opening day no discounts are given. If a person wishes to leave a written bid on something, he may. He should be told that he will have a small chance of making a deal with an offer much below the asking price.

At the end of Day One, records of the day's sale are reviewed with the owner or executor and decisions are made:

1. Should any prices be lowered?

2. Should any offers extended on the first day be accepted?
3. Should any of the displays be changed or rearranged?
4. Should offers be directly accepted on the second day, and at what maximum discount?

Day two proceeds just like the first day. At day's end, there should be very little left. People who made offers are called and the deals closed. Whatever remains is hauled off to the dealer's place of sale or to an auction house. Settlement with the owner or executor is made. Your payment, except for that from any items you must still dispose of, is completed. The owner gets most of his money.

It's a lot of work, and unless there's pretty good value in the complete furnishings, it might not be worth it to you to run an estate sale. But it forms an interesting alternative to offer to a seller.

Mail Order Buying

The prime source for buying antiques by mail for resale in flea markets and antiques co-ops is *Antique Trader*, a weekly newspaper of about 100,000 circulation that's comprised of almost 100% advertising. The few articles it publishes are interesting but of little value in pricing decisions. They mostly describe collectibles you might want to know about.

The *Trader's* classified and display advertising, however, is something else! There are thousands of offerings of everything under the sun every week. I have had some success buying from the *Trader*, but far more success advertising in it for people who want to be on my catalog list for toy soldiers. I was able to build a strong, profitable list within a year by running a $4 classified ad each week. For less than $300 in advertising, I was in business!

Many of the items offered, particularly the "warehouse find" type, seem misleading. Once I had to write the publisher to seek his help in getting an advertiser to fulfill his promise to send me a display case I had bought in good faith. This was after a wait of many weeks and several letters to the advertiser. When it arrived it was exactly what I wanted, well worth the money, and I used it to good purpose in my retail display. If I had not had a bad experience I would have ordered at least a couple more.

Antique Trader Adventures

However, that kind of advertised product is not the most important one carried by the *Trader*. The real action is from hundreds of classified ads on antique specialties. Your *Trader* is supposed to arrive on Monday, but, due to the slowness of the postal department, it can be as late as Thursday on the East or West Coasts. My *Trader* arrives in The U.S. Virgin Islands two weeks later, but of course that's to be expected. The total response to all *Trader* ads must be enormous! Subscribers sit down with it immediately and pore through all the offerings.

There it is—an ad on toy soldiers offered for sale! I pick up the phone and immediately call the lady in Texas who's offered them. My call, for once, is in time, and I promise to send $120 plus ten bucks for postage immediately. I've bought 40 soldiers made by Mignot of France at a decent price. I send my check, and the next week the soldiers arrive. They're great. I'm very satisfied and write telling her so.

A month later my Texas friend phones about some more soldiers she's bought! That's the way it works when you find a professional who wants to do business. Once you and another dealer get to know each other by phone and mail, the seller doesn't wait for the check. The items are sent immediately.

Another ad—again, toy soldiers. I call—they've been sold and I've wasted a buck or two in long distance money.

Next week, my *Trader* is three days late. I make three calls Thursday and everything I call about has already been sold. General rule: Never phone a *Trader* advertiser later than Tuesday morning!

The next week there's another supplier—new to me. I call, the item is still available, but I worry because the dealer doesn't know enough about toy soldiers to describe the ones he has. I make the deal and send the money. The following week the stuff arrives, condition: terrible. I send it back and the advertiser refunds my money immediately. Nobody's feelings are hurt.

I get a phone call from Illinois. It's an auctioneer who has some soldiers coming up in an auction and he's seen my "Wanted to Buy" ad in *Trader*. He's looked them up in O'Brien's *Collecting Toys* and gives me the catalog numbers.

I sit down after his call and make up a list of what I would pay for the pieces and phone it to him as an absentee bid. Two weeks later I get a letter from the auctioneer telling me which pieces I bought in the auction, I send him a check and he immediately ships the soldiers—two extremely rare figures!

A month later the same auctioneer calls. This time he has Arcade iron doll house furniture. I've never sold any, can't find any price guidance, my dealer friends know nothing, so I call the auctioneer and tell him that I'll bid up to $10 per piece. Two weeks go by and I get a letter from him telling me that the pieces sold in his auction for from $30 to $50 each! Can't win 'em all!

Mostly, mail order sellers sell with the guarantee that you'll be 100% satisfied. If you're not and return the items in *exactly* the same condition in which they were received within a few days, they'll refund your money. In my own mail order business I have followed exactly that practice. It pays for both buyer and seller.

Mail Auctions

Mail Auctions provide a way to buy specialized items, but I generally lose out to collectors who can afford to pay more than I can offer.

You get on the auction list by sending a small fee to cover the cost of mailing and Polaroid prints of the items. The auctioneer sends you lists, photos, and bid sheets of each auction, usually monthly or bimonthly. You write your bids on his bid sheet and return it. Then he sends a final result sheet, showing the amount of the successful bids on all items. If you're a high bidder on anything, a bill is enclosed. You send your check and he ships. I've never returned things and would not do so unless the item had been grossly misrepresented.

Much paper material—catalogs, books, labels, posters, prints, store advertising, and autographs—are sold in this way. I know of three mail order toy soldier auctions, all of which I have taken part in as a bidder.

Mail order auction dealers try to do business with one hand on the Bible—they don't want to get into hassles on returns, so they take pains to describe each item completely, defects as well as good points.

Drop-Ins

Drop-ins are people you've never seen before and will probably never see again. They produce ten Gorham place settings in sterling or a handful of 18-K jewelry from a wool sock. You buy at your own risk. It's well to remember that you cannot take good title to stolen goods. If you purchase a hot item and it's later discovered that you have it, you must give it up. You could be out quite a bit of money.

One rule I try to follow is never to buy from children if I have the slightest suspicion that the item might be lifted either from another flea market stand or from home. It's hard to believe that the carpenter's measuring tape a youngster shows me came from anywhere but Dad's toolbox. It might even be a good thing to ask "Is that your Dad's?" He might be shamed into returning it to the toolbox.

Most dealers, including myself, do not wish to be a part of dealing in stolen merchandise. You can ask the seller where he got the item, but usually if it's stolen he'll have a prepared speech which you could then judge on the basis of its probability. It will sound logical, even when it's a lie.

If you do decide to buy from a drop-in, ask for his name, address, phone number, and driver's license number. If it's stolen merchandise, he'll probably say he left his ID at home and go away quickly. Interestingly, most of my drop-ins have been women whom I've seen shopping around the flea market and who I know to be okay. Some of them have been customers too.

CHAPTER FIVE

All about Auctions

Reading Guide. The first part of this chapter is an introduction to auctions. If you're an habitual auction goer, read on to get new insights from an "insider." Be sure you understand:

- The main advantage of the estate auction.
- Auction Survival Rules #1 and #2.
- How to bid.
- Protecting yourself against unethical auction practices such as pooling, puffing, taking bids "off the wall."

Forty years ago, I attended my first auction. I had always wondered what a real auction would be like since my interest was stimulated by scenes in a motion picture that portrayed the excitement of an auction room. I can't remember the name of the auction house although I remember it was in Fairfield County, Connecticut, not far from our Westport home. It was in the 1950s.

The sale room was so small merchandise came from another room as needed. Lighting was dim, chairs uncomfortable, and ventilation nonexistent. Those who didn't find seats stood in side aisles.

The auctioneer was personable and got the job done. That night I placed my first bid and had the time of my life! I opened the bidding for a brass chocolate pot for a buck, bravely stayed with it and finally bought it for $3. It's still a prized possession, more for the memory of the occasion than for the pot itself. I wondered if I had paid too much. It would sell for $20 today, not a great deal above what you'd expect by adjusting for inflation, so it wasn't that much of a bargain.

A vivid memory is of a couple who nervously bid on a small oil painting which could have been from the eighteenth century. They went through hell with each bid, and finally won their prize for $50. As the crowd cheered, I found myself wishing I'd had the nerve to compete with them for the painting.

We were hooked, and while attending auctions in New England during the next ten years, the idea occurred that someday I would like to be an auctioneer. It appealed to the ham in me, and I thought it would be an exciting way to make a living.

Professional Auctioneering

Twenty years later I attended the Mendenhall School of Auctioneering, apprenticed to a licensed auctioneer, took the Pennsylvania state auctioneer's exam, and, at an age when most people think of retiring, began an auctioneering career. I was right—auctioneering is a great profession. I wish I'd started earlier, but what I've had of it has been fun. I've learned about the auction business and even more about myself under the stress of running the auction.

Some of what I'll share with you in this chapter you may not find anywhere else because auctioneers don't want to talk about practices that are illegal or unethical. My feeling is that if you're going to attend auctions, you should know the inside story.

The Auction Method

The auction method, practiced by honorable and skillful professionals selling to knowledgeable and honest buyers, is close to the theoretical market perfection found only in economics textbooks. A willing seller faces anxious buyers who compete to buy at the lowest possible price. Supply versus demand, raw and uncluttered. Well, sort of. Read on.

In many sections of the country the auction method has become preeminent in sales of cattle, tobacco, machinery, farm goods, real estate, and antiques. In my short career, my partners and I have sold houses, vacant property, airplanes, antiques, gold and silver coins, toys, dolls, and all kinds of collectibles. The auction gives the antiques dealer an important means of building an inventory of antiques. It also offers him a way quickly to liquidate stock he no longer wishes to carry.

Estate Auctions

Before the physical assets of an estate can be divided, everything must be turned into cash. The auction is the quickest and most efficient way to do it. Furniture, fixtures, machines, automobiles, household goods, tools, antiques, and hundreds of pieces "too numerous to mention" get sold by the auctioneer. It can be your golden opportunity for buying at a decent price, or your downfall if you don't set rules for yourself.

Large estates are often sold on the premises of the deceased. Smaller ones are moved to the auction house where they are offered in a combined sale along with other consignments. In either case, the auctioneer prefers to name the estate in his advertising to stress the level of quality of the sale.

Fig. 5-1 One of the hottest toy items in recent years has been the pedal car, particularly examples from the twenties and thirties. Here's a highly collectible variation, the pedal plane, artfully restored. An item that can be expected to bring a high price at auction.

In farm areas, auctions are held to dispose of the usual estate items with farm machinery, animals, lumber, guns, land, and buildings.

Whether on-site or in the auction room, the estate auction draws a huge crowd of people with wide-ranging interests and fills a full day or even two or three days or evenings.

Dealers and collectors carefully follow auction listings and sometimes travel great distances to attend sales that offer material within their fields of interest. Truly outstanding sales result when the estate of a public figure goes under the hammer. Recent examples include the estate of the late actor, Steve McQueen, an incurable collector, and the bankruptcy sale of the much admired John Connolly of Texas.

Antiques dealers always find something of interest in such a sale. Even where no noted person is involved an audience of 500 is not uncommon. About half the total audience will remain until the end of the sale, and even a couple of hundred people provide enough competition to insure spirited bidding.

Consignment Sales

Consignment houses take merchandise from anyone and schedule sales on a regular basis, often weekly. The auctioneer also conducts specialized sales and usually is also an "itinerant" auctioneer which means he'll contract to sell merchandise at the owner's location wherever it's located.

A typical consignment auction might consists of lots from three or four households, a few boxes of stuff from dealers, and inventory from a collector or dealer. There might also be local produce, eggs, and plants if the auction house is located in the country.

There will be junk along with the better stuff, but normally the auctioneer tries not to mix the two in the same lot. He may even have an assistant conduct a separate sale of junk while he conducts the auction of better merchandise.

Before the Bidding Starts

Before the first bid, there's time for you to go through all lots carefully. Before one auction my son pointed to a box in which were four old lithographed tin toys. I checked them out, put them in the bottom of the box and covered them with layers of worthless junk. I saw another fellow go through the box down to the bottom, then bury what he found there just as I had. I knew he would be my competition!

Bidding on the box started at fifty cents, quickly went to four dollars, then took off in two dollar increments, fives, and finally tens until I bought it for $140! The four toys were worth about $400. People who witnessed the bidding expressed wonder at what those two crazy coots were fighting over.

Selling at Auction

In addition to buying there, you can use the auction house to dispose of your mistakes. Don't expect to make money on them. You couldn't sell them, so how can the auctioneer do better? Whatever you get for them is found money because, by the time you've given up on these tired items you've learned they won't sell for a decent price. The beauty of the auction is that *everything sells!*

Beware of the other side of that coin and watch out for tired items from other dealers! If it didn't sell for them, it probably won't sell for you. I've seen items show up on different tables at the market, then go to the auction and back into circulation! Some items, worn from handling, end in the flea market dumpster through which some dealers search at the end of the selling day. Round and round goeth the junk!

Buying at Auction

It's important to know how to buy at auction, so I'll outline principles that pay off for me. First, don't get carried away. A collector might want an item badly enough to bid until he wins, but a dealer can't afford to do this. Your target is to pay no more than half of what you believe you'll resell it for.

Your best bet for fresh merchandise is the estate auction. If you've ever been first to go through an unexplored 100-year-old attic, you know the excitement of finding fresh merchandise. The estate sale taps into such troves. From deep in boxes, dresser drawers, pantries, and old chests in barns and storerooms are found the gems—antiques we're all hunting but seldom find. Contrast that with tired dealer stuff.

The tenure of one family in a house can extend back to times when everyday items that became unfashionable were tucked away—a bonanza of collectibles waiting for the auctioneer to find in boxes, dressers, and old chests.

Even though heirs sometimes raid the treasure trove, unless they're experts, they won't recognize the value in many mundane looking objects that will go up for sale.

Prior to an estate auction for which I was auctioneer, two sisters who were to share the proceeds of the auction spent three days going through the attic. They removed family nostalgia plus some valuable collectibles. Auctioneers plead with heirs not to do this since it waters down the sale, but one can't blame people who wish to keep tender reminders of earlier days.

Among items that remained after the sisters' blitz were a half dozen "Snow Babies," super little two-inch white fuzzy figures of little fat kids in winter poses. The oversight resulted in a good commission to us, as well as a good sale for the estate, when the little figures sold for more than $30 each!

At a crowded estate auction, you'll have trouble seeing everything before the auction starts. Faced with thousands of items, the auctioneer often can't unpack everything prior to the sale. A box will be carried to the podium and as items are removed great finds can be revealed for the first time.

You've got to be alert if you're buying at this kind of auction. It's hard to judge condition, particularly if one is seated far from the podium. Sometimes an object turns out to be something different than it looks to be when it's held up. That keeps prices low because everyone in the audience is in the same boat and nobody wants to take a chance. However, your courage may be more than rewarded by a dozen or so great buys at low prices, more than enough to make up for your mistakes.

You don't have to keep the mistakes, either, in most cases. The auctioneer will usually take back and resell an item that was falsely described or has a flaw he failed to point out. I've returned many items because of undisclosed flaws and never gotten more than a low grumble from the auctioneer.

The auctioneer rightly objects to the buyer who waits until the auction is almost over to return an item. Inspect each piece immediately and if it has an undisclosed defect return it without delay.

How To Survive

☞   Auction Survival Rule #1—Inspect each item carefully.

Don't be afraid to open packages, pull drawers, and rummage through boxes. One country auctioneer I know makes up what he calls "rootin' boxes" for buyers to dig through. He makes them up with care, sometimes placing something of good value at the bottom so buyers will think they've discovered something great.

Sometimes, of course, the value of an item is disguised by its accidental inclusion in an otherwise undistinguished mixed lot. I was searching through what looked to be a bunch of cheap stuff tied together with string. Untying it I found a cheap fishing rod, an aluminum cane, curtain rods, yardsticks, and a cased split-bamboo antique fly rod worth at least $150 to a collector. I carefully replaced the valuable rod in its beat-up case and retied the bundle perhaps a little tighter than when I first found it. Later I saw several people struggle with the knots and give up. I bought the whole thing for $2.

To check everything, regard each display table as a separate field of action. Scan from one side to the other, with each sweep taking in a narrow band of view, like reading a page of print. Closely examine anything of interest and replace it on the table.

Be sure to look under tables where there may be goodies stored for lack of room, some hidden behind other items. Open cartons, move things, test moving parts, and try spring-wound motors. Plug in electrical devices to check their operation.

Use a magnet to test for iron and brass. Held to an item that looks like solid brass, the magnet will stick if it's plated and refuse to stick if it's solid brass. A magnifying glass will help you read marks on merchandise, discover small defects, and detect signs of natural wear. A jeweler's loupe attached to an eyeglass frame makes a convenient inspecting tool.

Look at things on the walls. If you're afraid to remove pictures or prints that are hanging, get one of the auctioneer's helpers to get it down for you and hold it while you take a look. Ask for information about items, but be prepared for helpers who don't know very much.

Choosing a Location

Arrive early to select a good location in the audience area. A couple of cardboard boxes with your last name on them will reserve seats while you take your pre-auction tour. Where's the best place to sit? If you're concerned about having your bids seen by other bidders, go to the rear of the house. The problem with that is that you may have to turn hand springs to get your first bid in. Once you're in the bidding the auctioneer will come back to you.

I like to sit in the center of the house, a few rows from the front where I can see everything and easily get the auctioneer's attention. The auctioneer can find me when he has something he knows I'll be interested in. Auctioneers catch on quickly to your specialties and will look to you when your items come up, obviating the need for frantic waving. Once he knows you, the auctioneer will take a nod of your head as your bid.

Many dealers stand at the rear or side in order to see who's bidding against them. I've found it hard to bid while trying to watch other people. If you follow Rule #2 (below) you won't bid too much, so what's the difference who's bidding against you?

☞   Auction Survival Rule #2—Decide in advance what to pay.

As you preview the merchandise, write down the names of items you want to buy and the top price you will pay. Then *stick to your prices*—no matter what!

It's good to jot down prices that were paid for items you lost to others. Review of these results will keep you abreast of the market.

Most of the clunkers I've bought became mine when I cheated and went higher than the price I intended to pay. Instead of stopping when my opponent raised to my cutoff point, I figured, what the hell, one more bid won't matter. Then I made not one, but two, three or five more bids, shooting my budget for overpriced things I can't make money on. Dumb!

Another Day!

I'll always remember a Victorian iron Christmas tree fence, perfectly cast and still clad in its original green, red, and gold paint, with all pieces in a box, a beautiful and desirable piece designed to go around the tree or around the Pennsylvania Dutch "Putz." Actually I wanted it, not for resale but for my own collection of Christmas decorations. I stayed with the competition until the bidding hit $90 then realized my opponent would go much higher to get the fence. I signed off with misgivings. Golly, I thought, maybe just one more bid and I could have had it!

A year later, at another estate sale no more than ten miles away, the fence came up for bids. Not a similar one, the same one. I recognized the box and a couple of ornaments still in the box with it. I bought it for $32. You see, it can happen. Decide on your price and stick to it!

How to Bid at a Country Auction

You've carefully inspected each item, written down the names of things you want along with the maximum price you're willing to pay, grabbed your first cup of coffee and settled back in your chair. The auction is ready to start.

Usually the auctioneer warms up the audience, welcomes everybody, describes what he'll sell, and gives his ground rules. If it's an estate auction, he'll say something about the deceased as an appeal to people who recognize the name.

And Now, the Auctioneer

"This is an absolute auction folks, and that means the highest bid gets the item. There're no 'floors' or reserves.

"I'm Herb Brown, the auctioneer, and I'll be assisted by (*names of helpers*), and my assistant auctioneer (*name*), who'll call some of the bids for me. The pretty lady sitting to my right is Mrs. Brown who's my auction clerk as well as lifelong companion. Pretty, ain't she? Bid by raisin' your numbered bid card and wavin' your hand. No winkin', blinkin' or noddin'! And if you scratch your ear it's 'cause it itches. It ain't a bid! 'Nother thing—I won't take bids from behind me. You gotta be out in front where I can see you.

"All items are sold on a 'where is, as is' basis. That means you take your own chances when you buy. No guarantee on anything, *unless* I tell you some-thing' 'bout the condition of the item. If I say the motor works, you count on it workin'. If you buy it and it don't, bring it back *during the sale*, and we'll cancel the deal and put it back on the block. We can't take a thing back after the sale or even toward the end.

"On glass and china, I'll describe defects like cracks and chips. If I fail to do that and the item's badly chipped, you bring it back to me or to an assistant auctioneer and we'll take it back and cancel your purchase. But, please folks, don't nit-pick with teensy scratches.

" 'Where is' means you take possession when you buy an item. You're responsible for watchin' it before you take it home. I don't think there's any dishonest person at this auction, but, face it folks, somebody might make a mistake. So watch your items after you buy 'em.

"And, since we're all liable to be forgetful at times you won't mind my remindin' you if you bought anything, go to the cashier's table before you leave. I've got a good friend in the sheriff's office who helps me track down forgetful folks.

"We'll take your check so long's it's a bank in this state and you've got money in it. The cashier'll need your ID *before the auction* if you're gonna pay by check.

"We'll, that's about it, folks. Good luck and good biddin'. Pay what you can and enjoy the sale . . .

"Now whatamlbid, willabid fitty dollar f'this lamp . . . wallen, willa give forty . . . thirty . . . mansez 30, now 35, willa give 40 . . . ,"

The auction is off and running!

During the next three to eight hours, hundreds of items will be sold, dozens of purchasers will go home with good buys, and you, if you've appraised right and bid according to plan, will have additions to your flea market inventory on which you can make money.

If It's Your First Auction

Assume this is your first auction. You know what you want to buy, but you're nervous because you've never been in such a pressure cooker atmosphere. Hands shooting up. The auctioneer started slow, but now he's going like lightning. He knocks things down before you can get your wits together.

Right now, the thing to do is *relax*. Take a few minutes to get used to the auctioneer's chant. Some auctioneers are easy to understand, some difficult. *Listen for his numbers*. You needn't understand his words at all, just his numbers! He'll run words together between numbers (they're called filler words) like "whaddalabid" and use nonsense words to smooth out his chant to make it easy to perform for the better part of a day without tiring. After you listen for a while you'll know exactly where the bid is, and the rhythm of his chant will tip you off as to when he's about to drop the hammer and sell.

Generally you'll find the pattern of the auctioneer's chant gives you the number (in dollars) that has just been bid then the number (again, in dollars) he's looking for. In between are filler words. It goes like . . . "Twenny-five-willagive-thirty-twenny-five-thirty." Translated, that means he has a bid (somebody raised his hand or bidding card) of $25, and he now wants a bid of $30.

There's a reason for the shorthand! If he didn't use it, the auctioneer would be lucky to sell his 500 lots in a week! With it he can do it in a few hours and keep the audience interested enough to wait for the items they're interested in. After you've heard several complete pitches, from opening to "sold," and understand what the amount of the bid was at every stage, you've got it! Now you're ready to bid.

If you still don't feel confident, hold off until you can bid without panic. After a couple of auctions you'll wonder why you ever felt intimidated. By holding back at first, you may miss a few buys, but you've gotten along without them this far in life so why rush? You're getting an education in values and learning how to handle buying at auction, and it's costing nothing. Besides, it's kind of fun *not* to bid and just watch other people do their bidding.

You'll notice that the expert auctioneer *always* tells you what to bid, or, more properly, he asks you what you're going to bid by suggesting an amount. It's the sign of an amateur auctioneer at a charity auction when he asks, "What am I bid?" The audience sits on its hands until the auctioneer finally asks for a specific number: "Willamakit 60?," or whatever his style might be. You either bid it or you don't. Bid or let somebody else bid. If you bid and then hold back, somebody else will probably take over and continue the bidding, and you can get back in later if you wish.

At the start of an auction, most auctioneers speak more slowly than they will later in the sale. They know there are a few people who have not attended an auction before and they start slowly out of courtesy. Also, it takes the auctioneer a few minutes to get warmed up. Once he gets going and the audience is tuned in to his style and chant, he'll seem to be going like the wind. Actually, he's not speaking much faster than he would if he were saying the same things in ordinary conversation. It just seems, with his chant and filler words, that he's going fast. Soon you'll be fully confident that you understand every number and will feel comfortable as you bid.

How To Bid

How to bid? It's really easy. You were given a buyer's card when you registered at the cashier's desk or window. On it is your bidding number by which the clerk keeps track of your purchases. To place a bid early in the auction, raise your card high and wave it to make sure the auctioneer sees you. If the auctioneer doesn't see your bid, wave the card faster and higher. Later in the sale the auctioneer will look for your bid.

When you've made the high bid and the item is knocked down to you, *then* you raise your bidding number again to indicate to the clerk who sits somewhere near the auctioneer that you're the winner. The clerk writes down your bidding number plus the amount you agreed to pay, and, if the sale consists of numbered lots, the lot number. That information is communicated to the cashier on a sheet or ticket so your bill can be figured when you to check out.

When you decide to leave, go to the cashier's table, give your bidder's number, and the cashier will tally your bill. Be sure to check the prices on the receipt against your own record of what you bid. Professional clerks and cashiers seldom makes mistakes, but it's always possible.

The Bidding Increment

During the bidding the auctioneer will continue to ask for a raise in the amount of the bid until he believes he'll get no more. He then "knocks down" the item to the highest bidder. As bidding progresses, the difference between the last amount bid and what he wants as the next bid is called the "increment."

Say someone bids $10. The auctioneer will then ask for $11, or maybe $12.50, perhaps even $15. Generally the lower the value of the lot the smaller the increment. Most auctioneers are consistent with their own system of increments, something like $1 below $10, $2.50 up to a $25 value, $5 up to $50 and $10 over that.

If the auctioneer thinks the item should sell for several hundred, he's liable to start out raising the amount in increments of $25 or even $50.

He could be mistaken in the amount he thinks the lot will sell for. If you think the increment is too high, you can make a bid of half the asked for increment by holding one hand in a horizontal position, palm down with the other hand held under it, fingers up and touching the palm that's down. Then move your palm from side to side—in other words, you're saying, "Cut the bid in half." If he ignores your signal, it's not because he hasn't seen or doesn't understand it. He believes the item will sell high and won't waste time with small increments. Of course, he may accept your bid and lower the increment.

Sometimes, if the auctioneer has started too low (a dozen people scream to get into the bidding!) he'll jump the increment higher. He's admitting he underestimated the value of the lot and now wants to get the bidding going faster so as not to waste time.

Auctioneer's Techniques

The professional auctioneer tries to *help* people, not discourage them. His living depends on having satisfied sellers and happy buyers. He wants you to feel comfortable so you'll bid, get good buys, and come back to his next auction. He doesn't want you to feel intimidated or afraid that if you make a mistake you'll be stuck with something you don't want.

At the same time, the auctioneer wants to keep you on edge and aware of the intense competition that surges within the audience for each desirable offering. He works to make you know that if you don't make decisions quickly you're going to lose out to somebody else.

Sometimes the auctioneer will knock a lot down quickly just to teach the audience a lesson. This usually happens at the beginning of an auction before the audience warms up and gets competitive. He's trying to tell you to stop sitting on your hands and bid!

Correcting Mistakes

If you happen to wave at a friend and the auctioneer takes it as a bid, just wave your hand to get his attention, then tell him by shaking your head that it was no bid. He may lightly chastise you for confusing him with your greeting, but he won't make you stick with it.

The bid-handling technique practiced by most auctioneers is to pit two bidders against each other until one drops out, then find an additional bidder who will enter the bidding and go against the bidder who's left "in." It's difficult for an auctioneer to handle more than two bidders at once, particularly if they are located in widely separated areas of the audience.

For example, an item goes up and Buyer A opens the bidding for $20. Buyer B raises the bid to $22.50, and the two go head-to-head until Buyer B is high at $32.50 and Buyer A retires. During that period of bidding from $22.50 to $32.50, two other buyers tried to get in. The auctioneer stayed with Buyers A and B until A dropped out. Then, without missing a beat he goes to Buyer C who had tried to get in, asks him for a bid, and if he doesn't want to get in, Buyer C probably shakes his head to mean "No, I don't want in." The auctioneer remembers there was a Buyer D and looks for him. Buyer D nods or waves, meaning "yes I'll go $35." The auctioneer goes back to Buyer B who may raise the bid to $37.50 and the competition is now between Buyer B and Buyer D. They go on until one drops out. There may be a buyer E to take up the competition, or buyer A or C might re-enter the fray. Buyer A, B, C, or D— whichever one survives without a further bid being made by anybody else— is the buyer.

Can You Trust Him?

Auctioneers do not mean to misrepresent items they sell. Their business is successful only if they honestly represent merchandise and have happy buyers at the sale's end.

Auctioneers will not let you bid against yourself. Beginners often make this mistake in the excitement of the auction. You might bid $10, then when the auctioneer looks over the audience asking for $12.50, you may forget you're "in" and offer $12.50. The auctioneer will say: "You're in at ten," looking directly at you.

If he thinks you might not realize that someone else's bid is "in," he'll look at you and say, "You're out." It's your turn to raise the bid if you wish to.

Disputes between Buyers

Sometimes a bidder will believe he's bought an item when it was the bidder sitting directly behind or in front to whom the auctioneer gave the nod. In such a case, the auctioneer, upon hearing a protest, will back up the bidding to the point of dispute and continue it between the two contesting bidders. Everyone's entitled to make a mistake occasionally, and this is one that's easily made by the best of auctioneers.

Multiples

When there are two or more identical or very similar items being offered together as one lot, be sure you understand what the offer is. If you do not clearly understand the offer and wish to bid, ask the auctioneer. He will gladly explain.

One way to offer multiples is for the auctioneer to announce, "Here's a set of four chairs—all for one money." You know you're bidding a single amount of money that will buy all four chairs for one total amount.

Or he may say, "Four chairs—by the piece, take 'em all." That means that whatever you bid is multiplied by four if you're the buyer.

"Four chairs—by the piece, take one or more," means that if you're the successful buyer you may buy one, two, three, or four at the per-piece price you have bid. "Four chairs—by the piece—buyer's choice" means the same thing.

When four items are offered in a lot "by the piece—take one or more," and only one is chosen, the auctioneer then presents the three remaining chairs as the next lot. The next buyer may choose one or more, and the sale continues until all chairs are gone.

When there are a great many identical items the auctioneer may offer them "by the piece," get the highest bid, and ask the first buyer, "How many do you want?" After the first buyer states his choice, the auctioneer then addresses the audience, "Anybody else at the same price?" People raise their hands to buy without bidding, and the clerk records the buyer number and quantity bought by each additional buyer.

Sometimes a tray of small pieces is offered as "buyer's choice." Buyers then buy at the "per piece" price in competitive bidding. If the auctioneer thinks it's going too slowly, he may *change* the offer and say, "Now—all that's left for one money," which means the remainder go for one purchase price. Be sure to listen carefully in order to catch such changes when they occur.

How to Attend an Auction

Often there will not be seating provided at backyard auctions, so it's a good idea to keep folding camp stools in the car trunk along with empty cardboard boxes and packing materials in case you come upon an auction in your travels.

I get great pleasure from attending an auction away from home, partly out of professional interest and partly to be a buyer if there's anything in it for me. One of the first things I do when I'm going to be in a town for a couple of days is to check the local newspaper to see if there's an auction scheduled.

One of the greatest auctions my wife and I ever attended as buyers was a Saturday night sale in a Grange Hall on Cape Cod. We were driving home and just happened to see the ad in a local paper. We bought so much we couldn't load it all into our car for the trip back to Connecticut. The auction wasn't over until almost midnight, but the auctioneer gave us permission to leave the stuff in the hall until the next morning. We had a terrible time locating a rental trailer on Sunday morning, but we finally found one, loaded up and started for home.

The Learning Game

It's a good idea to have a pocket calculator, a notebook, and a pencil to write down your intended bids and to keep track of what you bought along with the prices. In that way you'll have a record to compare with the cashier's figures at the sale's end. It will also give you the chance to play a learning game. As an item comes up, write down the price you *think* it will sell for. Then, record the amount it *actually* goes for. Save the sheets and you'll be able to track your progress in "instant appraising," a key skill to develop.

Bidding Technique

I've heard and tried out a lot of theories on bidding, and don't believe there's a sure-fire method that influences the auctioneer or intimidates competition. My question is, "Who am I trying to scare off?"

You can't fool the auctioneer. He's not going to knock down anything quickly because you bid fast, slow or any other way. And most legitimate bidders are too busy trying to figure out what they're going to bid to worry about what you're saying. I'll cover price-puffers and crooks later.

Some people like to stay out until the "psychological moment," just after another bidder has placed what he thinks is the winning bid. The idea of this theory is that when you think that guy's last bid's been given and before the auctioneer hammers the sale done, throw in your bid. It's supposed to shock the bidder so he won't bid back and the auctioneer will knock the item down to you immediately. I've tried it and it doesn't often work. I've also had the auctioneer knock something down to somebody else while I was waiting for the "psychological" moment! Mainly, I advise getting into the bidding early and going as far as your budget allows on the item. Then stop.

It sometimes seems that an experienced auctioneer can hypnotize two bidders to the point of carrying on beyond the point either of them is happy with. At least that's the way it seems when I'm one of the bidders! As an auctioneer, I can't remember being that good a hypnotist!

Inside and Outside

At country auctions, junk is often piled in boxes, lined up, and sold by an apprentice auctioneer who walks the line selling mounds of plastic hair curlers and torn table cloths. It's good practice for the apprentice who warms up the crowd before his boss starts on the important merchandise. These boxes often contain tools and other items you can use at home and in your business. Lighting fixtures, garden equipment, electrical cords, and pots and pans are typical items for sale in box lots. And, occasionally there's a sleeper of real value!

Know Your Auctioneer

The auctioneer is interested in doing a professional job. His auctions are his life's blood—the same as plays to an actor. He's deeply committed to gaining the good will of members of the community. Without it his business can't survive.

But auctioneers are human. Each operates differently. Does he start high or low? Does he really know his merchandise? (Careful on this one—many auctioneers want you to think they're country bumpkins!) Will he quickly close out the bidding when the number of competitors gets down to two?

Time is important to the auctioneer. Unless he can sell between 60 and a

100 lots an hour, he won't do well. If he's a fast closer, it's important to get into the bidding early enough so as not to be left out when he sells. Sometimes a good piece gets knocked down at a bargain price if you wait too long to get in your bid.

The most important thing may be to go at your own pace. Don't let the auctioneer hurry you into a decision. Most auctioneers have characteristic signs that indicate they're about to sell. Watch for them. And if you miss an item now and then, so what? There are plenty more coming up!

It often seems that an auctioneer treats a member of the audience with favoritism. If it's true, I'd rather be a favorite than not! I find that when I know the auctioneer personally I seem to get items knocked down quicker.

It's difficult to know when this happens, but at day's end if I have boxes full of stuff I've bought at low prices, I can't help thinking somebody up there on the auction stand seemed to like me! When I'm a stranger at an auction, I don't do as well. I don't know whether this seeming favoritism is conscious or unconscious. I know that, as an auctioneer, I assiduously try not to show favoritism to any member of the audience. I make my friends work hard!

The auctioneer constantly sells, not only items, but himself to members of the audience to convince them they're having a great time and getting good buys. At the same time, his first and primary responsibility is to his consignor! He wants members of the audience to come back again and again. They will if they're convinced they've bought well. He also wants anyone in the audience who may become a consignor in the future to remember how well he did for sellers. It's a neat balancing act!

The auctioneer's success depends on cementing the relationship of both seller and buyer to himself so that he has a good audience at every sale. Most friends of the auctioneer will have their own permanent bidding numbers and the auctioneer knows them. They can bid almost in secret if they wish, particularly if they deal with a ring-man.

When the auctioneer knows you, he'll look for your bid when he holds up one of your specialties. If he has a collection within your field coming up, he'll call you or drop you a card to remind you to attend.

It seems as though some auctioneers reward good customers with quick knock-downs. I think they sometimes don't realize they're doing it. At least the steady customer has the edge over a new bidder so that when the day's over it may amount to lower prices and eventually to increased resale profits.

Use of the Ring

The "ring" is an auctioneer's team of assistant auctioneers who stand between the principal auctioneer and the audience. They take bids and relay them to the main auctioneer. The ring is particularly effective when there's a large audience. I attended one charity auction in a sports arena in which there was an audience of over 10,000 people. There was a ring man in each major section of the stadium who could take a bid and relay it to the main auctioneer via a hand signal. Through use of a good ring, the auctioneer is able to sell items to people whose bids he cannot see.

Even in a smaller room the ring is invaluable to the professional auctioneer. Typically, in an audience of 800 people there will be four to six ring men spread out to take bids. Many regular auction customers get to know a ring man and depend on him to bid for them. Prior to the sale of an item, a bidder may tell the nearest ring man how much he'll go on the lot. He can then sit back and relax, confident that the ring man will try to get it for him at a price no higher than his specified maximum. It's a fine system that speeds up the auction and helps both auctioneer and bidder.

Tricks of the Trade—the "Puffer"

One thing to be aware of is the "puffer," a consignor who bids on his own merchandise to keep the prices up. He or she is usually a "regular" who knows the other "regulars." He's much more apt to "puff" when he sees a new person bidding.

It's possible sometimes to identify consignors even at an auction where you're a stranger. Tip: Regulars who consign to auctions usually stand, not sit, in back of the seated audience. You'll see them chatting with lots of other people who also stand in back. If you're bidding and getting stiff competition from the back of the house, it could be the owner of the goods who's "puffing" against you.

Beware of puffing at auctions of Oriental rugs, guns, and furniture more than at auctions of any other kinds of merchandise. Occasionally heirs will puff at an estate sale, but they might be bidding for themselves.

Your best protection against such antics is to decide before the bidding on exactly how much you can afford to pay for an item and not go over that total. Then it doesn't make much difference who's bidding against you. You won't bid too much. Of course, you might get angry because it seems that you would have gotten things much cheaper if the sellers weren't making protective bids. But if they were not, there would be competition from other buyers instead.

If protective bidding irritates you, you might consider reporting it to the State Auctioneer's Board. Your complaint won't get far if you don't have hard evidence including testimony from others who know puffers by name. That's going to be hard to get.

Tricks—the Pool

Pool bidding is neither instigated nor sanctioned by the auctioneer. He knows when it's going on, but there's little he can do about it. The pool is a group of bidders, usually dealers, who conspire to lower prices in unlawful restraint of trade. They designate one of their number as bidder on behalf of their consortium on items they would normally compete for.

Pooling is more prevalent in furniture-buying than in other specialty bidding. Instead of six or eight dealers competing for furniture, the pool eliminates competition among members, resulting in lower prices—to the detriment of both auctioneer and consignors. The practice is unethical, illegal, and in violation of the Sherman Antitrust Act. It is, therefore, a federal offense. The FBI has been prosecuting where strong evidence is found.

After the auction is over pool members get together to hold a private auction among themselves. They bid on pool-bought items, dividing any cash left over. The losers are the consignors, who receive lower prices than if there had been pure competition, and the auctioneer, whose commissions are reduced.

Can't the auctioneer recognize pool members since they are regulars? Doesn't he realize that out of all those dealers present, only one is bidding? Isn't it obvious there's collusion? Since the obvious answer to each of the above is "yes," why doesn't the auctioneer put a stop to the practice?

Ethical auctioneers deplore the practice of pooling, but they're forced into a difficult position by the fact that pooling dealers are also their most regular customers. They do not wish to offend them.

Case of Mistaken Identity

About a year after the FBI inquiries started, I was selling furniture in my own auction when a dealer, whom I didn't know too well, placed the high bid on a suite of furniture. He grabbed the card with the bidding number of his friend standing next to him (a man well-known to me as an habitual pool member) and held it high for my clerk to record the purchase.

I had no prior knowledge of the buying practices of the bidder, but the use of another man's number (particularly that of a man I knew to be a pooler) seemed conclusive evidence. I shouted, "You know the FBI's lookin' into this?"

I can't believe it, but I had accused two men, without very good evidence, in public, over a P.A. system, with sixty witnesses watching and listening, of committing a federal crime! What a set-up for a slander suit!

The man who bought the furniture shouted back, "You bastard—this is the last auction of yours I'll ever come to!"

He stomped out. I could see his wrath was real! I later made my own investigation and learned the bidder had come late. He plunged into the bidding to buy the furniture suite having no time to get his own bidding number, so to uncomplicate matters, he had borrowed his friend's card. The whole thing was perfectly innocent and I became convinced that no pooling had been involved.

I felt terrible about making such a public accusation. That night I phoned the accused and apologized, explaining how my mistake had been made. He accepted my apology and became a steady customer. It always pays to admit when you're wrong.

I understand that some pooling dealers have been indicted and some auctioneers investigated as accessories. Unfortunately, there are many auctioneers who not only allow the pool to operate but are themselves members of pools at auctions other than their own. There haven't been many foolish enough to yell out in righteous indignation against the practice!

Your Defense

It's difficult to understand why collectors who want to buy furniture cheaply don't realize they can always beat the pool! Pooling dealers are buying for resale and won't pay more than half of retail. If the collector hangs back and buys later at retail, it'll be at twice the price he could have bought it for at the auction where the pool was operating!

The weird thing is that people seem intimidated by the pool and don't bid. Perhaps they've heard of instances of pool members teaching bidding opponents a lesson.

The punishment is to bid such a person up to a ridiculously high price and leave him there. I have had the satisfaction of turning this trick back on a pool member who had the nerve to approach me after the auction and ask if I wanted to buy the item from him. Of course I did not. I told him he won it fair and square. (For about twice what he should have paid!)

This leads naturally into the entire question of ethics in the auctioneering profession. There are several unethical practices specifically forbidden by the code of ethics of the National Auctioneers Association.

False Advertising

An auction advertised as "Absolute" should be without reserve bids. The auctioneer is under no instruction to protect the items offered by making a "house bid." The items sell *absolutely* to the highest bidder. If the word "absolute" is not used in advance promotion, there may ethically be a reserve or floor bid to protect any or all items. The auctioneer should announce if the auction is absolute or with reserve. Reserve bids must be clearly defined as such.

Auctioneer Purchase

It has long been held to be unethical for an auctioneer to bid in his own auction when he is on the podium selling. It's simple for an auctioneer to take a bid from himself without revealing to the audience that it is he doing the bidding. Or, he might have a friend in the audience bidding for his account.

The reason this is a bad practice is that some auctioneers might be tempted to knock down items quickly to themselves and not allow further bids. If anyone complains, the auctioneer can always say he didn't see the bidder's signal. If I suspect the auctioneer is bidding for his own purchase, I leave the auction. The tip-off is when runners, after items are knocked down, take them to a back room and don't deliver them to a member of the audience.

This is not to mean that anybody should object to mail and phone bids that are ethically handled. They're quite common and should be explained by the auctioneer as bids that are being placed by members of the auction staff, who represent bidders unable to be present but have written or phoned their bids to the auction hall. These bids are placed by members of the auction crew, even by the auctioneer himself, just as though they were placing bids for themselves.

Sometimes the auctioneer has the absentee bid written on a sheet of paper and makes a conspicuous display of the fact that it's not his own bid but from someone taking part in the auction as a bidder on the outside. Once the absentee bid is exceeded, the auctioneer should announce, "The house bid is off." Then the audience knows that the only bidders are the ones seated in the audience.

Most country and itinerant auctioneers allow their employees to bid for themselves on items in the auction. Thus, a bid might be placed by the auction clerk, cashier, ring man, or runner. The auctioneer usually explains before the auction that his employees may make bids, but that he will not.

I've seen an auctioneer, faced with a crowd that keeps its hands in its pockets, get so fed up with stingy bidding that he'll yell, "Well, heck, folks, this piece's got to be worth more than $3! I hereby bid ten bucks myself. Now— who'll go $12.50?" I wouldn't pronounce him guilty of anything worse than good showmanship even though it's technically a violation of the auctioneer's ethical code.

"Off the Wall"

Sometimes with a slow audience, the auctioneer speeds things up by taking "bids" from nonexistent bidders. He gazes over the audience, to the right, then to the left and suddenly seems to see a bidder on each side of the audience. One, two, three competing bids are taken, and one "bidder" seems to drop out. The auctioneer looks around for a new bidder and usually finds one. Often the single bid from the "third" bidder (who is actually the *first*) is the winner.

One way to know if you're facing phantom competition is to be aware of how many items get sold to the third bidder for a single bid, then delivered to a bidding number that keeps repeating itself while the items are delivered to the back room. If it happens a lot, you know your auctioneer has a brilliant imagination.

Every auctioneer has occasionally employed fictional bidders. It's a practice that can get a slow auction going and doesn't hurt anyone if it's not carried to extremes. But, it is quite unethical.

CHAPTER SIX

Profit: How to Make It and What to Do with It

Reading Guide. In this chapter you'll find suggestions for policies that will lead to profit as well as ideas for using your profit to make your business grow. You should know how to:

- Set prices and market-test your line.
- Handle markups, margins, turnover and profit.
- Sell antique value.
- Use price guides, and do market research.
- Determine a markdown policy.

Along with buying right, pricing is a key to producing the cash margin you need to pay expenses and invest in an expanding line of merchandise, with a bit of a cash cushion left over. In the beginning, the cushion won't amount to much. After your business is in full swing, you'll use less of your margin for expansion, leaving more for profit. It's important to price for a decent margin but based on a true market value that encourages people to buy.

Market Value

Every item you put up for sale has a true market value. The problem is that at first you don't know what that true value is. Don't throw up your hands and quit the business because you don't know market values and therefore can't price anything. I'm going to tell you how to price things even though you think you haven't the slightest idea what their prices should be! Magic? Not really. It's a matter of playing the averages. If you follow my "Market Testing" technique you'll come out all right. You'll "win a few, lose a few," and you'll average out fine.

Take that Old Chair There

Start with the *fact* that there's a correct market value for every item even if we don't know *yet* what it is. Would it be easy to price that old chair *below* market value? Sure it would. Is it worth more than $10? Of course it is. A third of the problem is solved. You now know something—$10 is a price that's too small.

What's too much? How about fifty bucks? Would *you* pay that for your crummy chair? No, of course you wouldn't. See how easy it is to solve two-thirds of the problem? Now you know a second thing: $50 is too much. Now for the third act: a price to put on the tag.

Ten dollars is too little and $50 is too much. Imagine two price tags—one for $10 and one for $50—each one hanging on an arm of the chair. Start marking up the $10 tag and ask yourself if your first markup—say $15—is too little. "Hmmmm," you say, "$15 is just a little too little." Go to the other label. Mark down from $50. Go to $40. Nope—still much too much. (I hope you're looking at the chair once in a while.) Then, imagine a price tag that reads $35. Would you pay that for the chair? No—it's still too much. Down and down she goes. You get to $20. How's $20? Sure, I'd probably pay $20 for the chair, if I needed a chair.

What do we have? A fifteen dollar price tag that's a little less than we think we could get and a $20 tag that's a little too much. Now take the final step and print the chair's price of $18 on the tag. See how simple it is?

First, it's better to err on the high side. You can always mark it down later. One thing to consider: $18 for a chair is so little people may wonder what's wrong with it. Consider what you paid for the chair. Let's say you paid $5.00 for it. You'll make a decent profit at any price over $10. So why not price at $10? Because the price you'll get, somewhere between $15 and $25, will make up for mistakes you'll make on other items.

Now, here's where the trial and error—the "price testing" comes in. You've just priced a chair. Later you'll sell it and write down what it sold for. Regard the sale as a test case.

The important thing is to keep track of prices people have paid for things you've sold. Next time you get a similar chair, you'll price with more confidence. If the next one is of the same type but in better condition, go higher with your tag price. If it's in worse condition, shave the price.

If you price too low and then give discounts to dealers or tough customers, you'll cut your average margin to the point where you won't be generating enough cash to make purchases. Your inventory will dwindle, and you'll be out of business.

On Very High Pricing

Since I've indicated it's okay to go high when you're unsure because you can always come down in negotiation, I think I'd better caution against pricing ridiculously high.

Recently, I answered an ad that offered the type of computer I use at $1250. Market value is $400. The advertiser priced it high, knowing he'd have to do some haggling. Fine.

I know parts are no longer available for this model. To keep mine going a few more years, I decided to buy any working one I could find *at market price*. To my offer of $400 the seller replied, "Oh no, I won't take $400!"

"But you say you don't use it any more. I *know* the market because I'm dealing in it constantly. I've bought three of them. I'll pay *full market value* for your machine—$400."

He replied, "Yes, but somebody without your knowledge will pay $1,200!" I couldn't believe my ears. The man intends to *fleece* an uninformed buyer of three times the value of the machine. Incredible, worse than my trying to get it for $50 by building a story on obsolescence, a tactic I didn't resort to.

What I mean by all of this is it's foolish to price ridiculously high, hoping you'll find a sucker. P. T. Barnum was right about a sucker being born every minute, but that's no basis for building anything but a sideshow business!

Boss and Worker

Remember, you're both Indian and Chief! It's one thing to set policy, another to follow it. You won't be in an ivory tower dictating policy to employees scared to death to break your rules. *You* both set rules and follow them, a tough assignment. After you've set the policy (in your Chief role), you're the Indian who carries it out. Some people find it hard to develop this kind of self discipline.

Selling Too Low

You can't imagine how many people I've seen come into the market and leave it within a few months because they lack the discipline. They pay little enough when they buy for resale and even set their retail price high on the tag. But then they panic and reduce their price, either on the tag or in response to pressure from a buyer, without leaving the item on display long enough at the original asking price to give it a fair test.

Your first tag price should be at least twice what you paid for the item. That leaves room to pay fixed expenses such as rent and packing materials. Shave the margins too much and you're in trouble. None of this is meant to say that you should never markdown or haggle. It is meant to enforce the idea that *whatever* your markdown and bargaining policies are they've got to be realistic from your Chief point of view and you've got to get your Indian side to follow them once they're set up.

Investing the Margin

You'll be tempted to pocket the margin as profit. Don't! Forget about profit for now. What you're going to do is spend *most of of your margin* for new merchandise. Think of it as investing to make your business grow. You're investing in *yourself*. Can you think of a better person to invest in?

Turnover

So far in this chapter we've talked about setting price and producing a proper margin (sale price less cost). But profit depends upon more than just pricing.

It also depends upon how long an item spends in inventory while you spend money to rent the space it's hanging around in!

The measure of "in and out" in inventory is called turnover. Retail success comes from the proper balance between price and turnover. Ideally, your cost of goods sold and pricing and markdown policies should produce a margin of 50% (that's a markup of 100% over cost) and a turnover of at least twice a year.

To visualize the relationship of pricing, turnover, and profit assume your business has an inventory with a cost value of $10,000 and a retail value of $20,000. That's more than you're going to start with, but within reach in a year or two. If your inventory turns twice a year your sales will be $40,000. If you've doubled your cost on the average, your gross margin will be $20,000. If you hold your overhead to $3,000 (and that should be easy in a flea market), you'll net $17,000. Not bad for a part time business, right? You can see that your profit will be cut if turnover is less than twice and increased if it's greater.

Conventional retail stores have expenses that you have in small doses—costs like payroll, advertising, and utilities. Each time the doors open for the day's business there's a fixed cost to be covered before any profit is realized. It's a sobering thought for the boss to realize he doesn't make a profit until after lunch, probably around four in the afternoon!

The amount of fixed expense that must be covered is often called the "nut" (that must be cracked, before the meat is reached.)

Fig. 6-1 Enough variety—in this case, every size and shape of brass pot, planter, and kitchenware—ensures fast merchandise turnover.

You'll make money (profit) in your flea market business long before lunch because your fixed expenses are so low, and that should make you feel better about those frantic early morning hours! You might even think of treating yourself to a lunch and then using the afternoon to make money to spend on purchases for inventory.

Costs and Sales

Another way the conventional retailer looks at his business is to compare his fixed cost (overhead) for each square foot of his establishment with how much in gross sales each square foot produces.

Depending on how large his store is, he'll calculate how much each square foot must produce to cover operating costs. Such an analysis may not seem to be necessary in the case of your flea market business, but it's good to know the principle and think of items you sell in terms of how many square feet they occupy, how long it takes to sell them, and how to find items that turn over more rapidly. It's something to think about.

Markup and Margin

Before going on, let's deal with other retail terms that will come in handy. We've seen that the amount you add to your cost to determine selling price is called the markup. When you sell an item the difference between its cost and

Fig. 6-2 A combination of high-priced, low-turnover items, and small, inexpensive, quick-turnover items makes a good balance.

what you sell it for is called margin. When you have paid $15 for an item and sold it for $30 you have:

1. Doubled your investment.
2. Realized a gross profit of 50% (based on sale price).
3. Sold that item at a 100% markup (based on cost).

Remember in using these terms that margin is always based on the sale price and the markup is based on cost. You won't find yourself thinking too much in terms of percentage of markup or profit, but you will think in terms of dollars. When these dollars are set against your fixed costs, you'll know what you have in terms of real or net profit.

Creative Pricing

So far we've talked about pricing in cut and dried terms without considering creative pricing which means setting price at what the market will bear.

You can go *beyond* doubling your cost in setting price, and in fact most experienced antiques dealers try for three times their costs. Believe me, I'm not referring to ridiculously high prices as in my computer example earlier. What I'm talking about is taking advantage of a good buy you've made by setting price at three or even four times the cost of the item to you without exceeding true retail market value.

Your profit is made more in the buying than in the selling, so your first rule is to buy right. One way to do it is to buy in quantity. When you make a house call and the owner has 100 things to sell, you're going to get a better price *per item* if you buy everything.

When you sit down with all the things you bought out of that house, you're going to price each one individually. If your buying was done right, you'll be able to mark some things up (the most expensive ones, I hope) in multiples of three or four. Remember, there will be *some things* that you won't make much on, so others must be marked higher to make up for them.

If creative pricing needs ethical justification, just remember that you've completely solved the problem of the seller who wants to get rid of *everything*. Your economic justification is that you've got to make up for the losers within the pile that contains only a few big winners.

Think in terms of the principle of turnover, discussed earlier. Try to price each item so that it will be sold at the highest possible price (maximizing margin) without hanging around to eat up its margin in rental cost. It's hard to say what the maximum time should be for items to hang around, but it's easy to make a judgement on any one item. Generally, if it's still around after three months, I'm concerned and consider marking it down 10%. At six months I worry and mark it down 25% and deal from there. After ten months I take it to the auction and am happy to get anything at all back for it!

I try to think of an unsold item in terms of how other dealers are pricing similar things and what's happening to items I see on their counters. This is a reason to shop prices constantly in the market and in shops.

Moving the Item

Price sometimes isn't the only answer. You may not have the thing displayed properly. It may be surrounded by unrelated merchandise that competes for attention and keeps the right people from looking at it. To test, move it to another spot in the display. Every week you should move a few things, and once a month completely shake up your displays and move everything around. That always gets things selling again.

My space tends to have things grouped in "men's" and "women's" departments. Feminists might hate me for this, but it seems to help get attention. My ladies' counter might contain a sewing kit, glass and porcelain, scissors, jewelry, and a miniature postage scale. My men's display usually consists of tools and guns, among other men's playthings. In between there might be a display of candles, toys, prints, and antiques.

These displays vary seasonally. Toward summer, I show old fishing tackle and pack away most of my candles until fall. It's important to give thought to grouping items. Don't be afraid to make radical changes when things don't move.

Changing with the Seasons

During my first year in the market, I stocked hand-dipped, dripless tapers from Williamsburg Soap and Candle Company. (If you call them, ask for Belinda— tell her I told you to call. She'll remember me.) These have proved to be the best-selling candles for an antiques-oriented display. The Williamsburg name is magic, and I was pleased with sales in my first fall season.

From the start, candles sold strongly up to Christmas, and I expected them to stop moving after the holidays. You can imagine my surprise when candle sales continued strong. By mid-January my inventory of candles was badly depleted. I ordered 50 dozen more candles and found that January sales were off from December. Not too surprising. The colors people wanted were different, fewer reds and greens, but the totals held up better than I had expected.

In April I ordered another large amount, having discovered that the more I displayed the more I sold. Eventually I owned a mountain of wax with steady sales that kept up almost to June 1. After that date I believe I still would have made enough sales to make the inventory worthwhile, but that flea market building got so hot during the summer that I was afraid the candles would melt during the week. I took them home and stored them in the cellar until the following September. A last 25% off sale closed the season before summer.

Even during summer, I took a few boxes to the market each week, partly to remind people that I was still in the candle business, and partly because they continued to justify the space given to them. When people asked about other sizes or colors, I invited them to my home where they could choose candles from boxes in my cellar.

A Matter of Choice

Most dealers I've talked with follow the principles of pricing I've given here—some more, some less. First, there's the idea of doubling cost. I know a few dealers who swear they only markup 40%, but I tend not to believe them. Most say they double or triple their costs. Of course, some won't discuss the subject, treating it as a deep, dark secret!

Some dealers point out that markup depends on how they plan to resell. If they have a special client in mind, somebody who regularly contacts them for a special item, they're content with a smaller markup. They don't have to hold the item for a long time, eating up overhead, waiting for a random buyer.

One of my good friends found an unusual retail store display piece for selling coffee, a huge aluminum coffee pot. She bought it and then phoned the company that had made it about 50 years ago. They were delighted to buy it and paid her enough for it to enable her to deliver it by taking an auto trip from her home in Pennsylvania to the factory in Tennessee, having a dandy vacation along the way. Sometimes there are unforseen rewards in this business!

A problem with buying for a client is that he might stop buying due to loss of interest or a financial reverse. Then you're stuck with an item for which you have no prospect. To head this off check with the client before making the purchase.

Only Buy to Sell

Occasionally I ignore my own advice and buy something intriguing or beautiful because I admire it, only to regret it later. My inner man warns me I'll have a tough time selling it at a decent markup within a reasonable time. But, I rationalize and justify it as something that will dress up my display, a crowd-stopper, so to speak. Believing it will eventually sell, I'll buy it anyway. Ignoring the fact that it'll take too much space to display and too much time to sell. If you buy for customers, not for yourself, you'll avoid this pitfall.

Sometimes a box-lot buy will yield both a profit and personal bonanza. Once I picked up a box lot in the outside sale line at a country auction because there were a couple of picture frames in it I wanted. I got them cheaply enough. Under the frames and some linens, the bottom of the box was packed with extra-fine coat, pants and skirt hangers, the hardwood kind with spring closures that you'd pay a couple of dollars each for in a store. I think I sold more than 50 of them for $1 each and took 20 home for my closets!

Antique Value

The trickiest pricing problem you'll have is with old items. Some dealers call anything old an antique because they've seen inexperienced buyers put old before quality. Such buyers have been conditioned by antiques columns and news stories of huge prices paid for rare antique finds to the point where it becomes implanted that old means valuable.

Antique is almost as wobbly a term as old. For years, dealers, collectors, and the U.S. Government have not succeeded in agreeing on a definition. In 1930, U.S. Customs said an antique was "anything made in 1830 or earlier." One hundred years became a convenient criterion for defining exemption from paying duties on antiques imported from foreign countries. The tax exemption is still in effect but the definition has changed.

As the year 1930 receded into history the Customs Department definition of antique became "anything 100 years old or older" from the date of importation. That's still the present day definition.

Dealers, especially in upper-scale antiques, welcomed the ruling. It made good sense. But, as collectors of lesser stuff began to form lines at garage sales and flea markets, dealers and collectors began to invent new definitions. Today there is no firm definition. Even specialists in high-style, very expensive antiques are quick to call a late Victorian piece that isn't quite a hundred years of age, an antique. The distinction between old and antique gets more and more shaky.

Toy soldiers are called antique if they're pre-WWII. Antique automobile meets exhibit cars made in the 1950s! Early twentieth century furniture and art deco are called antiques.

All of this is moot for the collector who knows what he, the dealers he deals with, and the writers whose stuff he reads, call antique. Even though there's no universal agreement on the exact meaning of the word antique, it is useful to think in terms of "antique value," in describing how items are valued by buyers and hence priced by dealers. It's best to think of antique and antique value as relative terms.

Antique value, in a broad sense, attaches to any object that's old, scarce, and sought by collectors. Size, color, design, and historic connotations all influence the value. Depending upon how badly the collector wants an item and what the supply of it is, the price is set in negotiation between buyer and seller. If there are great numbers of potential buyers, and the object is one that comes on the market often enough and is written about frequently enough, a price scale is established in the minds of knowledgeable people. That is the scale of antique value.

To deal in such objects, you must be in the network that knows what these scarce items are worth. That means going to markets, visiting antiques shops, attending auctions, reading antiques magazines and papers—all of this even though you may not yet be in a position to buy the objects of your study. Your ears, eyes, and mind must constantly be open to information on values in your field. It's never too early, never too late to learn. Fortunately, it's not all that difficult since, once in the field, you're constantly exposed to the history, use, supply, and value of antique objects.

Handmade vs. Manufactured

Not all collectible antiques are handmade. It's true that the most valuable and sought-after objects are the works of individual craftsmen. Period furniture, paintings and sculpture are outstanding examples of this.

But machine-made objects can be valuable, particularly if they were made by famous companies no longer in business or whose production has switched from wood and steel to plastics.

Big names, natural materials, and good design are the attributes that count. Winchester is a big name in weapons and cutlery. Stanley is a collectible name in tools, Marx in toys, Fenton in glass. There are thousands of late nineteenth- and early twentieth-century manufacturers whose products form the basis for the market in present-day collectibles.

Though machine made, design is important. On many machine-made things there is some handwork, which, along with design, has an influence on price. There are some collectibles virtually without handwork that, because of rarity and nostalgia are highly valued and collectible. Marx Playsets, which are boxed collections of little plastic figures sold to kids in the 1950s and 1960s so they could play out the action of various movie and TV dramas, are valuable. A set that sold for a couple of dollars in 1955 can be worth between $100 and $200 today.

Collecting Cycle

Phase 1. When a person starts collecting in a field, he at first uses little discrimination and even picks up duplicates of commonly available examples. If there are many makers in the field, he'll collect them all. Super customer for you!

Phase 2. As he progresses, the collector studies his field, attends shows and collector meets, subscribes to a fan magazine, visits and talks with other collectors, and probably joins a club. His collection is improved during this phase and he may even begin to specialize. You must learn to keep up with him.

Phase 3. Unless he wants to outfit a museum, our collector now finds he must begin to specialize—on one type, one company, one period, or one style of the collectible he seeks. In this phase he begins to exhibit the taste and discrimination which comes with study and buying. Tough to sell to, but he'll buy high-priced stuff.

Phase 4. Our collector is advanced. He has almost every example he wants for the collection—is proud to show it off even to other advanced collectors. He sells or trades off some of his duplicates at collector meets or to other collectors he's met by correspondence. He may lack one or two of the rarest items in the field needed to complete his collection. Often a phase 4 collector resigns himself to having an incomplete collection and virtually gives up the search for all but the rare pieces to fit into his collection like the one missing from the jigsaw puzzle. You can sell him the "rare piece."

Phase 5 (the end). Our collector either puts his collection up for auction or builds walnut cases for it while he writes it into his will. One thing for sure, the phase 5 collector, who once bought almost anything you came up with, won't buy another thing. As a collector he's kaput. By now he's a good friend, but unless he starts again in a new field he's no longer a customer.

Specialist Dealing

The dealer who's attracted to fields in which he'll cater to collectors of highly prized items should know a lot about the items he's going to be searching for and selling. Throughout this book I've told you that to succeed in a field you must learn all about it. Should this deter you from a field in which you have little knowledge but a great interest?

My answer is a resounding NO. It is not only possible but highly probable that, if you have a natural interest in a field, you can begin dealing in it before you're completely knowledgeable. However, be prepared to take some knocks. I did, I persevered, and in the end I had a glorious few years dealing in toy soldiers. This is a highly specialized collectible field of which, at the time of my entry, I had *absolutely no knowledge!* My case history could give you heart to do something you really want to do but from which you are deterred by your lack of knowledge.

The most important thing in starting to deal in a specialized collectible is to have *an established outlet for your items*. You should be set up in a flea market or antiques mall, have mastered at least the basics of dealing with people, and have an inventory of general collectibles to carry you while you make your mistakes in your new field. That field might be china and glass, antique tools, period furniture, or paper collectibles. Whatever it is, regard it at first as a sideline no matter how important you want it to become to you.

As you begin to deal in your new field, start learning everything you can about it as I did in toy soldiers—a specialty I had thought about for years. I entered it only after buying a few figures at an auction and offering them for sale along with my other stuff.

Starting in a New Field

My first purchase of toy soldiers consisted of Barclay figures of the pod-foot type, made after World War II. With them came some unpainted lead figures like the ones I poured as a child in the thirties. These are World War I figures I have since come to know as semi-flats. They have no collector value.

I hadn't the slightest idea how to price them, so I consulted Richard O'Brien's book, *Collecting Toys, 3rd Edition*, in which I remembered there was a section on American Dimestore soldiers. In it I found all of the Barclay figures I had bought as well as guidance on pricing according to condition.

I couldn't believe anyone would pay from $3.00 to $7.50 *each* for the little soldiers I held in my hands! But that's what O'Brien said, so I priced them at just a little below his assigned values.

Within a week I sold all the figures I bought except for the homecast semi-flats. Even at 50 cents apiece they hung around for months! Finally I sold all 25 or so to one person for $1. I was learning. And, I hadn't lost money.

On a house call in which I bought a number of tin toys, an area I knew a lot more about than soldiers, I found a dozen or so soldiers of pre-World War II vintage that I recognized as having seen in O'Brien's book. I didn't have the book with me, so I couldn't be sure of the values. I figured I would pay $3 each for them and take a chance.

Once home, I looked up the little men in O'Brien. They were in excellent condition, and most listed for $10 or more. Since I had only paid $3 a piece for them I had done okay. I could hardly believe my luck when I found one of them listed at $50 in excellent condition which mine was!

I didn't have the courage to put $50 on the three little men on a raft. It was made to look as though they were rowing across a river, but it was unrealistic. The soldiers are so large their craft would have capsized as they strenuously wielded their paddles! Kids in the '30s probably thought it was dumb and didn't buy it, so it's now a scarce figure.

I priced it at $25, knowing that if it sold for close to that I'd have made a handsome profit. It did sell, the very first day I displayed it for $25, to a man who identified himself as a "collector," although I've come to know him mostly as a dealer since that time. He introduced himself as "Chick."

Here's my card," Chick said. "Call me any time you get dimestore soldiers. I'll be right over—particularly if you find rare ones." I promised to do so and did before another month had gone by.

I advertised, "WANTED: TOY SOLDIERS" in classifieds, a daring step since I hadn't mastered identification and pricing, but I had to start somewhere!

As a result I was called by a family, interestingly enough, in Chick's town. Sitting in the dining room of their home with soldiers marching across the snowy white table cloth, I chuckled to myself that if Chick had known about the bonanza of 133 beautiful dimestore figures I was looking at, he'd be there today instead of me! The figures were cast iron and some were painted O. D. (olive drab). I had indeed found rare pieces!

I made the deal at $330. It was a lot of money, but since I had been doing well paying $3.00 per soldier up to now, and since I had a collector with his tongue hanging out waiting for me to make buys like this, what could I lose?

The next day I called Chick, and a week later he was standing in front of my case, looking at the soldiers I had bought. He reached in and took out a couple.

"Didn't you know these were repaints?" he asked.

My heart sunk. I had wondered why the World War I uniforms were painted olive drab, but assumed that it was a color variation to bring the figures up to date for World War II!

"Bob," Chick said, sympathy showing clearly in his eyes, "these figures were never painted O.D. at the plant. They're Grey Iron figures made in Mount Joy, Pennsylvania in the late '30s. At that time uniforms were khaki. These are not rare although some of them, if they had 95% or more of the original paint would be worth about $15 each."

"If they were all 95% original," I asked, trying to push back tears, "what would the whole thing be worth?"

"Oh, maybe a thousand or a bit more. But, even if they were in original paint, you couldn't sell many to one collector since most of them are common and there are lots of duplicates. It'd take you a year to sell them—maybe a $1,000 to $1,200 gross in a year—*if* they were in near original condition, which they're not. As it is most of them are worth nothing to a collector."

Defeat—pure, unadulterated, horrible, heart-sickening defeat! I swore I would never again make a buy unless I was completely, absolutely, positively, totally, and conclusively sure there was nothing wrong with what I was buying. I decided to continue to display the army for sale and be completely forthright with anyone who asked about the O.D. paint job.

The Army *Almost* Nobody Wanted

A couple weeks later a man stopped and stared for a long time at the parade in my soldier cabinet. He offered me $750 for the complete set, O.D. paint and all! He said he wanted to buy the figures, not for a collection, but to display in a museum in Western Pennsylvania. He offered a $250 cash down payment if I would put the figures on layaway and promised to come back with $100 each Sunday until the entire bill of $750 was paid. I agreed to his terms, carefully wrapped each figure, packed them in boxes, and locked the boxes in a cabinet where they would be safe and out of sight.

On each of the next two Sundays the man came and paid $100 in cash. I now had $450 against my original $300 investment, and it looked as though I was dealing with an honest man and a good profit.

Four months passed and I didn't see the man again. No visit, no money, and I still had 133 soldiers fast asleep, resting for their next war. I mentioned the incident to a friend who said she had had a similar experience at about the time my soldier buyer had first made contact. We found in comparing notes that her customer, who had put $300 on a layaway of antique Christmas decorations, was the wife of my soldier buyer!

Curiouser and curiouser!

I tried to call the man long distance but the line had been disconnected. I sent a letter by registered mail to tell him that in two weeks I was going to put the collection up for sale and that when they sold I would refund $200, keeping the remainder as damages for time and trouble. I told him if he came in before they sold and paid $400, he could have the soldiers. The receipt came back, but I could not make out the signature.

Meanwhile, my friend, following my lead, wrote a similar letter to the man's wife. She received no response.

Two days later came a phone call from the man's son who pleaded with me not to sell the figures. He said his father and mother (the ornament customer) had separated, and he wanted to get the soldiers for his father as a present. He promised to come to the market the very next Sunday and pay the remaining $400. This was agreeable, so I kept the gang off the market for another week. Nobody ever showed up.

Happy Ending

Now comes the strangest part of the story. Since it was apparent nobody would show up, I decided to experiment with a couple of the figures to see if I could remove the offending paint using a new detergent. I found by immersing a figure in a hot solution of the detergent for three seconds the O.D. paint came off almost miraculously leaving the original khaki paint! Two seconds more and even the original paint disappeared. I ruined a couple before I got the timing right.

The end of the story is that I sold almost all of the figures within a month except for the ones I left in the bath too long. I repainted these and offered them as "restored," a category I discovered sold well at half the price of original figures. I marked the tags of all of these "R," meaning restored and always explained what they were to customers.

Following that experience I began to advertise heavily for figures to buy— not only locally but nationally through *Antique Trader* and the toy soldier magazines. After a year, I published my first soldier catalog and began to sell figures by mail, an exciting experience you'll find described in Chapter 8 on mail order selling.

Knowing Your Lines

In the toy soldier story you see why it's dangerous to enter a field without knowing something about it. However, it also shows that if you can stand the blows that come with inexperience and make a profit on most deals while you learn, (and maybe have a little luck as I did!) you'll learn faster than if you relied only on books and talking with people.

At the same time, when you decide to specialize, it's good to start cracking books and going to shows. If you don't, sellers and customers will have the advantage. There are books on every collectible, some from major publishing houses, some little more than pamphlets by super-experts and sold privately. Every collectible from art to zoological drawings is covered by some sort of literature. In the appendix entitled "Collector Books", at the end of this volume, you'll find a number of recommended volumes on the most collected fields.

Many collector books are revised often enough so that you can rely on their advice, and some go even further. Coin guides, for example, give you the quantity of each coin minted so that you have an idea of relative scarcity. In the end though, regardless of what the books say, what really counts is whether someone else wants the item. You'll find that out only when you put it up for sale.

Values Change

The values of items can change rapidly. There's a collectible coin known as the "California Fractional." It's a tiny, wafer-thin gold coin in such improbable denominations as 50 cents and $1. They were made, I'm told, by jewelers in the gold rush days, and entered into commerce as officially approved legal tender. I had a couple of them which I took to a coin dealer since I know little about coins. I had heard that their values had gone up rapidly in the last few years and I wanted to check that out.

As the dealer searced his Fractional price guide, I noted a picture of one that looked identical to mine. There was a recommended price of $15,000 under the picture of the little gold disc. "Isn't that my coin," I asked, trembling with excitement.

"No," he replied, "See—that one has a star directly under the forward part of Liberty's chin. On yours the star is a bit to the left."

Because one star was slightly off, my coin turned out to be worth a mere $160. I would presume there are only one or two of the $15,000 fractionals in existence. It would have been nice to have the second or third one! The dealer told me that the value of fractionals had increased enormously in the preceding ten years. When I asked whether I should sell mine—presumably to him—he gave me a straightforward answer, "No, if I were you I'd hang on to them. They're bound to go up more. There just aren't that many." A very honest dealer indeed.

Price Guides

I use price guides constantly, and every dealer I know does the same. Their editors warn that the information is to be used only for general guidance and not taken as gospel. One should use information from the guides as only one part of determining price.

Contributors to guides get prices from actual transactions and report accurately. However, sales that give rise to such observations take place in such a variety of circumstances as to make them incomparable. Some prices are from auctions, some from store sales, and some from direct mail. Moreover, they come from all over the country and it's often impossible to apply values from one area to items in another.

Usually, but not always, the effect of condition is dealt with in price guides. Often the best that can be discerned is an approximation. What's "extra fine" to one person may be "very good" to another. Moreover, each collecting hobby has its own system of grading, the most exact being that of the coin field.

I bought two banks at $6 each, then found listings in an antiques guide for "Mulligan the Cop" for $100 and "Elephant on Drum" for $80. They both had pretty fair paint so I put a $75 price on each of them, knowing that my flea market customers are looking for bargains. It was almost a year and several markdowns later before I sold the two banks for $35 each. I had made decent profit, but much less than the price guide had led me to believe possible. Due partly to the advice I took from the guide, it took a year to sell them. Every market is different, and experience in your own will be your best teacher. But price guides are still an indispensable tool.

Markdowns

After something's been on sale for a while and doesn't move, when do you mark it down and by how much? The answer to this depends upon whether you're more interested in getting rid of it fast or marking it down in small increments in order not to lose too much money. My choice is an active markdown policy, not a when-all-else-fails policy.

An extreme example of the active markdown policy is Filene's Department Store in Boston where, during the days I shopped there and perhaps still for all I know, the marketing strategy in their bargain basement was based on scheduled markdowns.

When Filene's basement puts an item on the rack it has a price of about half what you would expect to pay at another store or even upstairs at Filene's. After a few days it's marked down, then a few days later it's marked down again. This continues until the item is sold.

Actually it's a Dutch Auction—an auction in reverse. A swanky item that may first have been offered for $400 in a designer shop might start off in Filene's basement at $200, then made subject to successive markdowns until it sells two weeks later at $30. I'm not suggesting such an extreme policy for your collectibles business, but it gives you the idea. I believe you're better off to mark down and sell rather than to hold for a long time.

Price Research

You can get ideas on prices by examining tags in other dealers' displays. Of course, this advice is useless if dealers in your market don't tag their items with prices. You can ask for advice and, as I've indicated elsewhere, most dealers will oblige with advice to a new entry in the market. However, don't overdo it. If you constantly take the time of another dealer to price each of the items you've bought in, he'll wonder when you're going to get smart enough to do your own pricing. I've been on both sides of this equation, and my advice is to ask for advice at first, but don't keep it up for long if you want to have friends in the market.

Professional Appraisal

Occasionally you will come into possession of an article of great value. You're not sure what it's worth, but you're afraid if you price it, even at what seems to you like the high side, you might make a mistake and sell it quickly at a lower price than it should command.

Your best bet in such a case is to go to a professional appraiser, an expert in his or her field, and pay for a market appraisal. Chances are the appraiser has a fixed fee for appraising one item on which he does not have to do extensive research, and this can be as little as $25. Make sure you make it entirely clear to the appraiser that you're after a *market appraisal*, not an evaluation for insurance or legal purposes. Tell the appraiser that you're going to make a pricing decision based upon his advice. Ask if he gives a special rate to professional dealers.

Appraisers are often certified by some type of organization, either a state dealer group or a national appraisers' association. There is no such thing as an official appraiser certification in personal property fields.

Inflation

A few years ago the value of antiques seemed to be going up at an annual rate of 15% to 20%, due to the high rate of inflation in the '60s and '70s. Financial advisors counseled clients to invest in antiques as a hedge against inflation. That advice is now seldom given.

Don't be fooled into thinking that because you paid $10 for something in 1965 it's worth $100 now. One sobering thought is that you might have been stung and the item was only worth 50 cents in 1965 and perhaps nothing now! Remember, there can be a fine dividing line between second hand and antique.

Price Negotiation

Always leave some room for haggling. It's the very soul of antiques dealing. If you conclude that most people won't pay more in an antiques market than 90% of a tag price, why not include that 10% in your original pricing and stand ready to take it off? The few that pay full price will give you a 10% bonus!

Dealers always want a discount, even if they think your item at $50 will sell for $200 in their store. As far as dealer sales are concerned, the best policy is to accommodate any dealer with 10% or 15%. This is standard and will satisfy most of them. I know dealers who will not buy from another dealer if no discount is allowed—no matter what! It's a matter of professional courtesy and easily factored into your pricing strategy. Since 80% of the sales you'll make will be to people in the trade, why not face facts and accommodate them?

It's amazing how many new dealers start off with a no discount policy and soon learn how foolish that is. What they didn't count on is that the vast majority of their sales will be to someone in the trade!

Most people who are not dealers themselves but who do a lot of antiques buying know they can worm discounts out of you. Here's where the 10% factor comes in. Build 10% into your pricing. Let's say you've bought a lamp for $45. You price it at $95. Along comes Mr. Smartguy who says, "Whaddaya want for that ol' lamp?"

"Ninety-five," you say, and he backs off. If you'd priced it at $120, chances are he'd have offered you $90 or $95. Customers usually won't make an offer at much less than 80% of your tag price thinking they'll offend you. Set your discount policy at a level to make it easy for dealers to make an offer.

Asking Price/Sale Price

It's been said elsewhere in this book, but it bears repeating.

    The key to the flea market sale is to get the customer to make you an offer!

No more than one out of ten of your flea market sales will be at your asking price. "What's your best price on this?" or "What's the best you can do?" or "What's your best dealer price on this one?" are all ways in which the customer tries to get you to lower your price so that he can then decide whether or not to buy. But if you can get him to make you an offer near your acceptable price, you've got a sale.

"Give you $10.50" is a definite offer. If $10.50 is a price at which you will sell, you've made a sale. Even if it's not quite enough, he's pretty close. All you have left to do is close the gap. Your response of "Well, I'll take $15" probably won't turn him away.

So the idea is to turn the first question the prospect asks into an offer. When he asks the question such as "What's your best price?," reply "What's your offer?" It's usually as simple as that. Your main task is to display and set prices so as to encourage him to ask that kind of question.

CHAPTER SEVEN

andling Prospects and Customers

Reading Guide. In this chapter you'll find ideas for turning prospects into customers and dealing with unique flea market happenings. Make sure you know:

- How to use active and passive selling techniques.
- How to develop and use a sales pitch.
- How to develop customer confidence.
- What to do with free-loaders, kleptos, displaced persons, and information seekers.
- How to handle offers, discounts, markdowns, checks, charge cards, and layaways.

We've become so accustomed to poor service in the supermarket or drug store (more of a discount department store nowadays) that we forget how wonderful it was to get service from owners, managers, and clerks. When I ask a store employee for information, I get the impression he was trained to make me feel I should buy or go away—anything but ask for service!

Salesmanship
Selling has been eliminated from modern retailing, except for specialized retailers such as automotive outlets. We're trained to get our information on a branded product through advertising, then go to a selfservice outlet and buy it without bothering anybody.

I'm amazed at the store clerk's reaction to my asking him to take a packaged product out from under a counter. He seems to find it incomprehensible that I want to see, feel, and look at the product. He's astounded I haven't learned about it on television! He's dumbfounded if I examine the product and decide *not to buy*! I'm supposed to be *presold*. He's accustomed to handing over the item and taking money. The very idea of having to impart information or do a selling job is alien to the person whose position once called for salesmanship and customer service.

If you want to be a product supplier and silently stand by waiting to collect money, don't go into the antiques business! It's dreadfully old-fashioned. People ask questions and a lot of them even expect you to do a job of selling!

You don't have national image advertising to back you. Unless your product is the type that's occasionally featured in *Early American Life* or *Colonial Homes*, your prospects may become exposed to it for the first time as they pass your table or enter your shop. Your display methods, the condition of your items, your sign language, and your pricing all help spark the shopper's interest, but you must close the sale. Antiques and collectibles may be the last bastion of old-fashioned selling.

Both active and passive techniques are important in working with customers. Arrangement of your merchandise and pricing are passive but important. A sales talk and a discount are active means of sales promotion, and they're critical.

The Sales Talk

Sometimes I get into a spiel about something in my shop that sounds for all the world like a canned sales talk. That's because early in my career as a salesman I learned the value of a prepared sales talk written by a person who knew the product and how to sell it.

Fig. 7-1 Baskets, glass, and textiles make up a typical flea market table.

If no sales talk had been written, I wrote it myself after learning everything I could about the product. I assembled facts into a logical sequence and rehearsed, building it to what the salesman calls a "close" that asks for the order.

Once I've handled something several times and talked about it to prospects, I'll have developed my pitch to the point where it becomes automatic. Automatic but, I hope, not boring. I don't want my sales talk to sound like a badly done telephone answering machine message.

The canned sales talk is best because you've built it to contain every important thing about the product, but it only succeeds when it's delivered as though it's spontaneous. If it's delivered in a fresh and enthusiastic style, your prospect will think your pitch has been created on the spot just for him, and that's what people react to!

Make it a practice to talk about newly acquired items you have the first chance you get. It makes no difference who you tell about them. Tell your husband, wife, boy friend, girl friend, or delivery man. As you describe the items, you'll construct a sales pitch in logical order. You're actually rehearsing what you're going to say to prospects, and as you do it over and over again it tightens up and becomes convincing. It's canned, but it's more effective than if it had been extemporaneous.

Develop the ability to turn a customer's question into a pitch for the product. For example, if my customer asks, "Will these candles drip?" I swing into my talk about the little ladies in Williamsburg who handdip the candles, how they're dripless and long-burning, and why they represent the best buy in candles available today.

You run a slight risk of telling more than the person wants to know. But, if you see your prospect's eyes glazing over, you'll know to turn it off. "Gee," one lady said to me, "all I wanted to know was whether they dripped. You've certainly got your sales talk down pat!" I hadn't meant to give her a long-winded pitch, but once into it I gave her the full story. She bought a dozen candles anyway.

If I were pressed to declare whether my candle sales talk produces a larger order than sticking to simple answers and letting the customer pick out her own candles, I'd say it does. I've tried both ways. When the customer sees I'm ready to answer questions and be of service she's more apt to buy from me. She'll buy with confidence because I've shown I know my product, and that gives the promise that I'll stand behind it.

Naturally, you don't bore repeat customers with the sales talk. When I see a first-time customer start making her selections, I spare her the pitch. People who've used the product pick up a box or two (about a $15 sale) and say— "Here, I'll take these."

I think of people who bought one or two candles, got my little sales talk, then returned a week or two later for a dozen. I've learned that building the story of quality around the candles is worth the time and effort.

I challenge the buyer to test me. She asks, "Do they drip?" I respond that they do not unless a strong wind is blowing. "Do they burn a long time?" I reply that they outlast any other candle. I challenge her to observe the results when she uses them. Only when she *proves it to herself* does she buy in quantity. Of course, such challenges should only be given when you're sure your claims will hold up!

Once in a while, to my long-burning, dripless pitch will come the answer, "Oh, I never burn them—they're just for looks." I try to convince her she should burn them, but it doesn't seem to change her mind.

Locking In

When a person walks past your table, neither looking to the left or right, not looking at anything you have for sale, there's no way you can make a friend by trying to stop her. If she does stop, wait until you can catch a glance, then say something neat like "Hello" or some other neutral greeting. "Hi" or "Good Morning" are both good. What you're trying to do is simply get her to acknowledge you're there. It's hard to sell something to somebody who doesn't see you.

Most people don't like effusive greetings and prefer to be the one to start the conversation, if any. A friendly "Hello" doesn't do any harm, and it encourages the shopper to ask for something she might have in mind or simply to return your greeting and go on looking.

If she picks up something for a closer look I try to maneuver myself nearer to make it easy for her to ask about the item. Generally, I do not volunteer gratuitous information. It scares people away. Often the shopper knows more about the item she's looking at then you do.

Before advancing information on collectibles find out what the customer knows about them. She might be an expert, and explaining the object can be an insult to her knowledge. Assume the customer knows all about it and wait for questions. You'll soon have a measure of the person's knowledge.

"How old is this?" or "Where was this made?" are two questions that often come at an early stage. To encourage the shopper's confidence, it's important to be absolutely honest. If you don't know, say so. If you believe something about age or origin to be true but are not sure, say so.

Sometimes you have information about an object from the person you bought it from, but you're not convinced it's reliable. People appreciate a statement like, "I'm not sure of the exact age of the scale. The patent date is 1910. I think it was made soon after that. Look—it gives a rate for a postcard as one penny so it must have been made before the end of WWII. My guess is 50 years old."

With that answer you've eliminated from the prospect's mind any consideration that the scale could be a reproduction without her having to ask that question. You've told everything you know about the object in an honest fashion. If the customer wants something made before 1900 you're going to lose her. But, isn't it better to lose the prospect (with her respect for your honesty intact), than have her find the 1910 patent date later, after you've made a wild guess that it was made in 1880?

Fig. 7-2 Always make the sale while your customer is holding the admired object in hand.

The Importance of Knowledge

It's important to learn all you can about your items. You'll be able to carry on an intelligent conversation about anything you have though it may often be quite a short one. You can't be the world's number one expert in everything!

It's amazing how much you can learn when you display a *learning attitude* to customers. People you don't suspect know anything about antiques will reveal amazing depths of knowledge if your attitude encourages them to help you learn.

Learning from a Customer

One Sunday a man I knew only as George came into the market. We'd never had a deep discussion about any field of collecting, and he'd never bought anything from me. He said, "I'm interested in buying lithophanes. Ever get them?" I'd known the guy for several years, but this was the first time he'd ever revealed any deep collecting interest. As luck would have it, his newly revealed specialty was something I had never heard about in my whole life.

Even after his explanation I couldn't visualize the thing, so he invited me to his home to see his collection. The lithophane is a porcelain technique that is hard to describe so unless he's sure a dealer might have a chance to find one, George usually skips the explanation. I learned something that day I wouldn't have known if I hadn't asked, "What is it?"

The point is that if I had said, "No, I haven't gotten any lately," I would have learned nothing. I must admit it's been several years since that visit and I have yet to see another lithophane! But when I do, I'll recognize it, thanks to my friend, George.

Another time a lady bought a wooden-handled tool, trimmed in brass with a hooked blade about four-inches long. As a tool collector I had never seen one like it. As I wrapped the purchase, I asked her, "Please tell me what this is—nobody around here seems to know." She told me that the instrument was used for threading wool onto a loom and that she had not known of it until a week before she saw mine. She was happy to find it and pleased to share her knowledge with me.

It can go the other way too, of course. A shopper will pick up an object without uttering a word, and look at me with a pleading expression as if to say, "Help!" My reply to this is, "Are you familiar with it?" He might reply that he has a thousand of them, or more likely he'll say he doesn't know but would like to.

I take it from there, trying to respect the customer's knowledge while filling in what he wants to know. The collector isn't interested in my showing off what little knowledge I have, so I try not to deliver a lecture. Some people want to feel superior, and if I can make customers out of them with a bit of ego massage, so be it! This dummy can respect their superior knowledge if it helps make a sale!

Your Prices

Without a photographic memory, it's hard to remember exactly what you paid and how much you decided to ask for everything. I use several sizes of tags and labels as much to help me as the customer. Good labeling is important. If I haven't handled an object for a week or two, I always feel safer if I have a chance to glance at the label before quoting a price.

It's helpful if the label tells you what you paid for the item. In order not to reveal this information to the customer, dealers employ a code that looks like a stock number printed on the reverse side of the label.

Customers are sometimes smarter than we give them credit for, and not a few of them make a hobby of deciphering coded cost symbols! They make quick work of the simple code some dealers use that's based on the alphabet: A for 1, B for 2, etc. The symbol, AB stands for $12, meaning that the item cost the dealer $12. Its advantage is that it's quick and easy to use. It's disadvantage is that everybody knows it's a code and calculates your cost before you even look at the tag. Gives them a decided advantage.

I thought I was being clever when I reversed the digits in my cost figure and wrote them, with a couple of nonsense symbols fore and aft. The tag might show a retail price of $50. On it would be the symbol, "G5–2H" The two numbers, reversed, recorded my cost price of $25.00. Dealers caught on immediately. You can figure out a usable code if you put your mind to it.

Another item that can be coded is discount information you wish to provide to someone who might be tending your stand in your absence. Let's say you have varying discounts but will give them to anybody who asks for one. One label might read, "$75—D15)" It's pretty obvious to anyone that what you mean is a $75 retail price discountable to a dealer ("D") by 15%. Be sure to tell your helper whether you mean percent or dollars off. This could be reversed as: "$75—D51." That's a little more concealing in that you've reversed the discount digits. A better way is to have a standard discount figure and tell your relief person that's as much as you'll give.

You can get quite fancy with a date of acquisition on your label in addition to cost data. Thus you'll be reminded of how long you've owned the white elephant, an indication of how deeply you might discount it. This can get a bit complicated, but at least it has the advantage of requiring the prospect to do a little studying to come up with a translation.

You could make up a stock number in digits to represent the month and year of purchase, the price (perhaps in reverse order), plus a couple of non-sense digits at the end. Thus 11–9012–15 would mean that you bought the item in November of 1990 and that you paid $21 for it (the reverse of 12). The 15 at the end means nothing—just a smokescreen to foil the enemy's intelligence forces!

Let's say that item 11–9012–15 is priced at $29.50 and that you paid $21 for it. You've had it around for a while and recently reduced it from $45. The margin of $8.50 isn't a big one, but you've decided you'll sell it at breakeven just to get rid of it since there has been so little interest in it. A customer examines the object and ventures, "Will you take $25 for this?" You check the price tag to make sure what you paid for it. Your quick look tells you that it cost you $21. Nobody has asked about the item for months, so your quick response (Hurry!—He might get away!) is "I'll wrap it up for you."

When a Mistake is Made

No matter how careful you are, a mistake will occur! If your mistake results in a huge advantage to the customer (and a serious money loss to you) it's best to point it out, admit it's your own error and hope the customer understands.

Misplaced decimal stories are legion. "How much is that cabinet?" the man asks you. "Twelve and a half," you blithely reply.

"Not too bad," the customer replies.

Oh wonderful, a twelve hundred dollar sale! It's all you can do to keep from leaping up and down!

"I'll just look around at these other things here first," your customer says.

"Yes sir, take your time." You count the money three or four times in your head. Let's see, that $1,250 added to my previous sales today—which were $10—I've racked up $1,260 already—boy oh boy!

Ages later, the customer has had his look around. He gets out his checkbook and begins to write. "Here," he says, "I'll give you a check—you said, twelve-fifty?"

"Yes sir," you reply, scarcely able to conceal your glee. He hands you the check. It's for $12.50. "I'm sorry, sir, but the price is $1,250," handing him back his check.

"I thought that was pretty cheap," he admits, tearing up the check and allowing little pink pieces of your dream to flutter in the breeze.

I was embarrassed recently when a $13.50 item in my display somehow got a second sticker placed over the first. Anyone who then picked it up saw $7.50 as the price. A couple decided to buy it. "Is this $7.50?" the lady asked. Quickly checking the label I replied, "Yes, it is."

"Okay," she said. "We'll take it." I started to wrap the item and suddenly remembered I had paid $7.50 for it. I peeled off the label revealing one beneath that read, $13.50.

Taking the object back to the counter I showed the original label to the lady and said, "I'm sorry, but my original price was $13.50. I just can't take as little as $7.50 for it."

The couple were incensed as I think I would have been in their place. "Well," the lady said icily, "I don't like being accused of switching labels."

"No Ma'am," I replied. "I am not accusing you of that. This is simply a mistake that somehow happened. Maybe someone else placed the label there or I did it thinking I was tagging something else." The couple turned and walked away.

Thinking about it later, I knew they could have transferred the label from another item, although that didn't occur to me when I first discovered it. Their protestations suggested it. If the couple were without guilt (as they probably were) they deserved to be angry with me. The result of the incident is that I lost them as customers. They may still think I tried to switch labels. Hindsight says I should have sold the item to them for $7.50 and said nothing about the mislabeling even though I was not legally or ethically bound to do so. The net result, if I had handled it right, would have been that they would have come back again to look for bargains like that one.

Handling Collectors

Be good to your specialized collector. Once he knows you offer things in his field, he'll make frequent visits to see if you have anything new.

He knows your temptation is to rate his interest so high you'll start marking up as though there's no bottom in his pocket! It's a mistake to succumb to the temptation. You'll stretch his resources and patience too far and lose him.

I know serious collectors who act downright stupid, as though they know nothing. I think they do this to see if you're going to try to exploit the relationship.

A collector will buy from many dealers to keep competition up and prices down. He often feels his best deals are with transients who know little or nothing and to whom he need not reveal himself as a serious collector. I've overheard conversations between a top collector and a transient dealer in which it would be difficult to tell who was the smart one and who the dummy! Each was trying to con the other.

Unproductive Conversation

You'll find yourself in conversations with people who aren't good prospects. When it begins. "Whaddaya git fer them kettles?" I can guess with 99% accuracy that he wants a free appraisal on kettles he has at home. He's curious to know what *them kettles* in *his* barn will sell for. The flea market is full of people looking for free appraisals.

My response to that type of inquiry, is a straight one. I give the price. What usually follows is "Yup, I got wunna them in the barn. Usta slaughter our own hawgs."

I ask at this point, "Could I come out and see your kettle. I might want to buy it." You'll probably learn he'll sell it to you for the price you have on yours.

You'll hear lots of remarks like, "Oh, my grandmother has one of these."

Or, "Look, Joe, remember those—we threw 'em away when we moved!"

"Do people really but this junk?"

Politely ignore them—or smile—or both.

You can't avoid unproductive conversation, especially if the person is interested in what you have for sale. But you must tear yourself away to take care of a customer. When you get trapped in an unproductive conversation, position yourself to keep an eye on the rest of your space to be able to respond quickly to the appearance of a genuine prospect, or inhibit the unauthorized exit of an item in the pocket of a shoplifter.

It's perfectly understandable when you say, "I'm sorry, but that lady seems to need help." Move on to the prospect and hope Big Mouth goes away. Don't worry about discouraging all the interesting people. Flea markets abound in talkers. They'll be back in droves to fill the hours between bona fide prospects.

Conversation Buster

For $29.95 you can now buy a *fake beeper* to attach to your belt. Secretly activated, it beeps loudly, acting for all the world like a summons to an important phone call, enabling you to make your escape from unproductive or boring conversations.

Handling Shoplifters

It's seldom one ever sees a light-fingered practitioner in the act of stealing. They're very clever at it, and this includes kleptos who are sick and can't help stealing. Sick or not, you don't want them to steal from you.

You can't do much more than be vigilant. Estimates on shoplifting loss as a percentage of sales run from 5% to 20%. I believe mine has not exceeded 5%.

It might be helpful to you to know the things I've had stolen, so you can make special provisions for securing these types of items. The first was a beautiful ivory and brass folding pocket rule. It was worth about $100 retail at the time and in an unlocked glass counter case. I believe the lid of the case was propped open so the thief had to reach around the slanted top and down inside the case to get to it. Also stolen from that case was a 14–K gold ring, with an airplane molded into the face, worth perhaps $75. Both of these instances of theft were in the indoor section of a flea market.

Later, in the antiques mall, I lost a tin mechanical toy worth $200 and a flintlock Pistol worth $700. I'm sure there were other items, but these are the ones that come to mind.

My toy soldiers are kept in locked cases that offer superior protection. I don't think I've ever lost a soldier to theft, although with so many it's hard to be sure. Of course, a thief might know he'd have trouble fencing soldiers, while more common items would give him fast turnover.

Any item is subject to theft by a kleptomaniac like the fellow I saw striding rapidly out of our market late one Sunday with a broad smile on his face and a World War II collectible under his arm. He had been described to me as a local business executive, and my only contact with him had been a couple of nonproductive conversations in the market.

The reason I remembered seeing him with his prize was that look of smiling triumph on his face. I thought, "He must have beaten somebody out of that one!" Boy, was I right!

Later, as we were closing, the dealer across the aisle pointed to the wall behind his stand and said, "Look—The fancy frame I had on that wall disappeared today. Some S.O.B. stole it." He described it and I knew it was the one I saw walking out under the smiling man's arm.

I couldn't very well accuse the fellow when he showed up a couple of weeks later, and the victim didn't feel he could make an accusation with only my memory as evidence. We always watched him closely after that.

Later, as co-owner of the antiques mall, I always had our guard follow Mr. Smiling Face from the time he came into the market until he left. There were other confirmed or suspected kleptos our dealer tenants had had experience with in other markets. All of them were followed when they came to our market.

Handling Freeloaders

In an outdoor market a man asked about a clock I had for sale. I replied by telling him all I knew about it. He looked at other things and then back at the clock as though trying to make up his mind. A second fellow picked up the same clock and two of them began to talk.

The second man told the first he had better clocks at home and cheaper. Incensed, I told the second man if he wanted to sell clocks he could damn well rent space, not use the booth I pay rent for. He and my prospect left, deep in conversation, intent no doubt on coming to a deal that had begun in my space.

Freeloaders see nothing wrong in using other people's space as a place to do business. I'd get angrier except that these people are often pickers who come up with things to sell. Once in a while they'll even buy something, so I can't be completely irate. Besides, they're fun. There were Crazy Ed, the gun nut, Cowboy Jim, a real expert in primitives, and Joe the Lurch, named for I don't know what. All great characters.

Being Helpful

You're in the market to do business, so you want to spend your time selling and buying and not on idle conversation. However, sometimes talk that seems idle can produce a further benefit. The Biblical idea of casting bread on the waters is the basis of every good public relations campaign. Your bread doesn't always come back with a diamond pin stuck in the crust, but it usually pays to be kind and helpful.

Some people are just looking for information. If they want something you don't have, it's easy to guide them to another dealer's display. There are displaced persons—small children or aging relatives of shoppers. Why not be friendly? If a moment of kindness turns into conversation that threatens to go on forever, you can always diplomatically find your way out.

Some people go to flea markets to find collectibles, some to scout for bargains, and some to locate an odd part or piece of something they haven't been able to find elsewhere.

A lady wandered through our market looking for a piece of convex glass for an oval picture frame and found the piece she needed at my table. She was overjoyed because a glass company had quoted $65 for a custom-made piece, while my price for the glass plus a better frame than the one she had was $35.

It's fun to give somebody a solution to their problem. My guess is that for every solution I come up with there are dozens of problems wandering around that never get solved. Because my display is such an eclectic collection, people think I must have anything, so I get lots of unusual requests and hear lots of problems. I steer people toward solutions in other dealers' booths when I don't have the answers.

Referring people to another dealer accomplishes three things: First, it makes the seeker happy because it directs him toward a solution. Second, it's good PR for the market. It could make a confirmed shopper out of the seeker, and that's good for everybody. Third, it improves your relationship with the dealer to whom you referred the customer. When I don't know who might have what the person seeks, I may have a catalog from which he can order the item, or I may know of a conventional retailer who might have it. I make these recommendations freely and take all such requests seriously.

When You Have an Offer

From the time the shopper shows interest, the important thing is to get an offer. The best offer is one you can accept. When you get an acceptable offer, you've made a sale.

Ridiculous offers get rejected without rancor or counteroffer. Offered $1 for something that cost you $10 and which you have priced at $20, you're going to reject it. Some dealers smile and say nothing. To a very low offer, say "No" and perhaps explain the value of the item without showing offense or anger. I doubt a counteroffer, say at $18 or $19, would be productive.

"No" is a good word. Why not use it? If you're asked to do a thing that's ridiculous for you even to think of, what could be better than saying "No," forcefully and positively?

If I'm offered $18 for an item that cost $10 and which I've marked $20, I answer something like, "Do you want it in a bag?" The customer named an acceptable price so I ask a simple, related question that closes the deal. Once the customer agrees to let you put it into a bag, you've made the sale.

If it's just gone on display and you don't feel you should take less than $20, by all means say so. You don't have to explain it. Taking an offer is related to how long the item's been in inventory. You'll always have another chance to sell it. And, of course, the person may come right back and agree to buy at your full price.

Walking away can be a buying strategy. When shopping, I always ask for a discount. If the answer is negative, I may walk off just to see if the dealer will stop me. Then, if it's worth full price I go back and pay it.

A more likely scenario is your customer asking, "Will you take less?" Or, he might be clever with "What's your clergyman's rate?" He's more likely to ask, "What's your best dealer price?" knowing most dealers have such a discount policy. You can ask to see a business card, but that just wastes time.

Any of these gambits adds up to the buyer asking for a gratuitous discount. He knows dealers build in 10% to 15% to accommodate it. Sound like we're playing games? I guess so, but it's habitual in the trade, so why fight it?

My usual response is to cut 10% from the price and if the customer is a dealer 15%. This does not always lead to a sale. In fact I'd guess that when I quote a price reduction, I've got about a 40% chance of making a sale.

A better way might be to respond to the question by asking a question: "It's marked $10, what do you offer?" If the offer is acceptable, wrap it up. If it's not, then counteroffer. This technique if it results in a reasonable offer is probably 70% successful in leading to a sale.

Another technique is when the shopper asks, "Can you take something off?"

"Try me," you respond. Doesn't work very often, but I don't care much for the people who ask if I can "take something off." At least it's better than removing my shirt.

Some shoppers (including some dealers when they're buying) will not make an offer. One dealer friend told me he believes the seller should set a price and as a buyer he won't suggest the price. I think he's found out he probably does better if the seller states his *best price*. Even then, one can always make a counteroffer.

The dealer, as you know, bases his evaluation of an item on what he thinks he can sell it for in his shop, so in selling to a dealer, you have little chance of playing on emotions or personal tastes. It's usually a pretty cut-and-dried decision-making process that leads the dealer to deciding what he can pay, plus a bit of stage-acting as he negotiates! His constant hope is that he'll find a real bonanza in the hands of a dealer who doesn't know his prices and asks for too little.

Negotiating

You'll mark down items that haven't sold after a reasonable time. Say you've had a lamp priced at $20 for four months. Then you marked it down to $12 and people still seem to hate it. At this point, toss your original cost-based price out the window and get whatever you can for the dog. (From an auction you might get $12, which, after commission will yield $7 or $8.) A customer asks, "What's your best dealer discount?"

"Big," I'd reply. He'll probably offer you $6. Take it and be happy you don't have to haul the item again. Win a few, lose a few. The chance to replace the loser with something that'll move fast is worth more than hanging on to your mistake. Counter offers can drive people away. If it's a new item you're convinced will sell at near your marked price, try to raise the offer. Three or four months later it's a different story.

Learning from Fashion Merchandising

You can learn about merchandising from the fashion trade, although you might reject comparisons because the product lines are so different.

First, it can be argued that fashion merchandise is subject to automatic obsolescence. Last year's garments are this year's castoffs. The product is seasonal and consumed within a year, discarded once it's out of style. That's not true, you may contend, in antiques where nothing is obsolete. Collecting is based on finding obsolete items. The more out of date they are the more they're desired. Whereas a swim suit is less valuable at season's end (has a lesser "utility," in the language of the economist, hence a lower value), the antique is worth just as much now as it was six months ago, maybe even more.

Second, buying fashion merchandise at wholesale tends to be seasonally connected with the announcement of new lines, while buying antiques for resale is a constant activity, since basically there is no seasonal factor.

My contention is that differences in seasonality and obsolescence cloud our thinking, and we would be wise to study the fashion field and adapt its ideas of pricing and markdowns in at least a limited way. I contend that markdown policy is related more to the dealer's need for cash flow and turnover than it is to the type of merchandise.

Take a look at how fashion merchandisers handle pricing and markdowns. First, the designer dress shop marks up by a large multiple. Example: A dress costs the shop $150. It's retail price becomes $600. At season's end its tag reads, "80% OFF," or even "90% OFF." The dress sells for $60 to $120. How can the retailer sell below cost and stay in business?

An antiques dealer rebels at the idea of cutting the price to less than he paid for the item. I admit the advice given earlier in this book would lead you to believe that is the *only* way to think about markdowns. It isn't.

Think about the designer line in its entirety. Each dress in the "Fall line" was marked up by a multiple of four. The store has two or three months to sell at full price. At season's end several hundred garments have been sold producing enough cash to pay expenses and recover *all of its investment* in the "Fall Line," *plus a profit.*

Now, just as autumn begins and the shop's stock consists of only 15% or 20% of the items that were bought several months before, *Everything in the Fall Line goes on sale at markdowns that range from 50% to 90%!*

How can they sell the $600 dress for $60 (90% off)? Aren't they losing money?

The answer is no. In cash terms, they make a gross *profit* of $60 on what's now a $60 dress because it's already been paid for in the large margins that came with earlier sales. Those early sales ran the shop, paid the bills on everything bought for Fall, and returned a profit. Now anything our little dress and the other remaining items bring in is *pure profit* and pays for the owner's Florida trip where she can wear the few swim suits left over!

To apply the fashion merchandising theory, think about a substantial buy (consisting of many items), say on a house call or at an auction. If it's a bonanza buy you can mark it up 300% or 400%, like the fashion people do! After it's been on display for several months and you've recovered your original cost plus profit, cut prices of everything left by 50%, 60%, or even 80%. Why not? Designer shops do great with the strategy! And, even if you don't literally follow it to a tee, the principle it teaches is a good one that can at least be adapted to the antiques business.

"Is it Old, Is it Antique?"

You know that old isn't necessarily good and doesn't always mean antique. Many people seem to think that anything old is valuable. I must admit I get tired of people hurling the word old at me when I shop in an antiques mall or flea market. Earlier we tried to come to a definition of the word antique, and here I'd like to comment on using both antique and old to your honest advantage in describing collectibles.

Generally, it's best to deal in the terms your customer uses. If he thinks of 1940s sheet music as antique, so be it. I'll sell him antique music.

A shopper might pick up a piece of door hardware from your table and inquire, "Is this antique?" Usually what he means is "Is this of modern manufacture or a reproduction that simulates the appearance of an older piece?" He won't use such stilted language, but that's what he wants to know.

Your answer could well be, "Depends on what you call antique. I'd say it's old, made before 1900. You could call it antique—see, it's handwrought. It came from Pennsylvania, and I believe it was made by a blacksmith there."

Argument against this elongated answer will point out that it's always best not to volunteer too much. Just answer the customer's question without taking a chance he'll hear something negative. Thus, if he hates Pennsylvania, or if he's looking for something made after 1900, you'd be better off to say, "Yes, it's old." You don't want him to put the piece down and walk away.

There's a neat bit of psychology here. Think of why somebody picks up something to look at. You're not suggesting he examine the piece. He reacted to something that interested him, and you haven't the slightest idea what it was. What you know is that he's probably in the market to buy something and is trying to decide how to allocate the amount of money he feels he can spend.

He looks at the object, and if his examination (plus what you say or what he reads in your attitude toward him and his interest) confirms his original thoughts, you've taken the first step toward a sale. But, only the first step.

Your prospect wants confirmation. Part of the confirmation is your positive answer to his question, "Is it old?" This should be answered according to his definition, not yours. That's why it's good to learn what his interest is and find out what he means by old. You can ask questions to find out what he's thinking. Then you can build on *his* interest in the object *he* picked up, or perhaps go to something else you have that fits his interest.

Special Prospects

In my flea market business I've had a "box lady," many "tool men," a "weighing scale lady," and lots of "toy buyers." One gal I thought of as the "zither-key lady" because she asked me for zither keys every time she came past. I haven't the least idea why she wanted them! These people show up in the market every week, right on schedule. My "Railroad Man" was the first to arrive every Sunday, always before 8:00 A.M. If I had anything in the train line, I always made sure I got to the market by 7:30 A.M.!

Whether or not I had what they wanted, I welcomed them and had a little conversation. If I had something in their specialties, I showed it and asked their opinion. They'd buy if they wanted the item. No amount of sales pressure would change them if they didn't.

Marketing Reproductions

I don't want people to buy things from me as antiques if they're not, and so I've come to the conclusion that every item that is a repro or a modern item should be so marked.

I made a pair of jumping jacks using lithographed illustrations printed in a modern book. They were printed in excellent colors and looked like ancient French toys.

To make them, I ripped a thin panel from a pine board and glued the parts of the paper dolls to it. After the glue dried, I carefully cut out the pieces with my scroll saw and articulated the legs and arms with thin black wire at knees and elbows. I attached strings to control their movements, and *Voila! La Mignonette!* I hung them above my table in the market, not thinking anyone would believe them to be antique. If anyone asked, I told them they were modern craft work. Incidentally, I've learned that nobody wants to buy anything made by the dealer! It's best they think it's made by somebody else! Just say it's craft work, and don't identify the craftsman!

Many people admired my jumping jacks which accomplished exactly what I had intended. They stopped people. I always showed the backs to reveal the new wood, because I didn't want to fool anybody into thinking the dolls were antique.

People walked away when they found out the dolls were new, and that was fine because I didn't want to sell my window dressing. A few people promised to "think it over."

An aside: People who promise to "think it over" never come back for small items. Sometimes they'll need thinking time on a larger purchase and will return. On small items, make your sale on the first visit or lose it.

One day I asked a friend to stand in for me. I gave him background on major items in the booth, but didn't mention anything as insignificant as the jumping jacks.

At the end of the day I dropped in to close the stand and my friend said, "A lady loved those old jumping jacks."

"Oh," I said, "what did she think they were?"

"Well," he continued, "she asked me if I thought they were old and I said 'yes,' I was sure they were. I told her I thought they looked like a couple hundred years old. She looked at them for a long time and told me I was wrong. She said they were made in the thirties. She bought 'em anyway."

I would have told the lady (who, if she reads this, may bring back the jumping jacks she bought in the Silver Spring Flea Market in Mechanicsburg, Pennsylvania in the late '70s and get a full refund—if she can remember the price she paid—I can't!) that they were not old but recently made after the design of old French toys. I didn't have the heart to tell my honest friend that he had accidentally told the lady a falsehood.

It's simply not possible to be an expert in everything! Museum curators who spend their lives in decorative arts consult other specialists in fields beyond their own expertise. When I don't know, I tell the customer it's in a field I'm not an expert in. I'll only say what I believe to be the truth about an item. If, in the process, I say anything that later proves to be false, the customer is welcome to bring the piece back for a full refund.

Refund Policy

The mail-order business taught me the importance of a "refund-on-demand with no questions asked" policy. Why not extend the same offer to the buyer of anything? I have always been liberal in making adjustments or refunds and it pays off. People have faith to buy when they know you stand behind your products. My statement that appears in every toy soldier catalog I have published is:

Minertoy Guarantee

"You're the boss," and if you do not wish to keep a figure you buy from this catalog, return it for a full refund. In addition, I'll buy back any figure I've sold you for the full purchase price you paid *at any time in the future*. No questions asked, provided the condition of the figure remains unchanged.
— MINERTOY

I've been asked only once to make good on that promise, and I did it cheerfully.

Accepting Checks

At first I accepted only cash and traveler's checks in the flea market. After a few weeks I had many steady customers and felt comfortable accepting personal checks from them without question. After that I decided to accept personal checks on local banks if a driver's license is presented for identification.

If an out-of-town dealer checks out in his ID and uses a company check, I'll accept it. I've never been burned. Among thousands of mail orders, at an average of $50 per order, I've only had one check bounce and it was eventually made good. My opinion is that it's not worth it *not* to accept checks. Just make sure you get a proper ID.

Some dealers demand a driver's license, a credit card (for ID, not necessarily to charge), and one other form of ID. I just don't think all that's necessary. Of course, your area may be entirely different than mine, and my suggestion is that you ask more experienced dealers to find out what their record is on bounced checks.

Charge Cards

The perfect solution to non-cash payment is the charge card, either MasterCard, VISA or American Express. You can get by with MasterCard and VISA which are both available in one transaction from your local full service commercial bank. They charge a smaller service fee than American Express.

The rate you pay (usually somewhere between 4% and 6%) varies from bank to bank even within the same trading area, so shop around. You must maintain a checking account with the bank in order to convert the charge slips to a deposit with instant availability.

The great thing about plastic money is that it converts instantly to cash. This alone makes it worth the commission. You'll lose some sales if you don't have charge card facilities. Many studies, including my own, have shown that the cost of the service is worth it in sales that are saved by selling to out-of-state customers who have no cash or whose checks you're reluctant to take. The bank guarantees any charge, but you must phone for approval for charges over a certain amount which varies. This means that you need access to a phone to dial the credit card company.

Layaways

Short-term layaways ("Hold it for me while I find my husband") without cash being paid down work about two-thirds of the time. No harm in holding for 15 minutes or even a half hour, but if the wait's longer, put the item back up for sale.

On long term layaways, get at least 50% on small items and 25% on items over $100. Draw up a layaway form and make copies. Your customer signs it at the time of the sale and gets a copy. People forget how long it's been since they promised something, especially when it involves paying money. The layaway contract form serves as a reminder.

dvertising and Promotion

Reading Guide. You've heard "Build a better mousetrap and the world beats a path to your door." Would you like to know what happens, no matter how good your mousetrap, if you don't promote it?

Nothing! In this chapter you'll get started with advertising and promotion. Make sure you give attention to:

- Selecting the name for your business.
- Writing and testing ad copy.
- Importance of emotional appeal in advertising.
- Selling by mail.
- Use of a guarantee.

When you trade products for other people's money, your success depends as much on how you market them as on the worth of your merchandise. In this chapter, we'll take a look at some of the principles of retail promotion and see how they fit what you're doing in the flea market, antiques mall, or co-op.

The Value of Advertising

Advertising does more than tell people what you have for sale. The way in which your advertising is constructed—in words and pictures—can build a favorable image of a product or it can do nothing for it. It can even produce a *negative image*!

Good advertising builds such a favorable image for the product that the consumer is willing to pay more for it. What other explanation is there for the high prices paid for designer items in direct competition with garments that are every bit as useful but lack the well-advertised name? How about those fashion sun glasses that for over $100 do no more than a pair of less well-promoted glasses at $20 or less? The difference in *market value* between designer products and lesser promoted ones is a measure of the worth of advertising.

As a hobby my professor of marketing at the University of Chicago made facial cream for the ladies of his family. His cold cream performed as well as, and was chemically identical to, brandname creams costing ten times as much as he could have sold his for. He made the point that without a $2 million dollar advertising budget he could never be a factor in the cosmetics industry. Fortunately, the antiques business doesn't require that kind of ad budget, just good, sound thought and decision.

What does advertising do for a product? How does it add to the product's value? And, most important, how can you use advertising in your own flea market business?

First, let's define what advertising is supposed to do. It should reach prospects and tell them what you have for sale (or what you want to buy), where they can find you, and offer salient facts about your business. It should be designed to give the reader or viewer a feeling that your product has either superior quality or bargain value, depending upon what you're trying to achieve. It builds an *image* of your operation and your products through repetition. It describes these things in the reader's terms. That's what selling is, and that's what effective advertising does.

Within the phrase, "Advertising and Promotion," let's include *everything* you do that's printed or broadcast about your offerings at retail and the way you do business.

Anything carrying the name of your business is an advertising message, not just the "Antiques Wanted" or "Antiques For Sale" ads you run in the local newspaper. That includes your sign, business card, letterhead and envelope, brochure, flyer, classified ad, even a story about your business success that appears in a local newspaper. They're all important.

Everything that's written or spoken about you and your offerings should advance the positive image of your business. Let's look at each effort, starting with the most important one of all, the name of your enterprise.

Your Business Name
There are lots of antiques dealers in flea markets and malls who do not put up a sign at all. I think this is a big mistake. As an individual dealer you deal directly with the customer, so the need is not so much to identify your company as it is to give your small operation character and meaning. It's your choice whether you'll use a name that's positive, negative, or neutral. At the very least make it neutral. What do you think of the following names? Look at each and decide whether it's positive, negative, or neutral. Then, read my thoughts on them. The important thing is to give thought to selecting a name for your business.

1. Country Cuzzins
2. Collectors' Connection

3. Maison Bleu
4. Elmer T. Smith, Antiques
5. Main Street Antiques
6. Dale's Treasure Chest
7. Minertoy

1. *Country Cuzzins* seems to say you'll be selling country store items and "folk art." It calls up a picture of you settin' there in the rockin' chair by th' ol' pot belly stove, rockin' back and forth, smokin' your corncob and adjustin' your bandana that's beginning to choke you a bit.

What happens when you graduate from rain barrels to expensive clocks or fine porcelain? Okay, you can change it then, or maybe you'll be so well known that you won't worry about the image. I think the name would be ill-adapted to most lines of better antiques and suffers from being overly cute. I'd call it neutral. It probably won't hurt you, but it won't help much.

2. *Collectors' Connection* is not bad. It carries a picture of you standing before crowded shelves of teensy china things that people buy for $2 each. I may be overly critical, since such collectibles can run into the hundreds of dollars. It might not cover high-style antiques too well, but generally it's a good name for a flea market type business, so I call it positive.

3. *Maison Bleu* tries to be ritzy by using a French phrase. It's so unmemorable as to make one wonder whether it stands for a French restaurant or a porno movie. I think it's a negative kind of name.

4. *Elmer T. Smith Antiques* (assuming Elmer T. Smith is your name) tells who you are, what you sell, and who stands behind everything. It's friendly, and people tend to respond to those they know by name. It covers all antiques. I like it. It's positive.

5. *Main Street Antiques* tells where it is and that's good. It sounds a little like a small town antiques shop (which it was). It represents a kind of friendly, old-fashioned, small town approach. Probably a pretty good name and an easy one to illustrate on a letterhead or a sign with a simple cartoon.

6. *Dale's Treasure Chest* is a successful antique jewelry business. It may not be too good to publicize to general buyers, but it suggests value and style to those interested in jewelry. Once someone gets to know Dale, the proprietor, the name sticks in the mind as an image that describes what she sells. It's positive for the right sort of business.

7. *Minertoy* is hard for me to be objective about. I used it for my toy soldier business and bimonthly catalog. It contains in one word the name of the owner and a definition of what's sold. Whenever you can, select a name that's only one word. Think of the money you'll save in signs and typesetting over the years! Easier to remember, too. I rate this a (biased) positive.

I usually go for the business name with the proprietor's name built in. So do a lot of people I've talked with on this subject. You can always use your name with a descriptive subtitle such as Elmer T. Smith, Nautical Antiques. It has class, tells the purpose of the store, attracts nautical buyers, and shows who's in charge. I think Mr. Smith will go further than Country Cuzzin and Mr. Blue House, don't you?

Logo, Sign, Business Card, Letterhead

Each of these has advertising value in your dealing with the public. Your first step is to get a commercial artist who, for very little, like $25 to $50, will design a logotype (heading design that can be used in all of the devices mentioned above) to represent your business's image. Pay a designer to get something distinctively yours. *Do not use clip-art*—syndicated art reproduced in books you buy in office supply stores. What you get from clip-art is a hackneyed image, such as a spinning wheel.

Your printer can use the logo on whatever you want printed. It's a good idea to shop for printers. Get quotes from three and look at samples before deciding who will print your business cards, letterheads, and envelopes. After you've used one printer for a while, shop for prices. You may find your first printer bid low to get the business then inched up his prices after he decided you're a solid account!

Dealing with the Printer

Depend upon the printer for printing only. Tell him you'll deliver typewritten copy, double-spaced and proofread, along with scaled photos, line drawings, and a layout. Ask for a type book so you can select type. If you don't understand how to scale photos and drawings to size, ask your printer to show you or get a book on basic graphic design. Correct printer's errors on proofs, but don't rewrite extensively if you expect the lowest prices.

Later, investigate the cost of having your artist do what are called *complete mechanicals* for your printing. They insure that the printer can make no mistakes, since the printed copy and illustrations will appear exactly as they do on the mechanical prepared by your artist. Most people think of printers as designers and typesetters. They are usually not good at these functions. Get the job the way you want it before you deliver it to the printer. It costs more, but the complete mechanical insures there will be no mistakes.

Find our what paper your printer can supply, and choose appropriate stocks and colors. For around $100 you can buy all your basic printed supplies. Don't overlook the possibility of buying printing by mail. *The Antique Trader*, for example, carries ads from printers who offer what seem to be great deals on business cards and letterheads. I haven't used them, but I have seen the same names for years, so they must do a good job, and their advertised prices seem okay.

But, you say, I'm only giving this flea market thing a try—I don't want to start with lots of printing expense. Why do I need letterheads, brochures, and flyers? The answer is that you don't need any of this stuff. I don't advise you to buy all that material for at least a year—except for the business cards. As your business grows, you'll find yourself answering ads by writing letters or sending orders to suppliers. At that point, you'll want stationery that's more professional than a plain sheet of paper. You'll get quicker and more positive response using a letterhead.

Business Cards

You'll use a business card quite often, even in the beginning, so I think it's a good idea to have cards printed right away. It's a kind of badge which shows you mean business. So, perhaps your first purchase should be a couple hundred business cards for $20 or $30, an expense that's easy to justify. By the time you need them, you'll have a cash reserve so it'll be easy to justify the investment in creating the image you want your antiques business to have.

If you want your card to reflect the specialties you sell, select an object that represents your product line or theme of your business. My first antiques card was illustrated with a chamberstick. It had exactly the right message to portray the style I wished my booth to have. Later it changed to a drawing of an old house (Main Street Antiques). After that, when I changed the business to one specializing in antique toy soldiers, the illustration became a drawing of a toy soldier. In each case, I tried to capture the essence of what my business was all about.

Put your phone number in a prominent spot on your card, and on other promotion you have printed, so people will know how to get in touch with you. Give the hours during which you may be reached at that number. Your tax license number is a good addition, since you can then use the card to establish your exemption from state sales tax.

I keep a stack of business cards next to my cash register ready for anybody who might want to get in touch with me for any reason. Don't place them on the front edge of your display case or front table, however, because you'll lose lots to kids who are business card collectors.

Letterhead

Use a larger version of your logo on your stationery. You'll be surprised at the attention you receive from suppliers and other correspondents when you write on a letterhead instead of a plain sheet of paper. The letterhead establishes your business as a going concern.

If you use a box number to speed up the delivery of mail, put box number and street address on the letterhead as well as on your business card. An explanatory slogan or motto can be printed below your business name. "Antiques Collector and Dealer" might be a good idea when you're getting started. Some people prefer to deal with a collector rather than with a dealer. They think you'll pay higher prices. "Call me from anywhere to look at dolls," is an example of a specialized message that explains your specialty and asks for a response.

Signs

I've used many different signs to name and describe my antiques business. The first was an actual antique, a child's alphabet trainer—a slate with movable letter blocks around the outside. I positioned the blocks to spell "Bob Miner Antiques Shop." It wasn't a large sign, but people commented on it.

After I became "The Candle Man" I had a sign built in the manner of an eighteenth-century trade sign. On it was painted, "Hand-dipped, Williamsburg

Candles Purveyed Here," all in eighteenth-century script (with the s's looking like f's). It's a real beauty and I attributed much of my success in selling candles to its professional appearance.

I've made my own signs for sales and specials using a felt-tip pen on white cardboard. One thing I learned from a master Pennsylvania sign painter (Mr. Jack Jaffe who had been in the sign business for sixty years), is that for best visibility, use black block letters on a white background. Jazzed-up signs with fancy scripts, wild colors, and special effects aren't nearly as effective!

Jack also taught me that you should not jam the letters and words together too closely. Most signs are painted with the letters very tight together, but he proved to me that words are easier to read when there is sufficient space between letters and words. It may not look as artistic, but what you want is a sign that gets readership and produces results!

Professional Help

I've concluded after many years of working with signs and printing, that it's worth the cost to hire a pro. If you're unfamiliar with printing procedures, get a book at the library or a graphic arts store that will explain it. It will seem complicated at first, but after you've dealt with a commercial artist and a printer a few times, you'll be an old hand at it.

Remember to insist on seeing proofs of the offset negatives before press plates are made. Read them carefully, word-for-word, and make necessary corrections.

The most obvious errors in typesetting are the ones you'll have the most difficulty spotting. Read *every letter* in the proof of your ad or printed piece. Sometimes you'll find a mistake in the bold headline of the ad where you least expect an error! The easy words—like the name of your city—will be the ones where errors occur. This results from your being so familiar with the word that your eyes glide over it without seeing each letter.

If you're a speed reader who skims without taking in every letter of every word, you won't be very good at proofreading. Get someone else to do your copyreading, somebody who reads slowly and concentrates on each word.

Newspaper Advertising

Since yours is mostly a local business, your main medium will be your local newspaper, and the section where most (if not all) of your advertising will run is the classified department. Good classified ads are important to the success of your business. You'll use them:

1. To locate people who have merchandise to sell.

2. To advertise a special item for sale at a location other than at your regular stand.

3. To advertise something exceptional at your stand or a special merchandising feature such as a sale.

Keys to classified success are choosing the right paper and creating a productive ad. One thinks of the paper with the largest circulation as the most responsive advertising medium, but this is not always the case in classified advertising.

Sometimes the major metropolitan daily will lay an egg, while a neighborhood sheet pulls a huge response for a specific category of advertising. The reason is usually that the smaller paper has become a marketplace for that category by pushing its sales people to sell hard in that field and offer inducements to advertisers, including large discounts, special position, banner heads for the classification, bonus advertising, and heavy co-op promotion.

Often the best puller will be a shopping giveaway that decides to build on its success in the supermarket and automotive categories and picks antiques or auctions to go after tooth and nail. If its strategy succeeds, the paper does indeed become a marketplace for a particular advertising specialty. It begins to work for advertisers when the paper starts carrying so much of the specialty that readers look to that paper to the exclusion of others for their needs in that field.

Choosing a paper for your ads deserves a lot of thought. Before you're ready to advertise, you should make a study of *all* the media in your area. Ask others where they have had their best results. Analyze, on a daily basis, the amount of advertising in various classifications that appears in each of the local media. Advertisers are not dumb. They try different media, then select ones where results are best. Some papers pull like mad for automobiles but are little better than fishwrappers for other categories.

If you haven't anyone to ask, make a careful analysis of the lineage (total quantity of advertising) carried in each paper in categories that are of interest to you. One paper may have three ads headed, "Wanted to Buy," another paper may have 30. There shouldn't be any question which is the marketplace for locating people who have things to sell.

Don't fall for the idea that the paper with fewer ads in your classification will be best for you because there will be less competition! That's the story that might be given you by the salesman who represents the number two paper. Go where your competition is—the marketplace.

Take a closer look at this marketplace phenomenon. Think about the flea market. Is there any place where you find more competition for the collector's dollar? If you're afraid of competition you would certainly shy away from establishing your business in the flea market. By moving your shop from the market to Main Street you eliminate competition. You also eliminate 3,000 people who pass your display each Sunday. On Main Street you'll be lucky to get 30 people a day into your shop.

Have you noticed how similar businesses (wholesale or retail), such as banks, wholesale florists, fish merchants, boutiques, and auto dealers, tend to bunch up along a single street that includes most of their competitors? Customers find it convenient to have a marketplace consisting of a number of competitors and go there to find sources that satisfy their needs. When a new firm joins the competition, it's because the owners know their best location will be near their competitors. That's where the customers go!

The same thing is true in mail-order advertising. If a magazine works for a few advertisers, within a few issues you'll see dozens of competitors. Because the marketplace pulls crowds of interested buyers, there's business for everybody. All competitive units will prosper. Those who eschew competition and go where there are no competitors fare poorly. You'll do best to place your ads in the marketplace publication pioneered by your competitors. Don't let personal preference for style or editorial orientation influence you. The important thing is results.

Your paper may not now use the heading under which your ad should appear, for example, "Antiques Wanted." Usually the paper will add the heading for you to get your account or for a slight extra charge. If you feel the heading is important, try to get it established. Normally the best headings for ads you will be running are *Wanted to Buy, Antiques, Miscellaneous for Sale, Household Goods for Sale,* and *Equipment for Sale.*

Timing

Timing is important. Think of days when people might be looking. If yours is a *Wanted to Buy* ad, decide on the best day, probably toward the end of the week or on the weekend itself. For a Sunday market your best *For Sale* advertising days are probably Friday and Saturday. Sunday might be okay, and if there's a special three-day rate it could be worthwhile to include Sunday in your weekly schedule. What you should do is test both Thursday-Friday-Saturday and Friday-Saturday-Sunday schedules. Find out which is best by testing and keeping accurate records of the results.

Shopper Newspapers

Often the best ad medium for flea market dealers is the local shopper, or free newspaper. Usually published in midweek, it's distributed free of charge to every household and business in the market area. The shopper's advantage is that it blankets the area with distribution since it's sent to everybody. Conventional publishers claim their paid circulation produces better readership, hence better advertising response. The way to settle it is to test. Find out which works best for you.

The shopper is usually a good puller for classified advertisers regardless of the day of the week on which it's issued. Often people save the paper for the weekend to be their guide to bargains on the days they're off work.

To find merchandise you can buy for resale, Monday-Tuesday-Wednesday could turn out to be your best advertising period. I've found that Sunday-Monday-Tuesday usually works best for me.

The Sunday paper deserves attention since Sunday is a great paper-reading day. People who might not go to the flea market spend hours with the Sunday paper, and lots love to read classifieds. They'll read your Sunday ad and call to arrange for you to see what they have for sale.

The Answering Machine

The phone answering machine helps put you in touch with people who call when you're away. Face it, you miss calls when you're at work, at auctions and yard sales, and at the market on Sunday. A $100 machine will help you get in touch with all these callers. It will more than pay its way.

It's worthwhile to practice recording a friendly outgoing message that will answer calls in your absence. Relax and make it sound as if you're answering the phone in person.

Remember, you're not recording the call for posterity or a nationwide audience. If it doesn't sound good, do it again and imagine you're talking *with*, not *to* another person. (Your new message erases and records over the last one.) Repeat it as many times as you wish until you get it the way you want it. Then make a new one once a week so people will look forward to it. The machine won't complain of overwork!

Advertised Specials

To promote traffic, it might be worthwhile to advertise, "SPECIAL: 10% OFF anything in my stand next Sunday, June 3 with this ad." It will be a good test to learn whether local advertising will stimulate business for you.

Writing the Advertisement

It's not possible to give a copywriting course here. If you wish to give it serious study, go to your local library where you'll find lots of books on advertising copy. Colleges give good extension courses in advertising. I can give only a few principles that have worked for me and hope they'll work for you too. We're talking mostly about classified, but the general principles hold for display advertising as well.

Headline Type: For your classified ad select the largest bold-face headline type the paper will let you use. Then build a short, grabby headline to snare the reader's interest. Make him stop at your ad and read it.

Thousands of copies of the earlier edition of the book you are now reading have been sold through an ad that had the headline, "WARNING: This Book Could Make You Rich!"

No Untruths is an important principle of advertising copy. Notice that I didn't say, "This book WILL make you rich." I used the word "could" which is truthful. I know for sure that if you heed the advice it contains you're on your way.

Plain English, in complete sentences, works best. No Buzzwords, no Advertising-eze. Use words that are easy to understand. Don't allow the paper to put abbreviations in your ad. In real estate it's okay to say BR for bedroom because people have come to expect that. But in your advertising, use complete words. Ad-takers are used to people who wish to economize, so they'll abbreviate and eliminate words from your copy, often at the expense of clarity, unless you tell them not to. Make it easy for the reader to get your meaning.

When you write advertising copy, imagine you're talking to a person. Write as you would speak with him across the table. Note I said speak *with*, not *to*. Think of your audience as a conversational respondent, an *audience of one*. Don't give a lecture or make a public announcement. Don't say, "Teddy Bears for all." Do write, "Come in for *your* lovable Teddy Bear." Focus on the individual reader. Use "you" a lot.

Always Test Copy

Have other people read your ad copy and ask them to explain its meaning to you. Don't expect them to be literary critics—advertising isn't literary anyway! You simply want to know whether you've made your point in such a way that people will understand it. Ask, "What does the ad ask you to do?"

Emotional Appeal is important to get people involved in deciding to get in touch. Appeal to the emotions by using phrases like, "You'll love our. . ." Try to put yourself in the position of the person reading your ad. If that person is a woman, don't be afraid to use words like "darling" and "cunning." If you're writing for a male audience, write your copy on the macho side, like you're selling Marlboro in Big Sky Country. Leave a little suspense in your message. Make sure there's something more the prospect must phone or visit you to find out about.

Wish Fulfillment is what great advertising is all about. If you can write your copy in such a way that the reader thinks visiting you will lead to the fulfillment of a strong desire, you've written good copy.

Use a Sales Close. This means using words like "Now," "Today," and "Hurry," or "Only 20 left." Don't forget to include basic things like address and phone number when they're important. Give the reader a way to get in touch!

What follow are ads that you might consider either good, bad or so-so. Remember that this is all a subjective matter. Mark a plus, minus, or zero (neutral) after each one and see whether we agree at the end of this chapter.

The final verdict on any advertising effort can only be what happens as a result of the ad. I'm not guaranteeing that I'm always right in my judgment, but I've done enough in the field of creating, critiquing, and analyzing results that I think I may be right half the time. Bat .500 and you can play in anybody's league, right?

1. BUYING ANTIQUES at guaranteed highest prices for wall or corner cupboards, tables, chairs, chests, trunks, quilts, or anything old. Day: 555–4738. Night: 555–3837.

2. HIGHEST PRICES paid for old oak furniture, dry-sinks, tables, baseball cards, slot machines, comic books. After 7 P.M.: 555–7385.

3. CUT GLASS WANTED. Paying good prices for perfect cut glass. Call 555–8374 before 10 A.M. or after 6 P.M.

4. FOR SALE: Star P.O. .45 Auto, new $200. Sterling auto Model 400: $160. 555–4837.

5. YARD SALE—3 Fam Sat 8 A.M. on 575 Wilford.

6. GIGANTIC YARD SALE: Sat., Feb 19, 10 A.M. 'til—Antiques, Furniture, dolls, glass collection. Everything goes. 867 West Dellwood (Left past IGA store heading west out of Smithtown.)

7. MUST SELL BEFORE SUMMER: Petunias, impatiens, zinnias, dozens of vegetable plants, perfect condition for planting. Half price, only 65 cents per six plants. Near entrance, Jordan's Flea Market. Sun, 9 to 5.

8. ANTIQUES, ART WANTED. Highest prices paid for old furniture, paintings, clocks, lamps, quilts, stained glass, pottery, toys, dolls, dishes. One item or entire estate. Cash on spot. 555–4847.

9. COME TO FLEA MARKET—Jordan's, Sunday Aug 11—see me at booth 114 for lowest prices on collectibles. Especially depression glass. Bring this ad for 20% discount.

10. WANTED—Marx electric trains & boxed sets of Marx/other playsets. Jones Box 289, Fairborn, Ohio 45324.

11. TWO STAMPS for list wooden primitives, butter & sugar molds. Proto Carter, 826 Redan, Des Moines, IA 50309

12. MOM WORE FRINGE in the 20's, I do now. Why not try it? Catalog of sketches $1. Martha, Box 738, Elburn, IL 60119

When You Sell by Mail

All of the antiques papers occasionally give special low introductory rates to induce people to try their classified columns, so you can get your feet wet in mail order without risking a fortune.

These publications have small circulations compared with general media. However, the specialized interest of readers is so intense that what they lack in numbers they make up in ferocity. Because their circulations are small, rates are relatively cheap.

Even the smallest ads get attention. The general rule for profitability in selling by mail in papers and magazines, is to use *only that space you need to describe what you're selling*. Unlike more general advertisers, you can't afford white space, fancy borders, and huge color illustrations. Readership is so intense you won't need these things.

The size of your ad is determined strictly by the number of things you have to sell. If what you offer is well known to readers you probably don't need an illustration. Your copy will be enough.

In my opinion, reproduction quality on the newsprint used by *Antique Trader* and other collectibles and antiques papers is poor, so if you can rely on readers' knowing what the item looks like, don't waste space and money confusing them with muddy pictures.

If your product is unusual or has special features that demand photographic illustration, use the best photography you can afford. Consider using a professional photographer. Highly important details of such a product should be shown close up.

Don't be tricky with headlines. Your best bet is to use the name of the piece in the largest type that will fit the ad.

You can try to sell directly from the ad, or ask for an inquiry and then send out complete information in the form of a picture or flyer. I favor selling directly from the ad, but if you follow that route, you must include complete information. Tell everything that will make it clear to the reader what you have for sale. I am amazed at how few advertisements for antiques do a full job of definitive description. A lot of long distance money is wasted by respondents who call to learn more about items that are not fully described. At least half the time when I call about an advertised item, I find out something over the telephone that eliminates it from my consideration.

Price should be stated since it qualifies people and separates buyers from lookers.

If you have many items, you should consider printing a flyer or price list. Offer to send it in return for a dollar, refundable with a reader's first purchase. This is the start of something larger, a catalog, which can be done by expanding the price list or flyer. I like charging $1 for the first list, then sending it free to the people on my mailing list.

Include your phone number, particularly when the price of the item is high. There's a good chance the prospect will want to talk with you about it before he buys, so make it easy for him. Some buyers just want to know how you sound before they send money in the mail.

Money-Back Guarantee

A money-back guarantee is so important to mail-order strategy that I wouldn't try to do business by mail without offering it.

Here's a sampling of ads from a recent issue of *Antique Trader* that will give you an idea of the kinds of things antiques dealers and collectors communicate about every week in that paper. (Names and addresses withheld to protect the innocent.)

AUTOGRAPH SALE! Giant Price List. 4,000 different autographs. Movie stars, political, sports. Send SASE—$.65.

WANTED: early Brass auto lamps, horns, brass clocks, Boyce meters, Trippe lamps, early auto accessories.

NATIONAL GEO MAGAZINES FOR SALE—1888–1920, old National Geo books, maps, brochures. Send wants.

WANTED: Old period fruit jars and lids.

POST CARDS SENT on approval. have 100's. Most categories. Send want list. You pay postage both ways.

NORITAKE CHINA—over 1,000 discontinued patterns in stock. Matching service—Noritake exclusively.

NEW, OLD Bradley Time Mickey Mouse watches, only $16.95 each. Ppd.

STEIFF BEARS: Teddy Rose, $229, Cinnamon w/leather paws (set of 4) MIB $395.

DOUBLE BARREL BOOT PISTOL, cap & ball, in fitted walnut case w/original maker label, ca. 1820, all original equip. & key, $1,500.

MUSIC BOXES WANTED—Buying disc and cylinder players, monkey organs, nickelodeans, Wurlitzer jukeboxes, mechanical birds, any antique mechanical music.

WAR SOUVENIRS WANTED. Paying top dollar for German, Japanese medals, daggers, swords, etc. NAME YOUR PRICE.

Good or Bad?

Here are my comments on the classified ads printed earlier in this chapter.

1. Good headline. No shortening of words or sentences. Completely understandable with details on exactly what's wanted. Good instructions for response. Good ad. Gets a plus.

2. Fairly good listing of specific items, but if the reader's possessions aren't included he probably won't call. Mediocre ad. Gets a zero.

3. Specialized dealer looking for only one type of item. If that's all he wanted it's a good ad. However, I think he could have described his wants a bit better. Still, gets a zero.

4. I don't know exactly what he has, although I've got to admit it sounds like guns. Gun guys will understand it, but it could be a bit more explanatory. Poor ad. Gets a minus.

5. A listing of just a few of the kinds of things for sale and directions would have improved this ad a lot. I think it's a poor ad. Gets a minus.

6. Good head, good list, good directions. Tells what, when, why, where. Excellent ad. Gets a plus.

7. Here's a good example of using a cut price as an inducement in a classified ad. Also, there's an attempt to solve the problem of having the buyer find the seller in a flea market. He has reserved space and gives good directions. An attention-getting sign, referred to in ad, might be an improvement, but this is a good ad as is. Gets a plus.

8. How could one say more? Excellent. Gets a plus.

9. Well-written ad directed to a specific market. Gets a plus.

10. This is an actual ad from *Antique Trader*, and is an example of the kind of short, inexpensive ad that pays off for advertisers in that publication. Gets a plus.

11. Here's a way to build a mailing list in order to sell specialized items. Two stamps (50 cents in 1989) is pretty cheap. Another idea is $1 bill, refundable with first order. This is a good ad. Gets a plus.

12. The One dollar approach to list-building. I'll bet this lady makes sales to the names she gets through this fine and amusing ad. Gets a plus.

CHAPTER NINE

eeping Records— The Easy Way

Reading Guide. Read this chapter to learn how to set up a simple system of records that will enable you to:

- Keep accurate financial records.
- Keep on the track of profit.
- Compare performance with past periods.
- Stay in the good graces of taxing agencies.

The information in this chapter falls short of a course in bookkeeping and accounting. You can get that from books available in libraries and bookstores, or you might look into courses offered by your local adult education program. If you use a personal computer there are excellent programs available which act as both teacher and accounting system.

As far as taxes are concerned, you would do well to buy the latest tax guide published by J. K. Lasser or the excellent volume on the same subject published by H & R Block. Either will tell you what you need to know to maintain records and do your federal tax returns. Every state that has a retail sales tax offers free literature.

At first, you won't find it necessary to employ the services of an accounting firm to keep your books, but if you have a professional tax preparer, it would be a good idea to ask for his advice on record-keeping. You might also inquire how much it will cost later to have him prepare a monthly operating statement and balance sheet. For a small business, this can be done very inexpensively.

However, for now *do your own bookkeeping—completely, from daily sales and expense entries to monthly statements.* There's a reason for this. Through keeping your own records and living with the figures, you'll have information

171

you need to make the right decisions and build the business. How easy it is to say to yourself, "This is probably going to be a profitable month, so I'll draw a little cash for myself." Handling the figures on a daily or weekly basis reminds you whether or not you can take a draw and keeps you honest with yourself. That's the first rule in making your business grow—be honest with yourself!

Your Basic Record System

Records are important to help you make your business grow and keep in the good graces of governmental taxing agencies. This applies to both income and sales tax. You should maintain the following systems, each of which we will deal with in detail:

1. Sales slips—one for each sale.
2. Daily journal of income and expense.
3. Checkbook.
4. Monthly summary—your operating statement.
5. Inventory records.
6. Voucher files (Receipts for expenses), by month.
7. Annual statement—helps prepare tax returns.

Sales Slips

If you dabble in the flea market for a couple of Sundays without keeping records, it's probable your state's sales tax department won't criticize you for dealing in cash without collecting tax or reporting anything. An occasional appearance in a flea market has been treated, until recently in most states, the same as a garage sale. You're allowed to sell personal possessions without collecting sales tax or reporting income.

But be careful! Some states have been cracking down on recreational flea marketers who sell every week for an extended period and do not report income. They're looking into residences that sprout garage sale signs (painted by a sign painter to last for years!) every month. They maintain this is evidence of a regular business and not just an occasional sale of second-hand family property. Look into this carefully, and find out how soon you must begin to collect state or local taxes.

Sales Books

When you decide you're ready to spend every Sunday flea marketing, go to an office supply store and buy a half dozen sales books—the kind with original and duplicate sheets for each sale and carbon paper built in. Buy the cheapest ones you can find—you can get fancy later and have sales slips with your name printed on them. Now, go the cheapest way on everything. (Be sure to save the receipt for the cash you've spent—this is your first business expense and it's deductible!)

The sales book has sets of serially numbered pairs of receipts—one of each pair for the customer, one for you. When you make a sale fill in the date on the top line, then write each element of the sale, one to a line. Strike the total at the bottom, and add the sales tax to produce the total amount which the customer will pay. If the customer is a dealer and exempt from paying sales tax, write "Exempt" and add his tax collection license number and home state.

Time-saving hint: Have a tax computation table (either one already printed— perhaps the office supply store has one—or one you've computed and printed) that will instantly give you the amount of tax for each sale you make without your having to compute the figure.

Tax License

Next, file for a State Tax Identification Number and what (in Pennsylvania) is called a State Sales Tax License. The licensing authority will assign your number and print it on a certificate (looks like a license to do business but isn't) that must be posted prominently where you do business. It's the notice to customers and others that you collect sales taxes and forward them to the State Department of Revenue. The Tax License is your evidence that you're a dealer, so that when you buy from another dealer you have proof that you're exempt from paying sales tax.

The intention is that retail sales tax should be collected only once—at the time of the ultimate retail sale. Thus when a retailer (who possesses a sales tax number) buys from another dealer or wholesaler, the retailer is exempt from the payment of retail sales tax. He'll collect it later from the retail customer and pass it on to the government. Normally, state regulations require that the *selling* dealer allow exemption from sales tax *only* to purchasers who have deposited a signed "Tax Exemption Certificate" with the selling dealer as evidence to a state tax auditor that the sale was indeed tax-free. The dealer must keep on file a tax exemption certificate for every exempt dealer he has ever done business with. The first time a dealer buys something from you, fill out the form and have him sign it.

Exemption regulations vary from state to state. Some states offer reciprocal tax exemption to licensed dealers from other states and some do not. You should understand your state's law on this in order to handle sales to out-of-state dealers who may not know your state's law. It's important to have blank tax-exemption forms to be filled out by out-of-state dealers who buy from you.

After you've filled out the sales slip and given the customer's copy to him, put your copy in a safe place. It's your permanent record of the sale, and whatever further records you keep of sales have their origin in your pile of sales slips. I have found it easiest to keep mine on an old-fashioned pointed spindle that sits on top of my antique cash register.

The idea of a cash register is not only to hold currency and coins but to keep track of sales—ring them up—as you punch the numbered keys. Unfortunately, mine was made in the early part of this century when nobody expected sales ever to go much over a $1.99. Its highest key is a dollar, so it isn't of much help in recordkeeping. But its merry clang announces to the world that I've made a sale, and it's consistent with the antique atmosphere I try to maintain. It's also a good place to park gumdrops, Lifesavers, and paper clips.

Be sure to record on the sales slip any information you wish to have on a permanent record. If you think you'll ever do direct mail to promote your business, or if you want to keep track of people who have specialized antique wants, be sure to take the name, address, and phone number and write it on the sales slip. Later, when you're copying the information from the slip into your journal, you can copy names, addresses, and phone numbers onto your list.

There may be specific inventory information you want to keep track of. In my candle business, I sold 20 different colors of four sizes in both scented and unscented varieties. Theoretically there were 160 different candle items to keep track of and re-order. It wasn't quite that simple since some items sell better than others, so reorder frequency varied from candle to candle. Some colors didn't sell, so I didn't re-order those.

I recorded candle sales by length, color, and scent to help with re-ordering every couple of months. When re-order time came, I called my friend Belinda at Williamsburg Soap and Candle Company. (Wish it were this easy on antiques!) So—if you have any items that you buy from a wholesale source—metal polish, buttons, calico by the bolt—use your sales record to set up an inventory re-order system.

Daily Journal

At the end of each working day (Sunday if that's the only day of the week on which you make sales), transfer the details from your sales slips onto a page in your Daily Journal. If you're in an every Sunday flea market, the Daily Journal is really a Weekly Journal, and either four or five of these sheets constitute a month's business.

The journal summarizes the sales activities for the day including taxable sales and the amount of tax collected, tax-exempt (dealer) sales, and totals of each. There should also be room on the page for any additional information you wish to record (such as my candle sales breakdown by size, color, and scent).

In addition to sales figures recorded first on the sales slips and then in the Daily Journal, deductible business expenses should be recorded and vouchers (receipts) filed away.

Let's say you arrive at the flea market early and do the rounds of other dealers. You buy three items. You should have either sales slips or memos jotted on pieces of paper as to what you bought and for how much. Attach these vouchers to your Daily Journal page with a paper clip, so that when it comes time to include them in your operating statement, you will have both the reminder to do so and the proper voucher to back up your record. If you buy by check, you'll have both a sales slip (or memo) plus the check register and canceled check.

Here's a very simple form for a Daily Journal. Use sheets for a ring notebook, or buy a bound ledger book that has accounting columns printed on every page with a wide blank column at left to enter the names of items sold. Add the figures entered under the headings, enter totals below, and you have your Daily Journal (which also includes items bought or sold for the week days following your Sunday Flea market appearance until the following Sunday).

The first illustration shows the blank page, the second one is filled in as it would be at day's end. This is not a big day—I've entered just enough to show how to enter the sales you've made. I hope your days will all be better than this!

(1) is the Flea market date, (2) lists items sold that day (and during other days that week), (3) shows what you originally paid for the item (Cost of Goods Sold), (4) records the sale price (money collected), and (5) is the tax collected on the item. (Assume tax of 6%.) Here's the simple Journal form:

DAILY JOURNAL

(1) Date	(2) Items Sold	(3) Cost	(4) Sale	(5) Tax
____	_____	___	___	___
____	_____	___	___	___
____	_____	___	___	___
____	_____	___	___	___

And, here's how the Journal page looks when it's filled in for one day's sales:

DAILY JOURNAL

(1) Date	(2) Items Sold	(3) Cost	(4) Sale	(5) Tax
Non-taxable sales (to dealers)				
____	_____	___	___	___
06/07	Brass Bell	$ 7.00	$ 13.50	—
	Indian Print	8.00	17.00	—
____	_____	___	___	___
Total dealer sales		$15.00	$ 30.50	—

DAILY JOURNAL

(1) Date	(2) Items Sold	(3) Cost	(4) Sale	(5) Tax
Taxable sales:				
	Box Lock	$ 6.50	$ 14.50	$ .87
	Toby Mug	18.00	36.00	2.16
	Washboard	27.50	55.50	3.33
Total taxable		$52.00	$106.00	$ 6.36
Grand totals		$67.00	$136.50	$ 6.36
Bank deposit (4) + (5)				$142.86

CheckBook

You should use a Company check to pay business expenses. Do not use your personal checkbook for this. A separate, business checkbook is much more impressive in the event you're ever audited, and if you decide to use an outside accounting service, a separate business checkbook is necessary as the source for your bookkeeper's entries.

Always write the purpose of each expense on the check to explain clearly why the purchase was made. For example, "Cloth to drape tables," or "Glass for picture frames in inventory." Get in the habit of being concise and complete early in the game. At the end of the month, use your checkbook to construct the expense side of your operating statement.

Monthly Operating Statement

Each monthly statement will probably fit one 8½-inch by 11-inch page and show four or five days' sales for the month. If you make a sale at some place other than at the flea market, it can be recorded in the Daily Journal the following selling day. In other words, your Daily Journal will record all sales made both on flea-market day and for the period of Monday–Sunday of the week. It's really a weekly record.

All expenses are listed for the month. Make sure you have a proper voucher, not just the check record, for those expenses paid by check. This gives double

MONTHLY OPERATING STATEMENT

Weekly sales and tax summary:

Week	Cost, Mdse.	Sales	Tax Coll.
06/07	$ 67.00	$136.50	$ 6.36
06/13	42.50	86.00	3.33
06/20	58.60	121.80	7.31
06/27—Closed—Vacation			
TOTALS	$168.10	$344.30	$17.00

Expenses:

Date	Item	Amount
06/07/90	Rent	$ 35.00
06/09	Bags	6.30
06/10	Price Tags	2.65

Total expenses for month: $ 43.95

PROFIT AND LOSS STATEMENT

Month: June, 1990

Total sales	$344.30
Less: cost of merchandise	168.10
Gross margin	$176.20
Less expenses	43.95
Net profit	$132.25

proof of your incurring the expense—your cancelled check and the supplier's receipt. It also gives you the means of double checking your records.

Sometimes you'll pay cash, so not every expenditure will be backed by a cancelled check. Some flea market people from whom you buy won't take anything but cash. Be sure to get a receipt. Otherwise your only voucher will be a note or memo from you to you.

Note in our illustration that the operating statement shows a gross margin. It's defined as total sales (before sales tax) to include both taxable and non-taxable sales. From that total, the cost (to you) of merchandise sold is deducted. The accounting term for this is Cost of Goods Sold, or CGS. Since you have recorded the cost of each item sold, your CGS can simply be the total of all CGS figures from your Daily Journal pages.

In a normal retail business CGS is calculated by deducting the closing inventory from opening inventory and adding purchases for stock. This is difficult to do in a flea market operation, so you can simply keep an inventory book with all items you buy for stock listed in it. Then, as you sell them, scratch through the items sold and transfer the CGS figure for each to your Daily Journal on the same line that tells what the item sold for and how much tax you collected on it. This keeps you on top of your business—you know much you made in gross margin on each item sold.

On your Monthly Operating Statement are recorded all the expense items for which you have vouchers (rent, telephone, supplies, etc.). These are then deducted from gross profit to yield the figure that is your net profit.

Last month's figures are shown for comparison to this month's, and space is provided for a running subtotal that shows year-to-date figures for this and last year's operations. You can make weekly, monthly, and year-to-date comparisons to find out whether you're on track in fulfilling goals you've set for your business. If you're not making budget targets, you'll know things need to be done differently.

At the end of the year, your monthly figures are totaled as the last year-to-date figure, and it's these that are used in preparing your income tax returns.

That may sound complicated, but the following form shows how easy it really is to do a monthly operating statement. Of course, yours will contain a great many more lines.

Inventory Book

In the Inventory Book you enter every item you take to your stand to sell. Each is recorded with cost price to you, date of acquisition, and the tag price at which you put it on sale. If you use a stock number system, that stock number should be listed with the item. I've found some problems with stock numbers on tabs, mostly with customers who think the number is the price or who take it to be a discount I'll give on demand.

At first I used a stock number that contained a code for acquisition data and the original cost of the item to me. Thus 80–03–0009 meant that I had bought the item in 1980 and had paid $90 for it. The last two digits were reversed. But sometimes in the heat of battle, I got confused or I'd make mistakes in printing the code on the tag. If it's not too difficult for you to remember what you paid for something, keeping your cost in your head and your inventory book is far easier.

At the end of each day, the items sold should be scratched through in the book, the sale date entered, and the price received filled in. That last figure also goes to the daily journal as mentioned earlier.

The Inventory Book is valuable for two reasons. At any time you can add up the cost values and sales values of all items in stock to get a total of both cost and sale figure. Such a document is an important record if you ever suffer a loss by fire or theft. You're probably not going to be able to get insurance coverage on inventory. At least I've never found an insurance company that would insure the stock of even a fairly well-protected and fire-secure antiques mall. However, losses by theft or fire are deductible at their cost value from your income tax return and that's some consolation in the event of loss.

There was a terrible fire in an antiques mall in Central Pennsylvania in which millions of dollars of inventory were lost. One friend of mine lost almost $100,000 worth of jewelry inventory. She later bought a huge, fire-resistant safe in which to store her jewelry from week to week. I remember her safe purchase very well. She bought it at one of my auctions!

Shoplifting losses can be entered in filing taxes at cost value as a monthly business operating expense. I am told that an alternate method is to write off a percentage (for example 5%) of gross sales. However, be sure to check on current tax law before taking anything as exotic as that on your simple operating statement. You'll try your darndest to prevent theft, but you've got to face the fact that it will take place no matter how vigilant you are.

Either your tax man, the J. K. Lasser Tax Book, or somebody in your local IRS office can be helpful in advising you what you can deduct. Things like mileage allowance for your car while on a buying trip or driving to and from auctions are deductible. Be sure to check for the latest allowance. It was over 22 cents a mile the last time I checked. Costs of repair and restoration of items for sale—lumber, screws, glue, glass, and depreciation on tools and the building itself—are deductible and should be included on the monthly operating statements.

Mileage cost for driving to and from your flea market is not deductible. That's commuting expense, and is never allowed. However, if you travel to an out-of-town antiques show and stay overnight, both mileage and living expenses (hotel, meals, telephone, etc.) are deductible. Be sure to include them. Get receipts, pay by check or credit card whenever possible, and keep a travel diary. Enter it all as you go along and keep your records up to date.

If you buy and maintain equipment of a permanent nature—such as a bench saw or drill press, a van that's used for nothing but business, or office equipment such as a computer that's used only for your work—depreciation is deductible. The amount you can take depends on current law and that should be checked as deductibility changes from time to time. Consult your tax advisor on anything that has to do with depreciation deductions.

Expense Voucher File

This is easy to maintain, but it'll fall flat if you don't keep up with it. The file consists of an accordion-style file folder with expanding compartments that are labeled 1 through 12 for the months. When you've made a payment, either by check or in cash, for a deductible business expense, an item for inventory, or any other business-related payment, toss the receipt, record or memo evidencing the transaction, into the appropriate monthly compartment. Then, at the end of each week you can summarize the expense items in your Daily Journal, and at the end of the month in your Monthly Operating Statement.

In the flea market business, you don't need anything fancy like account number systems. Just toss the receipts (vouchers) into the file and total them later. If you grow into a million-dollar-a-year antiques department store there will be plenty of time to set up a complex system. By that time, you'll have an accounting department and your controller will set up a system for you. In the meantime, for the first couple of years, the time spent thumbing through your month's vouchers will put you in good touch with your business, and it's not worth the effort to get over-complicated.

Keep It Simple!

Your record system should be as simple as you can make it while affording you the capability of recording all useful information you need to keep track of where you are and whether you're on target, pay your taxes, and take advantage of every legal tax break.

Using a Computer

There's not a business in the world today that can't justify a computer system of some kind. This is not to say that as soon as you decide to get into the flea market business you should run out and buy $10,000 worth of computer equipment. You probably shouldn't buy any for at least a year and maybe never. Wait until you're certain you want to stay in the business and until your operation begins to fall into some kind of pattern.

During the first year or two, it would be well to study what's available in simple computing systems in preparation for buying one. That's exactly what I did beginning in 1983 when personal computers were beginning to come down in price to the point where they made sense for small businesses. In addition to business, I try to write, and I knew that I could use the word processing function of a computer to produce such efforts as this book faster and better than with a typewriter.

My computer investigations took me to many New York City establishments that were competing for the rapidly expanding interest in PCs. I knew absolutely nothing about computers, just that I was sure I would have one some day—I hoped soon. New York, by the way, is still the best place in the world to shop for computers. Not only will you find every conceivable brand of hardware and software, but because of intense competition, great deals are always available.

The highest quote I got was for a complete IBM personal computer system at about $6,000. The lowest quotes were in the $4,000 to $5,000 range. This would buy me a simple diskette machine with 64K of RAM (operating memory) and a word-processing program. I don't remember exactly what additional software was included but it wasn't much. In addition, the price included a near-letter-quality printer. The price was too rich for my modest budget, and, I reasoned, I'd gotten along without it for a long time so why rush? Prices were already coming down, and I would probably profit by learning more about computers before making a selection.

A year later a neighbor told me he had a Kaypro 10 (that number meant the machine had a phenomenal quantity of 10 million bytes of hard-disk memory!), and that he had tried but found it too time-consuming to master the operating system. He had paid over $2,500 for it, used it very little, and would part with it for $1,000. I grabbed the opportunity.

In the five years since I began computing I've bought two printers, a switch box, and an uninterruptible power supply (a combination storage battery and surge protector to keep the computer and printer safe in the event of power outages, an almost daily occurrence in the U.S. Virgin Islands where this is being written). The point of all this is, I have a satisfactory system I've put together at a cost of less than $2,000.

One thing I was sure I would use the computer for is keeping track of inventory, but what I found through experience is that if inventory is composed of unique items—as antiques are, every piece being an individual—the computer is virtually worthless for inventory control. It's easier to write it down when you buy it and scratch it off when you sell it!

But when I got into selling toy soldiers by mail, my computer was invaluable in keeping track of inventory and doing my catalog using a data base program called D-Base II that allows indexing, searching and arranging by such parameters as manufacturer and type. It also keeps track of both wholesale cost and retail price on every soldier and will give me an instant inventory value at either retail or wholesale at the press of a button!

aking a Plan
for Growth and Profit

Reading Guide. In the last chapter, you read about your accounting system and how it helps you record quantified facts about your business operations. Now, we'll consider business planning with which you set a course for growth and eventual profit. We'll see how to:

- Set goals (objectives).
- Develop a one-year plan.
- Budget cash flow.
- Develop a buying plan.

Management means setting goals (objectives), outlining means of achieving them, and periodically examining results to see whether goals are being met. It also means the application of new thinking, new decisions, and corrective action to insure that operations get back on track when they stray.

Operating executives of big companies are required to make written plans as blueprints to future success. Usually there is a one-year plan and a five-year plan. The process has been called "Management by Objective." The idea is to identify key objectives that if accomplished, insure overall company success. Each manager has his own set of objectives. He sets them, with approval of his superior, and is judged frequently—monthly, quarterly, annually—on how well he's accomplished his objectives. He's rewarded if he makes them, fired if he misses consistently.

This system can profitably be applied to a small business. The major difference between the large and small business is in management organization. The big ones have rank upon rank of high, middle, and lower managers. You have but one—you. You set the objectives or goals. You will work to achieve them, and you're the one to analyze how well you've done and make decisions on corrective action. This takes personal discipline. We can only show you how to apply it. It has to come from you.

Where do you want to be a year from now? Five years from now? Ten? Come up with the answers to these questions, and your objectives can be pretty well set.

Your One Year Plan

Let's assume you start your weekend business with an inventory worth $1,000. That's what you paid for the items in it, plus increases in estimated value to allow for inflation. Of that group of items, some may be worth double what you paid for them, some more. Some, the ones you bought with emotion instead of common sense, may be worth less than their original retail price. Let's assume that after they're priced for resale, the price tags total $2,000. Using these assumptions, let's see what the basis of a first year plan could be.

Assuming 50 weekly flea markets (two out of the year for vacation) and a sale of as little as $100 per market, you calculate your first year's sales at a conservative $5,000. It's apparent you don't have enough merchandise to stay in business longer than 20 weeks and still have something to sell unless you add to inventory during that time. Therefore, one plan you've got to make is to buy merchandise for resale during the year. Planning's easy, isn't it?

Your Buying Plan

You've started with $2,000 (retail value) in merchandise and an estimated $100 a week sales figure for planning. You know you'll have to add to that about $3,000 more (retail) or $1,500 (the price at which you buy it wholesale), assuming you buy it for half the price you'll put on the tags.

So, if that's your objective—and it seems like a good one—to sell $5,000 worth the first year, you know you have to spend $1,500 for new stuff to achieve the goal. But, if that's all you did you'd have sold $5,000 worth and you'd be out of inventory at year's end. So, it's obvious that your buying plan must include spending $1,500 to replace goods sold, plus another $2,500 worth at 50% of retail value—a total of $4,000—to end the year with $5,000 in estimated retail value in merchandise and $5,000 in sales getting there.

If you want that to be your goal, the only way to accomplish it is to produce $4,000 in cash margin that you can turn right around and spend to make the business grow to that point. If you take out profit, you'll inhibit the development of your business and delay the day when you'll operate at the level you wish to achieve by year's end.

You must replace sold inventory on a steady basis as you go along. If you don't your inventory will dwindle as people buy your better stuff. Shoppers will become old friends and whiz by, giving your display no more than a quick glance.

At this point, we've developed two objectives for our first year plan:

1. Sell at least $100 per week.
2. Buy $2,500 (wholesale) as quickly as possible.

Importance of Turnover

Each time you add a significant number of items to stock, you'll get a flurry of activity. The best way to add a quantity of inventory is with a big "house buy" that adds a hundred or more pieces at one time. You'll be amazed how collectors and other dealers will flock to your resupplied stand. They'll see what you have, buy, and spread the word. You'll gain a reputation as an aggressive dealer who always has something new. This is a key, non-monetary objective to add to your plan.

Raising the Ante

By aggressively carrying out your plan to buy a steady flow of new stuff, your sales will soon exceed the $100 per week level, then exceed $200 per week. You'll constantly challenge yourself to achieve new, higher weekly sales totals. How high is up depends on how much stuff is available for purchase in your area. At some point you'll find you're consistently exceeding your objectives so it's time to set new ones. You'll be selling at a $300 or $400 weekly clip. Display more and sell more!

As your weekly sales grow, you'll have more cash margin to spend for new stuff. You must find sellers, auctions, and homes from which to buy. As inventory grows, you'll sell more and that generates more money for investment. The success cycle!

You're doing the flea market part time so you don't need income from your flea market activity. Plow most of it back into new inventory. That's what makes your business grow!

Growing inventory means you'll need more space, and rent will go up. Allow for that in your changing plan. If you manage well, your fixed expense total, rent plus other costs, will not increase proportionately, so that your margin as a percentage of sales will go up. The larger your space and the greater your inventory, the more cash you'll have available for expansion.

Investing in Yourself!

In your first year, plan on investing three-quarters of your total sales in new inventory. If your week's sale is $100, $75 will be "buy money." That $75 is earmarked for purchasing items you think will make you a profit.

Of course, some weeks will produce less and some more than your planned sale figure. Let's say your first month produces $400 in gross sales. Following your plan you would earmark $300 of that for inventory purchases.

Let's assume expenses total $75 per month including rent, supplies, etc.

Here's what your first three months would look like if sales stay at $400 per month:

CASH FLOW—FIRST THREE MONTHS

	Inventory at Cost	Inventory at Retail	Cash on Hand
Begin	$1,000	$2,000	0
1st month sale	−200	−400	+400
Replenish	+300	+600	−300
Pay expenses			− 75
End 1st month	$1,100	$2,200	$ 25
2nd month sale	−200	−400	+400
Replenish	+300	+600	−300
Pay expenses			− 75
End 2nd month	$1,200	$2,400	$ 50
3rd month sale	−200	−400	+400
Replenish	+300	+600	−300
Pay expenses			− 75
End third month	$1,300	$2,600	$ 75

Let's analyze what's happened during your first three months in your part time business:

1. Your beginning inventory, which cost you $1,000, has adjusted for inflation to a present-day value, has risen from $1,000 to $1,300 in cost value, an increase of 33⅓%.

2. Your inventory, figured at total retail value, has gone from $2,000 to $2,600, also 33⅓% up.

3. You have taken in $1,200 in cash, spent $900 for new merchandise and $225 in operating expenses, and increased your cash cushion from 0 to $75.

Your investment of $1,000 worth of merchandise and zero cash has grown to be worth, at cost value, $1,375. In retail terms it's worth $2,675 (267% more than your initial investment. Read it and weep, Wall-Streeters!

Now what happens? Now that you have an inventory a third larger than the one you started with, your sales are going to go up. (Remember, display more, sell more). Actually, they probably inched up during the first three months, but for the sake of simplicity, let's say they've stayed the same.

Now let's say sales go from $400 to $500 per month, a very conservative increase. To display more you need more space, so your rent will have to go up. Not much, just a bit. Let's say total expenses go from $75 to $100 for each of the next three months. Under the newly revised plan, your cash flow is going to look like this:

CASH FLOW—SECOND THREE MONTHS

	Inventory at cost	Inventory at Retail	Cash on Hand
End 3rd month	$1,300	$2,600	$ 75
4th month sale	− 250	− 500	+ 500
Replenish	+ 375	+ 750	− 375
Pay expenses			− 100
End 4th month	+ 1,425	$2,850	$100
5th month sale	− 250	− 500	+ 500
Replenish	+ 375	+ 750	− 375
Pay expenses			− 100
End 5th month	$1,550	$3,100	$125
6th month sale	− 250	− 500	+ 500
Replenish	+ 375	+ 750	− 375
Pay expenses			− 100
End first six months	$1,675	+ 3,350	$150

You're Building a Business!

Your original investment of an estimated $1,000 worth of merchandise (at cost value) has grown to an inventory sales value of $3,350, and you have a modest $150 as your "cash cushion." If you spent less for inventory replacement than in our example, your cash surplus will be larger, but unless you made some very good buys (thus preserving the retail value of your growing inventory), your inventory value at the end of the six months would be less.

At this stage keep cash down, inventory up. Your main objective for these first six months, and indeed for the first year and even beyond, is to increase inventory. That's your major asset and the basis of your business. Without it you can't increase sales and make the business increase in value.

Finishing Your First Year

Businessmen have been giving a lot of attention lately to cash flow, planning exactly how the *cash* will come in (as opposed to *sales* which often are quite different, what with charge accounts and deferred expenses). Let's assume some modest increases, and see how things could work out.

During the second six months of your first year, your average sale will probably jump again, not suddenly, but gradually. At the end of the first year it would be reasonable to set a goal of $200 per average week (including any sales you might make to special collectors during the week). If at the end of your first year, you are averaging $200 per week in sales and an annual sales rate of $10,000 (assuming two weeks off for vacation). If you continue to spend ¾ of your cash income, you'll add inventory at the rate of $7,800 per year!

During the second six months of your first year, you might enjoy a rise in sales to $600 per month. Why not plan for it, then work to make it happen? Even with the increase in inventory replenishment to $450 (cost) per month and an increase in expenses to $100 per month, you will see your capital (entirely generated by the business) grow to the following values by the end of year one:

Inventory, at cost	$2,725
Inventory, at retail	$5,450
Cash	$ 500

Here's how that works out:

CASH FLOW, SECOND 6 MONTHS

	Inventory at Cost	Inventory at Retail	Cash on Hand
End, six months	$1,675	$3,350	$150
7th month sale	−300	−600	+600
Replenish	+450	+900	−450
Expenses			−100
Totals, 7th month	$1,825	$3,650	$250
Monthly growth	150	300	50
× 6	900	1,800	300
End of first year	$2,725	$5,450	$500

Your Cash Cushion

Let's look at that $500 surviving cash balance. What's it for? To blow it on a vacation at the shore? Have a weekend in New York? Buy a new television set?

None of the above. Depending on your payroll deduction for income tax at your place of employment, or your quarterly payment of estimated federal tax due, you may owe some income tax to the Feds. In that case, your $500 cushion, or part of it, will go for taxes. Sorry.

I've purposely stayed away from involving federal income tax in our consideration of planning to keep it simple. But it's important to consider it early and keep payments up to date as you go along. Don't wait until year's end.

What's Your Business Worth?

At the end of the first year, let's take a look at the value of your business. An appraiser would take the cost value of the hard assets (inventory, fixtures and supplies, cash) and add to that an amount which, for lack of a better phrase, the accountants call "good will." Good will is really the amount of money it would take, starting from scratch, to get where you are in the business. What would somebody pay you to be where you are at the end of the first year? To that figure add the value of hard assets.

The sum of inventory and cash is $3,225. To that add at least $3,000 for good will. Your business could now be said to be worth $6,225. Not bad on an investment of $1,000 worth of merchandise and no cash in the beginning! If you've enjoyed the market, the people you've met, and the learning of new skills, it's been a rewarding year!

Reality

We've given a fictional example of a business plan and shown what happens if that plan is fulfilled exactly as laid out, on schedule with no setbacks, no bonanzas, no exceptions! The real world doesn't work that way.

REALITY: A $200 sale per week is not an unrealistic goal in the beginning but every week will not produce $200 in sales. Some will produce $100 and some $300 or even $600.

Seasonal Factors

We've given no consideration to the seasonal nature of the business. Bonanza weeks will occur, probably in fall or spring. Summers can be slow unless you do outdoor markets in productive areas.

If you live in the snow belt, you'll have winter days when customers can't get their buggies out of garages and you end the day with a big fat zero in sales because of the weather!

You can't predict any one week's receipts. What you can do is set a reasonable amount for an *average* weekly sales goal and try to achieve it. Budget for seasonal fluctuations after experience enables you to pin down seasonal patterns from your records. The minimum period for a reasonably accurate sales average is, I believe, monthly. Divide by 4 or 5 (depending on how many weeks you sold that month) to get a weekly average.

Following the Rules

Spending just ¾ of cash income for new merchandise forces you to plan and operate conservatively. It's easier to plan than operate, however. No matter what your plan, you'll be tempted to break your own rules and take a greater risk in buying than your plan dictates.

You'll be sorry later. But even your occasional falls from the straight and narrow are part of learning and developing the selfdiscipline that enables you to succeed in building the business. If you *mostly* stick to your plan, no matter how many bumps there are along the way, you'll reach the goal you've set!

Remember, the purpose of planning is to give you objectives—targets for success—as well as a route along which to proceed. If you follow a conservative and realistic plan, you'll be on your way to creating a rewarding lifetime avocation or occupation. You might even get rich, and that's what we want to happen.

I haven't seen anybody make it overnight, mostly because it's darned near impossible to amass an inventory that will support six-figure sales in just a year or two unless you quit your main job and devote full time to buying and selling. Even then, it's tough to put that much stock together. So relax, do your conservative planning, buy right, sell hard, and have a good time for five to ten years, by which time you are going to have a fine business going!

Planning Activities

Now, to close this, let's go back to the beginning of your first year and your first plan to develop the business and become a professional. Put together a written plan of activities that will cause your business to develop the way we've outlined it. Your plan might look something like this:

1. *Attend at least an auction each month*, better still once a week. At first you won't have much money to spend, but it's good entertainment and you'll learn a lot.

2. *Within the first two months, start placing "Wanted to Buy" ads* in the local newspaper. This is an absolute necessity so that your meager beginning inventory will be replaced as you sell it and begin to grow. Learn and practice the technique of successful house calls early.

3. *Visit as many flea markets and antiques shops as you can*. If you travel, plan to visit markets and shops in other areas. Open your mind to new ideas. Don't neglect junk yards and salvage yards if they sell antiques.

4. *Join a local antiques dealers' association or club*. You'll profit from learning from others in your field.

5. *Read trade literature*, including several of the magazines and papers mentioned in the appendices to this book.

6. *Make friends of other local dealers, pickers, haulers, appraisers, and auctioneers*. People enjoy being helpful and you can learn a lot from them.

7. *Make it a two-way street and offer to help other dealers in any way you can*. At first your help might consist of hauling cartons from cars into the market in the morning, but as you develop knowledge, you'll be amazed how other dealers will look to you as an expert in *your* fields.

Your Second Year

By the time you're in year two of antiques trading, you'll have learned a lot about buying and selling and about what sells in your area. And you'll have uncovered sources for buying. You may decide to broaden your lines or go into specialties.

Plan your second year just as you did the first. Decide, before the second year starts, whether you want to commit the full 75% of sales dollars to buying new stock for inventory, or whether, at this time, you want to start drawing a bit of profit from the business.

I suggest you stay with the 75% investment plan for at least another year—even better, two years. By the time another two years have gone by you'll probably have an inventory worth at least $15,000 at your cost value.

During your second year, if you've been able to build a good antiques inventory, plan to exhibit in at least one out-of-town antiques show and sale. Take only the better items to sell there. You'll discover whether your material sells in such a show and whether you like the nomadic show life.

Your "Antiques Wanted" advertising should be a weekly (if not daily) activity, and one or two house calls a week will produce an increasing number of good buys.

Don't forget to make provisions for having cash at tax time to pay taxes on your profits. If you do as well as I think you're going to do, you'll have to file quarterly estimates of federal tax and pay as you go on your business earnings.

After a couple of years, you'll want to make a decision on whether to stay in the flea market or to look for broader horizons. If you like doing shows and have the time it takes, that's a good route for expansion. Or, perhaps you're headed for a mall or co-op for antiques dealers. Make any of these steps when you think it will accelerate your growth and profits.

You may decide that your business can do more than create inventory assets or current income. It may provide the basis for an investment program in fine arts and period antiques. Instead of making all purchases for inventory you would then devote a part of your buying to selecting pieces that you would keep in your home so that future appreciation in value would add to your long-term retirement plan.

Whether you branch out and make antiques and collectibles a full-time occupation or are content to pursue it on a part-time basis, I think you'll enjoy the business. This kind of buying and selling is fun!

 **ollectors' Clubs**

Information on collectors' clubs is reprinted, with permission of the publisher, from the 4th Edition, *Warman's Americana & Collectibles*, Wallace-Homestead Book Company, Radnor, PA, Harry L. Rinker, editor; and from 23rd Edition, *Warman's Antiques and Their Prices*, published by Wallace-Homestead Book Company, Harry L. Rinker, editor.

For additional, non-affiliated, collectors' and antiques publications, see Appendix 2.

Advertising

The Ephemera Society of America, PO Box 224, Ravena, NY 12143.

National Association of Paper and Advertising Collectibles, PO Box 500, Mount Joy, PA 17552. *P.A.C.* (newspaper).

Tin Container Collectors Association, PO Box 440101, Aurora, CA 80014. *Tin Type* (monthly).

Akro Agate Glass

Akro Agate Art Association, PO Box 758, Salem, NH 03079.

Animal Licenses

The International Society of Animal License Collectors, 4420 Wisconsin Avenue, Tampa, FL 33616.

Art Pottery

American Art Pottery Association, 9825 Upton Circle, Bloomington, MN 55431.

Autographs

Universal Autograph Collectors Club, PO Box 6181, Washington, D.C. 20044-6181.

Avon

Bud Hastin's National Avon Collector's Club, PO Box 9868, Kansas City, MO 64134.

Banks
Still Bank Collectors Club of America, 1 Banker's Trust Plaza, 24th Floor, New York, NY 10006. *Penny Bank Post* (publication).

Baseball
Society for Baseball Research, PO Box 323, Cooperstown, NY 13326. *Baseball Research Journal*, *SABR Bulletin*, *The National Pastime* (publications).

Beer Cans
Beer Can Collectors of America, 747 Merus Court, Fenton, MO 63026.

Bells
American Bell Association, Rte 1, Box 286, Natronia Heights, PA 15065.

Big Little Books
Big Little Book Collector's Club of America, PO Box 732, Danville, CA 94526.

Bottle Openers
Just For Openers, 63 October Lane, Trumbull, CT 06611.

Buttons
National Button Society, 2733 Juno Place, Akron, OH 44313.

Cameras
American Photographic Historical Society, PO Box 1775, Grand Central Station, New York, NY 10163.

Canals
American Canal Society, 809 Rathton Road, York, PA 17403. *American Canals* (quarterly).

Canal Society of Ohio, 120 East Mill Street, Suite 402, Akron, OH 44308. *Towpath* (quarterly).

Pennsylvania Canal Society, Canal Museum, PO Box 877, Easton, PA 18042. *Canal Currents* (quarterly).

Candy Containers
Candy Container Collectors of America, Box 184, Lucerne Mines, PA 15754. *Candy Gram* (newsletter, annual convention).

Cartes de Visite/Cabinet Cards
Photographic Historical Society of New England, Inc., PO Box M, West Newton Station, Boston, MA 02165.

Cat Collectibles
Cat Collectors, 31311 Blair Drive, Warren, MI 48092. *Cat Talk* (bimonthly).

Cigar Collectibles
International Seal, Label and Cigar Band Society, 8915 East Bellevue Street, Tucson, AZ 85715.

Circus Items
Circus Fans of America, c/o J. Allen Duffield, PO Box 69, Camp Hill, PA 17011.

The Circus Historical Society, 743 Beverly Park Place, Jackson, MI 49203.

The Circus Model Builders International, 347 Lonsdale Avenue, Dayton, OH 45419.

Clocks
National Association of Watch and Clock Collectors, Inc., PO Box 33, Columbia, PA 17512. *NAWCC Bulletin*.

Clothing
The Costume Society of America, PO Box 761, Englishtown, NJ 07726.

Coca-Cola Items
The Cola Clan, 2084 Continental Drive NE, Atlanta, GA 30345.

Cup Plates
Pairpoint Cup Plate Collectors of America, Inc., Box A-2058, New Bedford, MA 02741. Quarterly newsletter.

Degenhart Glass
The Friends of Degenhart, PO Box 186, Cambridge, OH 43725.

Depression Glass
National Depression Glass Association, Inc., PO Box 1128, Springfield, MO 65808.

Disneyana
Mouse Club, 2056 Cirone Way, San Jose, CA 95124.

Dolls
Ginny Doll Club, 305 West Beacon Road, Lakeland, FL 33803.

Madame Alexander Fan Club, PO Box 146, New Lenox, IL 60451.

United Federation of Doll Clubs, PO Box 14146, Parkville, MO 64152.

Elephants
The National Elephant Collector's Society, 89 Massachusetts Avenue, Box 7, Boston, MA 02115.

Fans
The Fan Association of North America, 505 Peachtree Road, Orlando, FL 32804.

Fan Circle International, 24 Asmus Hill, Hampstead Garden Suburb, London, England, NW11 GET.

Fishing Collectibles
National Fishing Lure Collectors Club, PO Box 1791, Dearborn, MI 48121.

Flag Collectibles
North American Vexillological Association, 3 Edgehill Road, Winchester, MA 01890.

Frogs
The Frog Pond, PO Box 193, Beech Grove, IN 46107.

Games and Puzzles
American Game Collectors Association, 4628 Barlow Drive, Bartlesville, OK 74006.

Gasoline Collectibles
International Petroliana Collectors Association, 2151 East Dublin-Granville Road, Suite G292, Columbus, OH 43229.

Geisha Girl Porcelain
The Geisha Girl Porcelain Newletter (club), PO Box 394, Morris Plains, NJ 07950.

Golf Collectibles
Golf Collectors' Society, PO Box 491, Shawnee Mission, KS 66202.

Graniteware
National Graniteware Society, 4818 Reamer Road, Center Point, IA 52213.

Hatpins
International Club for Collectors of Hatpins and Hatpin Holders 15237 Chanera Avenue, Gardena, CA 90249.

Inkwells
The Society of Inkwell Collectors, 5136 Thomas Avenue, Minneapolis, MN 55410.

Keys
Key Collectors International, PO Box 9397, Phoenix, AZ 85068.

Marbles
Marble Collectors Unlimited, 503 West Pine, Marengo, IA 52301.

Marble Collectors Society of America, PO Box 222, Trumbull, CT 06611. *Marble Mania* (quarterly newsletter).

National Marble Club of America, 440 Eaton Road, Drexel Hill, PA 19026. Quarterly newsletter.

Matchbox Collector Cars
Matchbox Collectors Club, 141 West Commercial Avenue, Moonachie, NJ 07075.

Military Insignia
American Society of Military Insignia Collectors, c/o James F. Greene, 1331 Bradley Avenue, Hummelstown, PA 17036.

Motion Picture Personalities
Studio Collectors Club, PO Box 1566, Apple Valley, CA 92307.

Moxie Collectibles
Write Frank N. Potter, Route 375, Box 164, Woodstock, NY 12498.

Music Boxes
Musical Box Society International, RD #3, Box 205, Morgantown, IN 46160.

Nippon China
International Nippon Collectors Club, PO Box 230, Peotone, IL 60468.

Occupied Japan
Occupied Japan Collectors Club, 18309 Faysmith Avenue, Torrance, CA 90504.

Owl Collectibles
Russell's Owl Collector's Club, PO Box 1292, Bandon, OR 97411.

Padlocks
American Lock Collectors Association, 36076 Grenada, Livonia, MI 48154. Bimonthly newsletter.

Paper Dolls
United Federation of Doll Clubs, P.O. Box 14146, Parkville, MD 64152.

Pencils
American Pencil Collectors Society, 603 East 105th Street, Kansas City, MO 64131.

Pens
Pen Fancier's Club, 1169 Overcash Drive, Dunedin, FL 33528.

Phoenix Bird China
Phoenix Bird Collectors of America, 5912 Kingsfield, West Bloomfield, MI 48033.

Planters Peanuts
Peanut Pals, 3065 Rumsey Drive, Ann Arbor, MI 48105. *Peanut Papers* (bimonthly).

Playing Cards
Chicago Playing Card Collectors, Inc., 1559 W. Platt Boulevard, Chicago, IL 60620.

Playing Card Collectors Association, Inc. 3621 Douglas Avenue, Racine, WI 53404.

Pocket Knives
American Blade Collectors, P.O. Box 22007, Chattanooga, TN 37422.

The National Knife Collectors Association, PO Box 21070, Chattanooga, TN 37421.

Political Campaign Items
American Political Item Collectors, PO Box 340339, San Antonio, TX 78234.

Radios
Antique Wireless Association, 17 Sheridan Street, Auburn, NY 13021.

Antique Radio Club of America, 81 Steeplechase Road, Devon, PA 19333.

Reamers (Fruit Juicers)
National Reamers Collectors Association, Rte #1, Box 200, Grantsburg, WI 54840.

Rose O'Neill
International Rose O'Neill Club, PO. Box 688, Branson, MO 65616.

Scouting
Scouts on Stamp Society International, Carl R. Hallman, 20 Cedar Lane, Cornwell, NY 12518.

Soda Fountain Collectibles
The Ice Screamers, 1042 Olde Hickory Road, Lancaster, PA 17601.

Stereo Cards and Viewers
National Stereoscopic Association, Box 14801, Columbus, OH 43214. *Stereo World* (bimonthly).

Stuffed Toys

Good Bears of the World, PO Box 8236, Honolulu, HI 96815.

Teddy Bear Collectors Club, PO Box 601, Harbor City, CA 90710.

Tarzan Collectibles

The Jungle Club, 5813 York Avenue, Edina, MN 55410.

Thimbles

Thimble Collectors International, PO Box 2311, Des Moines, IA 50310.

Toothpick Holders

National Toothpick Holder Collectors Society, PO Box 246, Red Arrow Highway, Sawyer, MI 49125.

Toy Trains

Lionel Collector's Club: PO Box 11851, Lexington, KY 40578.

The National Model Railroad Association, PO Box 2186, Indianapolis, IN 46206.

The Toy Train Operating Society, Inc., 25 West Walnut Street, Suite 305, Pasadena, CA 91103.

The Train Collector's Association, PO Box 248, Strasburg, PA 17579.

Valentines

National Valentine Collectors Association, Box 1404, Santa Ana, CA 92702. Quarterly newsletter.

Willow Pattern China

American Willow Report, 1733 Chase Street, Cincinnati, OH 45223.

World's Fair Memorabilia

Expo Collectors & Historians Organization, 1436 Killarney, Los Angeles, CA 90065.

World's Fair Collectors' Society, P.O. Box 20806, Sarasota, FL 33583.

APPENDIX TWO

ublications, Periodicals, Book Sources

Periodicals, newsletters and books are in italics; book clubs and publishers appear in bold.

Advertising Trade Cards
Trade Card Journal, 86 High Street, Brattleboro, VT 05301. (Quarterly).

American Dinnerware
The New Glaze, PO Box 4782, Birmingham, AL 35206.

Antiques and Collectibles—Publishers
Books Americana, Inc., PO Box 2326, Florence, AL 35630. Noted for books on decoys, kitchen collectibles, and toys. All books on mail list of Collector Books. Collector Books, PO Box 3009, Paducah, KY 42002. Comprehensive list of antiques and collectibles books. Write for list or see weekly advertisement in *Antique Trader*.

Crown Publishers, Inc. and Publishers Central Bureau, 225 Park Avenue South, New York, NY 10016. Publishers and mail-order booksellers whose lists contain many current and out-of-print books on collectibles and antiques.

Currier Publications, PO Box 2098, Brockton, MA 02403. Publishes and sells direct art price guides and books on art collecting.

Greenberg Publishing Company, Inc., 7566 Main Street, Sykesville, MD 21784. Write for list of highly specialized collector's books in many fields. Examples: Super-hero toys, American Flyer sleds, marbles.

Hobby House Press, Inc., 900 Frederick Street, Cumberland, MD 21502. The major doll and teddy book publisher. Also sells material from other publishers.

House of Collectibles, 201 East 50th Street, New York, NY 10022. Publishers of "The Official" price guide series, a division of Ballantine/Random House.

Krause Publications, 700 East State Street, Iola, WI 54990. Specialists in automobile, baseball cards, coins, comic books, record, and sports-related magazines and books.

LW Book Sales, PO Box 69, Gas City, IN 46933. Reference books on antiques and collectibles. For list, call 1-800-777-6450.

Schiffer Publishing, Ltd., 1469 Morstein Road, West Chester, PA 19380. Publishes books on antiques in many fields, including period antiques.

Seven Hills, 49 Central Avenue, Cincinnati, OH 45202. Major distributor of foreign titles. Also publishes antiques and collectibles books.

Wallace-Homestead Book Company, PO Box 2165, Radnor, PA 19089. Publishes price guides, general list, and collectors guides, including Warman's guides. Distributors for Tomart Publications. Sells direct. For list, call 1-800-346-6767.

Appalachian Glass
The Daze, Box 57, Otisville, MI 48463.

Baseball Cards
Baseball Card News, 700 East State Street, Iola, WI 54990.

Baseball Hobby News, 9528 Miramar Road, San Diego, CA 92126.

Beckett Monthly, 3410 Mid Court, Suite 110, Carrolton, TX 75006.

Sports Collectors Digest, 700 East State Street, Iola, WI 54990.

The Trader Speaks, 3 Pleasant Drive, Lake Rokonkoma, NY 11779.

Black Memorabilia
Black Ethnic Collectibles, 1401 Asbury Court, Hyattsville, MD 20782.

The Black Book Club, PO Box 40, Farnwood, NJ 07023.

Bottles
Antique Bottle & Glass Collector, PO Box 187, E. Greenville, PA 18041.

Cameras and Photographs
Shutterbug Ads Photographic News, PO Box F, Titusville, FL 32781.

The Photographic Historian, Box B, Granby, MA 01033.

Candlewick Glass
The National Candlewick Collector Newsletter. 275 Millege Terrace, Athens, GA 30606.

Clothing
Vintage Clothing Newsletter, PO Box 1422, Corvallis, OR 97339.

Collector Editions, Modern
Collector Editions, Collector Communications Corp., 170 Fifth Avenue, New York, NY 10010.

Collectors Mart, WEB Publications, 15100 Kellogg, Wichita, KS 67235.

College Collectibles
Plate World, 9200 North Maryland Avenue, Niles, IL 60648.

College Athletic Collector, 10432 Haskins, Lenexa, KS 66215.

Depression Glass
The Daze, Box 57, Ottisville, MI 48463.

Dog Collectibles
The Canine Collector's Companion, PO Box 2948, Portland, OR 97208-2948.

Dolls and Dollhouses
Doll Reader, Hobby House Press, Inc., 900 Frederick Street, Cumberland, MD 21502.
Doll Times, 218 West Woodin, Dallas, TX 75224.
Dolls, The Collector's Magazine, Acquire Publishing Co., Inc., 170 Fifth Avenue, New York, NY 10010.
Miniature Collector, 12 Queen Anne Place, Marion, OH 43306.
Nutshell News, Clifton House, Clifton, VA 22024.

Farm Toys
The Toy Farmer, RR2, Box 5, LaMoure, ND 58458.

Fast Food Memorabilia
For Here or to Go, PO Box 162281, Sacramento, CA 95816.

Football Cards
See under Baseball Cards.

Geisha Girl Porcelain
The Geisha Girl Porcelain Newsletter, PO Box 394, Morris Plains, NJ 07950.

Glass Collectibles, Modern
Glass Review, PO Box 7188, Redlands, CA 92373.

Jewelry
Ornament, A Quarterly of Jewelry and Personal Adornment, PO Box 35029, Los Angeles, CA 90035.

Jukeboxes
Jukebox Collector Newsletter, c/o Rick Botts, 2545 SE 60th Street, Des Moines, IA 50317.

Kitchen
Kitchen Collectibles News, Box 383, Murray Hill Station, New York, NY 10156.

Lunch Boxes
Hot Boxing, PO Box 87, Somerville, MA, 02143.

Military
Military Collectors' News, PO Box 702073, Tulsa, OK 74170.
North South Trader, 724 Caroline Street, Fredericksburg, VA 22401.

Milk Bottles
The Milk Route, 4 Oxbow Road, Westport, CT 06880.

Motion Picture Memorabilia
Classic Images, PO Box 4079, Davenport, IA 52808.
Nostalgia World, PO Box 231, New Haven, CT 06473.

Owls
The Owl's Nest, Howard's Alphanumeric, PO Box 5491, Fresno, CA 93755.

Paden City Glass
Paden City Party Line, 1630 Colby Avenue, #5, Los Angeles, CA 90025.

Paper Dolls
Celebrity Doll Journal, 6 Court Place, Puyallup, WA 98372.
Paper Doll News, PO Box 807, Vivian, LA 71082.

Pens and Pencils
Fountain Pen Exchange, Hudson Valley Graphics, PO Box 64, Teaneck, NJ 07666.

Pinball Machines
The Pinball Collectors' Quarterly, RD#3, 46 Velie Rd., Lagrangeville, NY 12540.
(Publication now suspended, but set of back issues available).

Pocket Knives
Knife World, PO Box 3395, Knoxville, TN 37917.

Postcards
Barr's Postcard News, 70 S. 6th St., Lansing, IA 52151.
Postcard Collector, Joe Jones Publishing, PO Box 337, Iola, WI 54945.

Radios
Antique Radio Classified, 9511 Sunrise Blvd., Cleveland, OH 44133.
Radio Age, 636 Cambridge Road, Augusta, GA 30909.

Railroad Memorabilia
Key, Lock and Lantern, PO Box 15, Spencerport, NY 14559.

Records
Discoveries, PO Box 255, Port Townsend, WA 98368; *Goldmine*, 700 East State Street, Iola, WI 54990.

Scouting
Scout Memorabilia Magazine, c/o The Lawrence L. Lee Scouting Museum, PO Box 1121, Manchester, NH 03105.

Silver Flatware
The Magazine Silver, PO Box 22217, Milwaukie, OR 97222.

Slot Machines
The Coin Slot, 4401 Zephyr St., Wheatridge, CO 80033.

Soldiers, Toy and Dimestore
Old Toy Soldier Newsletter, 209 N. Lombard, Oak Park, IL 60302.
Toy Soldier Review, 127 74th Street, North Bergen, NJ 07047.

Stuffed Toys
The Teddy Bear and Friends, Hobby House Press, Inc., 900 Frederick Street, Cumberland, MD 21502.
The Teddy Bear News, PO Box 8361, Prairie Village, KS 66208.

Thimbles

Thimbletter, 93 Walnut Hill Road, Newton Highlands, MA 02161.

Toys

Antique Toy World, PO Box 34509, Chicago, IL 60618.

Model and Toy Collector, 15354 Seville Road, Seville, OH 44273.

Toy Shop, 700 East State Street, Iola, WI 54990.

Yester Daze Toys, PO Box 57, Otisville, MI 48463.

World's Fair Memorabilia

World's Fair, PO Box 339, Corte Madera, CA 94925.

index